BROWNSTEIN

BAYREUTH
African Studies Series

Publisher/Editor

Pia Thielmann & Eckhard Breitinger
Bayreuth University
D 95440 BAYREUTH
Germany / R.F.A.
www.breitinger.org

A catalogue record for this book is available from the British Library.

Bibliographic information published by Die Deutsche Bibliothek

Die Deutsche Bibliothek lists this publication in the Deutsche
Nationalbibliografie; detailed bibliographic data is available in the
Internet at http://dnb.ddb.de

First published by Bayreuth African Studies in 2006

Price per copy: EUR 29.95 (plus postage)

ISBN 3-927510-95-5
ISSN 0178-0034

Printed by Rosch Buch, D 96110 Scheßlitz

Sola Adeyemi (ed.)

PORTRAITS FOR AN EAGLE -

A FESTSCHRIFT IN HONOUR OF FEMI OSOFISAN

Bayreuth African Studies

CONTENTS

ACKNOWLEDGEMENTS

The initiative for this volume arose out of a desire to honour one of the most committed contemporary playwrights on his sixtieth birthday. This collection, however, would not have been possible without the support and guidance of certain colleagues.

I owe a considerable debt of gratitude to Harry Garuba, the grand mentor of modern Nigerian literature, who, in addition to reading the manuscripts, offered invaluable intellectual support and personal encouragement. My gratitude also goes to Akin Adesokan of Indiana University (USA) and Taiwo Sanusi in Perth, Australia for assistance in the initial screening of the contributions. And to Chris Dunton who always has a kind word. Martin Banham and Jane Plastow of the University of Leeds supported this project immensely and I cannot thank them enough.

My gratitude goes Biodun Jeyifo and Olu Obafemi who not only encouraged this project, but contributed to the success of it. I also acknowledge a huge debt to Eckhard Breitinger who, without hesitation and with much encouragement on his part, agreed to bring out this book under the imprint of Bayreuth African Studies Series. My appreciation and respect go to Dee for her support and constant push in the realisation of this project.

Finally, to the individual contributors, scholars and friends, my special thanks for their efforts and dedication in making this collection of essays and tributes a successful one.

PREFACE

An attempt to honour a person is always an overwhelming task. And when that person is a literary icon, a prolific playwright, essayist, poet, novelist and teacher, that task becomes onerous, especially if it involves bringing together a collection of essays like this. I expected the challenge as something that has to be accomplished. However, I did not expect the amount of essays and tributes that poured in from practically every continent to celebrate the 60th birthday of Femi Osofisan. As Biodun Jeyifo, his friend of almost forty years, illustrates in the Foreword, the ties that bind FO – as he is known to many – to these contributors is not just scholarship or the accessibility and relevance of his drama, but true friendship. Thus, it was a challenge deciding which of the contributions to include in this volume and which ones to leave out for, perhaps, inclusion in other volumes. In the end, I hope my decisions have contributed to adequately honouring our playwright and friend.

My first acquaintance with FO was almost thirty years ago, in secondary school. The school fare in those days consisted of James Ene Henshaw's *This is Our Chance*, Wole Soyinka's *Kongi's Harvest*, Ola Rotimi's *The Gods Are Not To Blame* and Zulu Sofola's *Wedlock of the Gods* as well as the usual Hardys, Shakespeares, Dickens, and the Romantic poets. There was no Osofisan on this list then. But the school library was progressive and one rainy day, Osofisan slipped into my hand in the form of a restless encounter, chocolate covered and brimming with eloquence, anger and 'revolutionary ethos'. However, my first experience of listening to FO and watching him work did not occur until 1985, when I was an undergraduate at the University of Ife, during the rehearsal of *Esu and the Vagabond Minstrels* at the University's famous Pit Theatre. The theatre happened to be sited between my hall of residence and my faculty, well, not exactly, but it made good excuse then to detour via the theatre for a spell of dramatic inspiration before the rigours of my studies. There I was, always, throughout the rehearsals, lurking among the pillars of the raised platform surrounding the theatre, or sitting on the concrete benches, gradually shifting from being interested in the theatre to becoming captivated by the directorial approach as well as the familiar personality of the playwright. After Ife, I made my way to the University of Ibadan to study Theatre Arts and FO became, officially, my teacher. This collection in honour of Osofisan's birthday therefore is a homage to the man who continues to create a radical shift in the psyche of our nation, whose drama staunches our open wounds and whose songs rouse us from our lethargy and set us 'ablaze'. So, Elereko, for all these and more, *ba re ní gboyè o!*

This book is divided into three broad sections. The first is a short section of tributes, followed by a candid interview where FO talks about his writing, his dreams about theatre and publishing in Nigeria and his frustration at the endemic corruption in the country. Though conducted eleven years ago, the interview is still relevant today for its topicality and the consistency of the playwright's view, a trait that has become synonymous with FO throughout his professional career. Included in this volume are a further fourteen essays ranging from analyses of Osofisan's adaptations of Greek classics to a comment on the rhetoric in his poetry.

My wish is that you will, if this is your first encounter with FO, come to appreciate his writing and his personality as closely as those who have had a longer association with his work. And if you are already familiar with the man and his work like the contributors of this festschrift, then join us in celebrating the new age of literary Africa.

CHRONOLOGY

1946 (June 16): Babafemi Adeyemi Osofisan aka Okinba Launko born at Erunwon, Ogun State, Nigeria. Father, Phillip Biobaku Osofisan, a lay-reader, choir master and headmaster of Epiphany Primary School, Erunwon, died three months after his birth; mother, Phebean Olufunke Osofisan, teacher (d. 2001). Brought up by uncle, Ebenezer Olatokunbo Osofisan.

1952-58 Primary School education at Ifo, Western Nigeria.

1959-1963 At the Government College, Ibadan where he obtained his West African School Certificate in 1963. Took part in dramatic activities organised by the school principal, Derek Bullock, who greatly influenced him. Edited the school journal in his final year.

1965 Higher School Certificate. Wins the 1st Western Nigeria Broadcasting Service (WNBS) Independence Prize with the essay 'Five Years Ago'.

1966 Wins the 1st T.M. Aluko Prize for Literature, Government College, Ibadan. Gains admission to the University of Ibadan to read French. Awarded the Western State and Federal Government of Nigeria's Scholarships (till 1969). Acts in James Ene Henshaw's *Dinner for Promotion*.

1967-68 Attends Universite de Dakar, Senegal, for the year-abroad French language programme and associates with the Daniel Serrano Theatre. Acts in Dapo Adelugba's *That Scoundrel Suberu*, an adaptation of Moliere's *Le Fourberies Scapin*. Produces Moliere's *The Doctor In Spite of Himself* and *The Imaginary Invalid*, and his own *Oduduwa, Don't Go, Behind the Ballot Box* and *You have Lost Your Fine Face*.

1968 Obtains Diplome d'Etudes Superieures, Dakar. Becomes the President of the University of Ibadan Dramatic Society. *The Cooling Spring* written.

1969 Graduates BA (Hons) in French, University of Ibadan. Premieres *A Restless Run of Locusts*. Enrols on the Graduate Studies Programme at Ibadan.

1971 Acts in the premiere production of Wole Soyinka's *Madmen and Specialists*.

1972 Weds Adenike Oyinlola Adedipe.

1972-73 French Government Scholarship for Graduate study. Attends Universite de Paris III, Paris, France. Associates with Jean Serreau. Appointed Editor/Translator for the Ford Foundation, Nigeria. Commissioned as Tranlator of Kourouma's *Les Soleils des Independences* and Alain Ricard's *Theatre et Nationalisme*.

1973 Appointed Assistant Lecturer, Department of Modern Languages, University of Ibadan.

1974 Obtains his PhD with dissertation, 'The Origins of Drama in West Africa: A Study of the Development of Drama from the Traditional Forms to the Modern Theatre in English and French'. Acts in Jean Genet's *The Blacks*, produced at Ibadan. Starts *Opon Ifa*, a poetry chap-book.

1975: Publishes *Kolera Kolej* (novel), *A Restless Run of Locusts* and *Somewhere in A War Period* (short story). Starts KOMFESS Artists with Kole Omotoso, Biodun Jeyifo and others.

1976 Premieres *The Chattering and the Song* at Ibadan (later translated into French by Nicole Medjigbodo and published as 'La Trame et la Chaine' in *Peuples Noirs, Peuples Africains*, no. 13, pp. 90-118; no. 14, pp. 133-157; and no. 15, pp. 163-171). Publishes 'War's Aftermath' (poem), 'Kijipa Ekun' (short story), 'Oduma: Two Variations – A Theme' (poem) and Wole Soyinka's 'Ogun Abibiman' in *Opon Ifa*. Stage adaptation of *Kolera Kolej* produced by Dexter Lyndersay at Ibadan.

1977 Assists Dapo Adelugba in directing Wale Ogunyemi's *Langbodo*, Nigeria's drama entry to the 2nd World Black Festival of Arts and Culture (FESTAC '77). Premieres *Who's Afraid of Solarin?* *The Chattering and the Song* published. Publishes 'Criticism and the Sixteen Palmnuts: The Role of Critics in an Age of Illiteracy' in Academic Literature, *Ch'Inbada* 3.19 (October-December 1977)

1978 *Who's Afraid of Solarin?* and 'Like a Dead Clock Now' (poems) published. Premiere of *Once Upon Four Robbers* at Ibadan. Promoted Senior Lecturer, Department of Modern Languages, University of Ibadan. Publishes 'Tiger on Stage: Wole Soyinka and the Nigerian Theatre' in Oyin Ogunba and Abiola Irele (eds.) *Theatre in Africa*.

1979 Starts Kakaun Sela Kompany, a semi-professional theatre group at Ibadan. Premieres *Morountodun* at Arts Theatre, Ibadan.

1980 Presents 'Beyond Translation: A Comparative Look at Tragic Paradigms and the Dramaturgy of Wole Soyinka and Ola Rotimi' at the Inaugural Congress and First National Symposium on Translation and Interpretation of the Nigerian Association of Translators and Interpreters (NATI), University of Lagos, Nigeria. Premieres *Birthdays Are Not For Dying*, *The Inspector and the Hero* and *Fires Burn and Die Hard*. Publishes *Once Upon Four Robbers*. Transfers his appointment from the Department of Modern Languages to the Department of Theatre Arts, University of Ibadan.

1981 Delivers 'Do the Humanities Humanize? – A Dramatist's Encounter With Anarchy and the Nigerian Intellectual Culture' at the 2nd Faculty of Arts Lecture, University of Ibadan. Visiting/Exchange Senior Lecturer in Comparative Literature, Department des Lettres Modernes, Universite Nationale du Benin, Lome, Togo.

1982 Awarded the City of Pennsylvania Bell Award for Artistic Performance for his role in *A Flash in the Sun* (an ensemble creation directed by Yinka Adedeji for the exhibition of Treasures of Ancient Nigeria in Philadelphia, USA). *Oriki* *of A Grasshopper* and *The Midnight Hotel* premiered. Publishes *Morountodun and Other Plays* [containing *Morountodun, Red is the Freedom Road* and *No More the Wasted Breed*]. Appointed Foundational Editorial Board Member and the Arts Editor of *The Guardian* newspapers, Lagos.

Writes and produces 'The Visitors' Series on the Broadcasting Corporation of Oyo State (BCOS), Nigeria with Unibadan Performing Company. The plays include *Behind the Ballot Box, To Kill A Dream, At the Petrol Station, Operation Abandoned, The New Cathedral, A Success Story, Operation Rattrap, The Audience Also Dances, A Debt to the Dead, A Date With Danger* as well as *Birthdays are not for Dying, Fires Burn and Die Hard* and *The Inspector and the Hero*.

1983 Member, the pioneering Editorial Board, *The Guardian* Newspapers, Lagos (until 1988). *Morountodun and Other Plays* wins the first Association of Nigerian Authors' (ANA) Prize for Literature. Appointed Professor of Drama, University of Benin-City, Nigeria where he designed a new and comprehensive curriculum and developed the library as well as Music and Dance studios. Directs *Farewell to a Cannibal Rage* at the University of Pennsylvania, USA (July-August). Publishes Alain Ricard's *Theatre et Nationalisme* (Paris, *Presence Africaine*, 1972) as *Theatre and Nationalism*, (Ife: University of Ife Press).

1984 *Esu and the Vagabond Minstrels* premiered at Benin-City. Leaves University of Benin.

1985 Appointed Visiting Professor of Drama, University of Ife (now Obafemi Awolowo University), Ile-Ife. Sets the record for a long run on a university campus in Nigeria with *Esu and the Vagabond Minstrels* at Ile-Ife (26 days). Promoted Professor of Drama, University of Ibadan. Visiting professor, Ogun State University, Nigeria.

1986 University of Ife Humanities Lecture – 'Wonderland and Orality of Prose: A Comparative Study of Rabelais, Joyce and Tutuola'. Returns to the department of Theatre Arts, University of Ibadan. Participates in the International Writers' Workshop at the University of Iowa, USA. Produces *Midnight Hotel* at Ibadan.

1987 Presents 'And After the Wasted Breed?: Responses to History and to Wole Soyinka's Dramaturgy' at the Jahnheiz Jahn Memorial Conference at the University of Mainz, Germany. *Another Raft*, a response to J. P. Clark-Bekederemo's *The Raft* premiered at Ibadan. *Farewell to a Cannibal Rage* directed by Sandra L. Richards at Stanford University, USA. *Maami* (novella) serialised in *The Guardian* newspapers, Lagos. *Minted Coins*, collection of poetry written under the pseudonym Okinba Launko wins the ANA Poetry Prize and the Regional Commonwealth Poetry Award for First Collection.

1988 Elected President of the Association of Nigerian Authors (ANA) at the Makurdi Convention. Presents 'The Challenge of Translation – Or Some Notes on the Language Factor in African Literatures' at the Symposium on African

Literatures Before and After the 1986 Nobel Prize, Lagos. Produces the Yoruba version of *Who's Afraid of Solarin?* as *Yeepa, Solarin Nbo!* And premieres *Twingle-Twangle, A-Twynning Tayle* at Ibadan. Wins the ANA Poetry Prize, for *Minted Coins*. Listed in *Contemporary Dramatists* for the first time.

1989 National Drama Consultant, Movement for Mass Mobilisation, Social and Economic Recovery (MAMSER), Abuja, Nigeria. Guest Writer, Annual Conference of the African Literature Association, Ithaca, USA. Serialises *Cordelia* (novellete) in *The Guardian* newspapers, Lagos and premieres *Aringindin and the Night Watchmen* directed by Sunmbo Marinho, at Ibadan.

1990 Resident Writer, Foundation Henri Clewes, La Napoule, France. *Wuraola, Forever*, novel, serialised in *The Guardian* newspapers. Directs the second ever production of Wole Soyinka's *The Road* at the Arts Theatre, Ibadan. *Yungba-Yungba and the Dance Contest* premiered. Publication of *Les Tisserins*. (Trans. of *The Chattering and the Song* by Eliane Saint-André Utudjian and Claire Pergnier). Paris: Editions Nouvelles du Sud.

1991 Founds the Centre for the Study of Theatre and Alternate Genres of Expression in Africa (CentreSTAGE Africa), a non-governmental trusteeship organisation. Guest Writer, Annual Conference of the African Literature Association, New Orleans, USA. Guest Dramatist, African Studies Orleans, USA. Guest Dramatist, African Studies Association, St. Louis, USA. Visiting professor, African American World Studies Programme, University of Iowa, and of African American Studies at Luther College, Decorah, Iowa, USA. Visiting Writer, British Council, London, England. Visiting Writer, The Japan Foundation, Tokyo, Japan. Performs, with the Kakaun Sela Kompany, *The Oriki of a Grasshopper* and *The Engagement* in six campuses in the USA. Becomes the Vice President (West Africa Region) of the Pan-African Writers' Association (PAWA). Grand Patron, Ghana Association of Writers (GAW).

1992 Ford Foundation Fellow, Africana Studies and Research Centre, Cornell University, Ithaca, USA. Fellow in Drama of Other Worlds and Visiting Professor of Drama, King Alfred's College, Winchester, England. Visiting African Writer, Inter Nationes, The Republic of Germany. Guest Dramatist, National Black Arts Festival and the Emory University, Atlanta, USA. *Aringindin and the Night Watchmen* published. *Abigail (Pirates of Hurt)*, novel, serialised in *The Guardian* newspapers. At the Annual ASNEL Conference on 'Defining New Idioms and Alternative Forms of Expression', Bayreuth, Republic of Germany. Grand Patron of the Arts, Pan African Writers' Association (PAWA).

1993 Fellow, Ragdale Foundation for Playwriting, Lake Forest, Illinois and visiting professor of Drama at the Northwestern University, Evanston, USA. Resident Faculty, The Ohio State University Center for African Studies. Appointed Principal Consultant, Atlanta Olympic Games Committee. *Dreamseeker on Divining Chain* – poetry (under the name Okinba Launko) and *Yungba-Yungba and the Dance Contest* published. *Yungba-Yungba* wins the

ANA Drama Prize. Relaunches *Opon Ifa* as *Opon Ifa Review*, a quarterly journal of the arts, primarily for creative writing.

1994 World premiere of *Nkrumah-Ni!...Africa-NI!*, National Theatre, Accra, Ghana. Commissioned by the Guthrie Theatre, Minneapolis, Minnesota, USA to write two plays. Writes and workshops *Tegonni, An African Antigone*, an adaptation of Sophocles' *Antigone* at Emory University, Atlanta, Georgia, USA and publishes *The Album of the Midnight Blackout*. *Ire Ni!* (poetic-drama) produced at the Arts Theatre, Ibadan for Wole Soyinka's 60th birthday. *Ma'ami*, a novelette published.

1995 *Nkrumah-Ni!...Africa-Ni!* directed by Neloufer de Mel at the University of Colombo, Sri Lanka. *Twingle-Twangle, A Twynning Tayle* published. Presents 'Medium of Change/Change of Medium: Reflections on Theatre Practice in Contemporary Nigeria' at the Africa Conference, Africa '95, London, England. Directs *Midnight Hotel* at the School of Performing Arts, University of Ghana, Legon, Accra, Ghana. Runs (With Alain Ricard) Playwriting workshops for AFRICREATION, in Lome, Togo and Accra, Ghana (until 1997).

1996 Visiting Professor, University of Leeds, England. Produces *Esu and the Vagabond Minstrels* and presents 'Warriors of A Failed Utopia? – West African Writers since the 70s' as the 2nd Annual African Studies Lecture of the Institute of African Studies Unit. *Reel Rwanda!*, the first play about the Rwandan genocide, produced at the Tricycle Theatre, London, England in March. British Council, Lagos commissions *One Legend, Many Seasons*, the stage adaptation of Charles Dickens' *A Christmas Carol*. Presents *Fiddlers on a Midnight Lark* at the Alliance Francaise, Lagos, Nigeria. Drama Consultant, Cultural Olympiad, Olympic Games, Atlanta.

1997 *Many Colors Make the Thunder-King* produced by the Guthrie Theatre, Minneapolis, Minnesota, USA (February 26 - March 30). *Andorra Goes Kinshasa* premiered in Lagos, Nigeria and *A Nightingale for Dr DuBois* is premiered at the W. E. B. Dubois Memorial Centre in Accra, Ghana. *Making Children is Fun*, a play for children, published. Resident at the Centre of African Studies, and the Institute for Higher Studies, University of Edinburgh, Scotland as part of the 'Africa 97' programmes. *Ònà Òmìnira, Ònà Èjè*. (Trans. of *Red is the Freedom Road*) by Ademola Aremu published by Hakuna Matata Press, London.

1998. Visiting Fellow, Tisch School of Performing Arts, NYU, USA. An adaptation of *Esu and the Vagabond Minstrels* by Cornerstone Theatre Company, Los Angeles, USA. *Ire & Other Poems for Performance* published.

1999 *Recent Outings I* (containing *Tegonni, An African Antigone* and *Many Colours Make the Thunder-King*), and *Recent Outings II* (containing *Nkrumah-Ni, Africa-Ni!*, and *Reel, Rwanda!*) published by Opon Ifa Readers, Ibadan. Directs *Once Upon Four Robbers* at the University College of Northampton, England. Made Officier de l'Ordre Nationale de Mérite, République de France.

2000 Project Director, UNICEF/Department of Theatre Arts, University of Ibadan Project on Theatre for Development for Children Survival and Development and Women's Empowerment (2000 – 2001). Appointed General Manager/Chief Executive Officer, National Theatre, Lagos, Nigeria (until 2004). Short-listed for the prestigious Neustadt Prize in the USA.

2001 *One Legend, Many Seasons* (drama) published. *Pain Remembers, Love Rekindles* (poetry) published. *The Nostalgic Drum: Essays On Literature, Drama and Culture* published by Africa World Press, New Jersey. *Insidious Treasons: Drama in a Postcolonial State* and *Literature and the Pressures of Freedom* published by Opon Ifa Readers, Ibadan. 'Ibadan and the Two Hundred Snails' published in Dapo Adelugba, Remi Raji, Omowunmi Segun and Bankole Olayebi (eds.) *Ibàdàn Mesiògò: A Celebration of A City, Its History and People.* 'Antigone in Yorubaland: Some Remarks on the Conception of *Tegonni, an African Antigone*' published in *The Performer: Ilorin Journal of the Performing Arts.* Vol 3, Anniversary Edition. 'The Political Imperative in African Dramaturgy and Theatre Practice,' published in Austin Asagba (ed.) *Crosscurrents in African Theatre Practice,* Department of Theatre Arts, University of Benin, Benin City. Conferred with the Award of Distinguished Alumnus, Faculty of Arts, University of Ibadan. Re-publishes *Kolera Kolej* (novel) and publishes *Kolera Kolej* (play) for the first time in one volume.

2002 *Restless Breed* (containing *A Restless Run of Locusts*, *The Oriki of A Grasshopper*, *No More the Wasted Breed*, and *Birthdays Are Not For Dying*) and *Seasons of Wrath* (containing *Altine's Wrath*, *The Engagement*, *The Inspector and the Hero*, *Flood!*, and *Fires Burn and Die Hard*) published by Opon Ifa Readers, Ibadan. *Bishop Ajayi Crowther: The Triumphs and Travails of A Legend* premiered in Lagos, Nigeria. 'Democracy and the Humanities Or, "Na who sabbe sef" for Nigerian Unity and Sustainable Governance?' FASS: Journal of the Faculty of Arts Seminar Series, Benue State University, Makurdi, Nigeria vol. 1, pp. 1-19. Chairman, Sub-Committee for Drama and Literary Events, Creative Task Force, 8th All African Games [COJA], Abuja, Nigeria.

2003 *Il était une fois quatre voleurs* [Trans. of *Once Upon Four Robbers* by Nicole Medjigbodo], *La trame et la chaine.* [Trans. of *The Chattering and the Song* by Nicole Medjigbodo.] and *Aringindin and the Nightwatchmen* published. *Wesoo, Hamlet!* performed. *Major Plays 1* (containing *Many Colours Make the Thunder-King, Farewell to a Cannibal Rage,* and *The Oriki of a Grasshopper*) and *Major Plays 2* (containing *Esu and the Vagabond Minstrels, Red is the Freedom,* and *Aringindin and the Nightwatchmen*) published by Opon Ifa Readers, Ibadan. Appointed the Lee G. Hall Distinguished Playwright-in-Residence at DePauw University, Greencastle, Indiana, USA, for the production of 'Wesoo, Hamlet'. Co-edits (with Remi Raji and Veronica Uzoigwe) *A Melody of Stones: An Anthology of New Nigerian Writing.*

2004 Guest playwright, Chipping Norton Theatre, Chipping Norton *Women of Owu* commissioned and premiered by Chipping Norton Theatre and Collective

Artistes, United Kingdom. Publishes 'Can the Humanities Survive? A Playwright's Odù for African Renaissance in the Age of ICE and Globalisation' in Akinrinade, Sola and Modupe Kolawole, Ibiyemi Mojola, David O. Ogungbile (eds.) *Locating the Local in the Global: Voices on a globalised Nigeria* (Obafemi Awolowo University, Ile-Ife). Also 'Eagles in the Age of unacknowledged Muse: Two Major Writers in Contemporary Nigerian Literature, Akachi Ezeigbo and Promise Okekwe,' in Ernest N. Emenyonu [ed.] *New Women's Writing in African Literature.*

Delivers the First Tai Solarin Memorial Lecture, titled 'The Individual and the Challenges of Commitment in an anomic Society' in Lagos (July 27).

Delivers 'Opon Ifa's Rebirth: Chaos and Creativity in Our Literary Compound' at the University of Lagos and 'The Humanities and Globalization' at Kogi State University, Nigeria.

Awarded the Nigerian National Order of Merit (NNOM) in the Humanities.

2005 Publishes 'Stirbt das Theater in Afrika? Uberllegungen aus nigerianischer Perspektive' (Translation by Jule Koch of 'Is the Theatre dying in Africa? Reflections from a Nigerian Perspective') in Arndt, Susan and Katrin Berndt (eds.) *Kreatives Afrika: SchriftstellerInnen uber Literatur*, Theater and Gesellschaft. Wuppertal: Peter Hammer Verlag GmbH. Delivers lecture – 'Is the Theatre Dying in Africa? – Reflections from a Nigerian Perspective' – in Bayreuth. Presents the first J. P. Clark-Bekederemo lecture in Lagos, Nigeria – 'Answering the Communal Call: J.P. Clark and the Allotropes of the Self'.

2006. Delivers the three part University Lecture – The City as Muse: Ibadan and the efflorescence of Nigerian Literature – at the University of Ibadan, Nigeria. Premiers *A Diary of My Father: A Voyage Round Wole Soyinka's Isara* at Ibadan.

Fiddlers on a Midnight Lark, Bishop Ajayi Crowther: The Triumphs and Travails of A Legend, Women of Owu and *Wuraola Forever* (novel) published.

Conferred with the Fonlon Nichols Award by the African Literature Association.

FRIENDSHIP - AND THE REVOLUTIONARY ETHOS
(FOR FEMI OSOFISAN; AND FOR OUR MOTHERS)

BIODUN JEYIFO

All the great philosophers, all the moral and spiritual traditions of the world place a great, priceless value on friendship. For some philosophers, friendship has a higher value than almost any other human relationship – ties of blood and kinship; comradeship in play, war or business; and love, be it amorous love or love of country. Indeed, friendship is considered by some philosophers as not only a form of love, but also the very highest of its forms. Which of the great philosophers was it who in fact vigorously asserted that if it ever came to the choice of betraying one's friend or one's country he hoped he would have the courage to betray his country before his friend? Friendship indeed has a long track record of the highest valuation possible in the reckoning of philosophers on the subject of the ultimate spiritual values of the human community. And in the heritage of the world's folkloric traditions, friendship is celebrated in innumerable songs, tales and proverbs. For this very reason, it is a daunting subject to write about with freshness, with originality. Thus, I do not know if anything I will say in this essay on my friendship with Femi Osofisan on the occasion of his attaining the age of sixty will be original, will have freshness with regard to the subject of friendship in general.

In my life, friendship has meant a lot to me, not in the abstract, but in the lived, concrete context of particular friendships to which I credit nearly all that has been fulfilling and sustaining in my experience. I suppose that from these friendships I could perhaps write a memorable essay on friendship in general, but that would have to wait for another occasion. What I aim to do in this essay is write about one particular friendship, one of two or three that stand far above the many friendships I have been fortunate to have in my life. Thus, though I may not write anything fresh and illuminating about friendship in general in this essay, what I can vouchsafe as the desired and attainable goals of the essay are unabashed sentiment and bracing, but hopefully gainful candour in acknowledging and celebrating what friendship with Osofisan has meant for me these past thirty-eight years.

*   *   *

The circumstance through which we became friends would prove both auspicious and defining for the type of friends Osofisan and I would later become in the years ahead, though neither of us knew this at the time. The occasion was a meeting we had after he wrote a response to a review I had written of the staging of one of his earliest plays titled *Oduduwa Don't Go!* My review, which was published in an undergraduate journal, had been rather sharply critical of the ideological underpinnings of the play and Osofisan wrote a rejoinder in which he sought to refute the meanings I had, in his opinion, misread into his play. Following his rejoinder, we both agreed to meet to talk things over and that was it: after that meeting, we became friends forever. But I am perhaps moving too quickly in this reminiscence.

At the time of this fateful meeting, we were both undergraduates at the University of Ibadan. He was a 'Katangese', and I was a 'Kutite'. 'Katanga' (the name of one of the breakaway provinces of the Congo during the crises which engulfed that country after the assassination of Patrice Lumumba) was the unofficial name for Independence Hall, one of the new male halls of residence of the University. That was why Osofisan was a 'Katangese'. The other new male hall of residence, Azikiwe Hall, was unofficially called 'Baluba' and its residents were called 'Balubites'. 'Baluba' was also the name of a province in crisis-torn Congo. I was a 'Kutite' because I was a member of Kuti Hall. This was one of the three oldest male halls of residence in the University, the other two being Mellamby and Tedder. Respectively, their residents were called 'Mellambites' and 'Tedderites'. Each hall had its own distinct identity and traditions and between the groups of older and newer halls, there was a clear divide in inherited traditions shaping the residents' *esprit de corps*. More precisely, the older and much smaller halls of residence were built in the colonial period and were initially named for the founding white principals of the college and, for the female hall of residence, Queen Elizabeth herself; later, two of these older halls, Kuti and Sultan Bello, were named for important figures in the country's nationalist project of anti-colonialist subject-formation. The alumni and alumnae of these older male and female halls of residence were the scions of the first generation of the country's homegrown intellectual and bureaucratic elite. From this, they lent a stamp of 'pedigree', a venerable or hoary status to their old halls of residence. The newer halls, 'Katanga' and 'Baluba', were literally and symbolically *postindependence* and were very proud of this fact. Like the postindependence nation itself, they were busy inventing new and distinct identities for themselves. For this reason, it was logical that some of the sarcastic epithets often used to describe the identities being forged in the new Nigerian nation were applied to the 'Katangese' and 'Balubites' of Independence and Azikiwe Halls: brash, volatile, uncouth, appellations which they embraced with pride!

Friendships were generally more easily forged within the same halls of residence or within the groupings of new and older halls, but it was true that friendships were of course forged across these divides. But this is not really what is at issue here. Rather, what is pertinent to my reminiscences here is the fact that friendships among undergraduates in those years were forged against the backdrop of the myths and social imaginaries of a decolonized, nation-building project that are indicated in these appellations and epithets:

'Mellambites' and 'Tedderites', 'Kutites' and 'Katangese'; the pedigreed 'colonial' halls of residence and the upstart, 'postcolonial' identities of the new halls. And of course, in the manner in which all social imaginaries are lived in actuality, these appellations and epithets were as often realized in being breached as in being confirmed. Thus, there were 'Katangese' or 'Balubites' who were thought to behave like 'Mellambites' or 'Kutites' and vice versa. These nation-building myths and social imaginaries, and not the epithets and appellations which encoded them, would later become the subject of never-ending discussions between Osofisan and myself when we became friends, but meanwhile, as respectively a 'Katangese' and a 'Kutite', we remained mere acquaintances, not friends.

We did meet regularly though as members of the University Dramatic Society. If my memory serves me right, Osofisan had the unprecedented record of being President of the Society for two years in a row. But I was far more engaged in the institutional and social politics of student life than I was in the activities of the Dramatic Society; I was a member of the so-called 'Pyrates Confraternity' and in my second year, I became Publicity Secretary of the Students' Union. Moreover, Osofisan was a member of the Class of 1966 and was thus a year ahead of my class of 1967. Finally, he was majoring in French while I was majoring in English. Thus, before that meeting to discuss my review of his play, we were generally aware of each other's existence on campus, but beyond the activities of the Dramatic Society, we had little contact and hardly ever were in the same circles of youthful camaraderie characteristic of undergraduate life outside formal studies towards graduation.

I cannot be entirely certain about this, but I think the distinctly *intellectual* nature of the circumstance in which Osofisan and I became friends, though not completely unknown, was very unusual in undergraduate life, then and now. It was true then - as it is now - that friendships among undergraduate students were often formed around formal and informal study groups, but it is doubtful that a truly intellectual dimension to friendship is formed on this particular basis of study groups. Definitely, when Osofisan and I met to discuss my review of his play and his response to my review, it was the only such encounter in my entire undergraduate experience. I am sure that this was true for him also. For we met to talk fervently about essays we had written, not for our teachers, but for the public, essays in which we were debating aspects of a larger national cultural and political history of which we were a part. In other words, it is perhaps fateful that at the very inception of our friendship was an *intellectual* companionship. This is all the more significant given the fact that at that beginning, we were not yet professional academics, we were indeed intellectual neophytes. This effectively meant that we not only cut our intellectual milk teeth together, in the course of the early years of our professional intellectual apprenticeship, we made the journey of self-discovery, of self-formation together, through both moments of misgivings and doubts and moments tremendous exhilaration and fulfillment. The most intense, the most taxing of such moments were to come after our 'conversion' to revolutionary socialism, after the radicalization we both experienced in the course of our graduate studies and the first years of our careers as young, junior academics, but that was way ahead in the future. Meanwhile, after that first meeting which 'launched' our friendship, we still had to grow together through the years of our young adulthood, with all the rites of passage associated with that phase of life – dating; getting married; raising a family; staying (he) or not staying (me) married; becoming distinct, known personalities in the public life of our country. An entire monograph of memoirs can be written on how much we shared, how much our lives were so intertwined in each domain of these big passage rites of life. One of these domains that proved almost as defining as intellectual comradeship for that early phase of our friendship was the matter of dating, of the male heterosexual hunt for members of the opposite sex. I should perhaps write only briefly on this topic, hoping that discretion will follow closely on the heels of an inclination to write unrestrainedly on the subject thereby helping me to avoid the risk of divulging too much!

The successes and the disappointments of dating were often negotiated through refractions afforded by our common interest, our common investment in literature, drama and the arts. Many of our partners we met through drama rehearsals for onstage and television performances. And as friends, we dated or paired off with friends; in a particularly significant instance, this entailed even sisters. Occasionally, and let me say *serially* not simultaneously, we dated the same partners.

And let this be told: Osofisan often carried out this dating game, this male heterosexual hunt for females, with poems! These were poems written to love objects that were sometimes never actually given to the persons involved as he debated with me whether or not to do so. This came about especially after he came to the realization, through bitter experience, that poems were not a particularly effective means of winning the hearts of desired partners. Or rather, once he discovered that while he was writing those poems, some other guy had gone off with young woman concerned! To this day, he still has rueful regrets about a particular damsel, the object of a fervent desire who also gave indications of a serious interest in him but whom he lost almost certainly because he relied too much on poetry while she, well, she waited in vain for more practical demonstrations of his affections! [For the scholarly pundits of Osofisan's plays, take note that this is the source of many of the love songs in his writings, this and the fact that he is so much of a songster, a talented composer of songs and music. Indeed, I opine that if he hadn't gone to all those prestigious secondary and tertiary institutions, if he had been a high school dropout, he would in all likelihood have ended up as a bandleader of one of the Nigerian highlife bands of the sixties and seventies and would have given the superior Ghanaian highlife bands a run for their money!] But let it be said also that poetry played a big role in winning the heart of the woman he was to marry and that even after they'd been married for more than two decades, he still continued to write love poems to her. Finally, let it also be known that I was about the only friend he had at this time with whom he could discuss these escapades of poetry and the pursuit of love objects, the only friend whose amusement was not unkind, was indeed sympathetic since I had had my own form of the same 'mania' in my high school days when I had been an avid writer of passionate love letters, many of which were never delivered to those to whom they were addressed.

In either case, there was of course the priceless fact of having a willing and sympathetic ear in one's bosom friend. But more than this was the fact that neither of us had any other friend who exactly could meet the unique demands of the roles we created for and found in each other in these rites of young, male adulthood. This is perhaps why I cannot recollect a more surprising and pleasing aspect of the experience of these years than the fact that in the perception of almost everyone who knew us, somehow, as we became more and more inseparable, we became fused into almost a single entity, a single whole comprising two near identical parts. This circle of those who increasingly saw us as *twinned*, as alter egos of each other, this circle included our respective siblings, our colleagues and associates, our ideological adversaries and professional interlocutors. And above all others, it also included, surprisingly on one level and unsurprisingly on another level, our mothers.

From the very first time that his mother met me and my mother met him, it was the same categorical pronouncement from each mother: 'Iwo ati ore e yi ma jo'ra yin ju o!' [What unbelievable look-alikes you and this friend of yours are!] Nor was this a one time only pronouncement; until both mothers passed away, they continued to lend this seal of discursive legitimacy to a near universal perception of Osofisan and myself as two minds and two bodies fused into one composite personality. This in spite of the fact that neither of us thought we had anything more than a vestige, a chimera of the physical resemblance that was vaguely insinuated by our lean, hungry looks, our full, flaunted beards, and our bespectacled visage of ardent proponents of nonconformist ideas and causes.

It is a banal fact of human existence that fate has an inscrutable logic in those areas of Being that are incapable of being directly or even credibly correlated to the determinate forces of material existence. For how else can one explain the fact that each of our mothers came in time to find in her son's friend the support to the demands of dutiful, loyal sons and daughters that most of her other children, the respective natural siblings of Osofisan and I, could not or would not meet with regard to a mother's right to emotional and spiritual sustenance in her declining years? Circumstances served to make me the far greater beneficiary of the role of loyal and supportive 'sibling' that we played to each other as compensation for both of our mothers' great ill fortune in having begotten some terribly disloyal children. I never would have wished to return the favour in almost exactly the same situation, but somehow it was fated to be and when the time came, I was there as a supportive 'sibling' in terms almost identical to the role Osofisan had played in my absence during the last year of my mother's life.

If so far I have given the impression that acts of 'doubling up' as a sibling in the respective eyes of each of our mothers was altogether an unprecedented or onerous experience for either of us, I must now dispel that impression. Like nearly all traditional African mothers, Yoruba mothers treat their children's friends like their own children, in effect like the siblings of their children. The word 'ekeji e' that my mother used for Osofisan and that his mother used for me means, literally, 'your twin, your double'. This is a word that all Yoruba mothers use for very close, intimate friends of their sons or daughters. What gave a special quality to the use of this word by our mothers was the fact that, as I have said, they, like nearly everyone who knew us, really felt that we were incredibly alike in so many things that it was as if we acted with one will, one consciousness, one sensibility. As I have also remarked earlier, by the special inflection which they gave that word 'ekeji e', our mothers merely gave a seal of legitimacy to a very widespread perception. This caused many acts and instances of mistaken identity, fortunately nearly all of them devoid of dire consequences. Two anecdotes will serve both to illustrate this point and to extend it to the discussion which will conclude this essay, the discussion of the period in the life of our friendship when it was tested to the utmost limits of its depth, its durability.

Let us give the first anecdote the title of 'Undeserved and Still More Undeserved Expulsion'. This happened in the period when Osofisan and I were graduate students at the University of Ibadan. Later, he would go to Paris and I to New York for continuation of our graduate studies. But at this particular time, we were both residents of the Tafawa Balewa Postgraduate Hall at Ibadan. One day, I found myself being continually distracted from concentrating on some work I was doing at the postgraduate section of the University Library. This was because the Deputy University Librarian, from an adjoining office to the main reading room, was having a phone conversation at the loudest decibel level possible at a public space. Finally, unable to put up with this distraction any longer, I decided on what I considered an appropriate form of protest. This entailed writing a short note on a piece of paper and placing the note silently on the Deputy University Librarian's table where she could easily read it. The note said that this *was* a library and some people were trying to work if you please! The lady was extremely angered by this action from a 'mere' graduate student and she demanded an apology from me. I of course refused to tender any apology. Following this refusal, she ordered me out of the Library. I also refused to obey this order whereupon the University Librarian himself was called to the scene. After he also failed to get me to tender an apology to his deputy, he had me physically ejected from the Library. 'Physically ejected' is perhaps too strong a term to use because in literal terms, what happened was the following rather dramatic and ceremonial expulsion: I was escorted out of the Library by two guards who walked on either side of me out of the postgraduate section of the building, through the long hallway linking that section to the undergraduate library, into the main foyer of the two separate buildings which constituted the library complex, and then out into the grassy lawn in front of the complex. As I was thus led out of the building, I was told that I could consider my library privileges suspended indefinitely as long as I refused to tender an apology to the big library administrator I had 'disrespected'. The next afternoon, I was having lunch in the cafeteria of Tafawa Balewa Hall when Osofisan came to me with a tale of what he called 'a bizarre happening' at the University Library where two guards had physically ejected him from the Library 'for no reason at all'. I was immensely amused by this story and this of course only served to exacerbate Osofisan's annoyance. I asked: 'You were ejected for no reason at all'? 'Yes', thundered Osofisan, 'yes'! Then as an afterthought he added, 'except that the guards and their bosses kept saying that since I had been warned the previous day not to come to the Library until I gave an apology for my misbehaviour and was formally cleared by the Librarian himself, if I dared to show up again I would lose all library rights and privileges for the remainder of the academic year'. Much later, I found out that it was the same set of guards who had walked each of us out of the library and even when they came to realize their error, they still swore that if they didn't see the two of us together in the same place and at the same time, they would make the same mistake again.

I cannot think of a better title for the second anecdote than 'Insider and Outsider in the Family'. This happened on the day of the wake for my father in October 1976, the day before his burial. This of course was the period of the intense and extreme radicalization of a significant segment of Nigeria's professional intelligentsia about which I will presently have more to say in the concluding section of this essay. There is no need to go into the details now except to say that on account of this radicalization of consciousness and sensibilities, questions logically arose for me concerning how far one *ought* to go in collaborating with friends and family in the act of giving a departed parent a befitting, dignified funeral. Osofisan was of course in near total agreement with me in my stand against some of the more ostentatious, more exhibitionist observances and practices associated with the burial of a 'big man' that some of my siblings wanted for our father. This apparently was the subject of a discussion that one of my maternal uncles had with Osofisan on the night of the wake for my father, all the time thinking that he was conversing with me. This was an uncle who'd known me all my life, who in fact sometimes came on visits to my house on the university campus and had met Osofisan several times on those visits. Going by what Osofisan later reported to me of this occurrence, what was so astounding about the event was the fact that until he gently pointed out his error to my uncle, the man was completely unaware that it wasn't me, his nephew, to whom he was talking, this in spite of the look of amused astonishment on Osofisan's face.

This phenomenon of being taken as the 'ekeji', the 'double' of a friend, no doubt immensely pleased us, as much as it also was a source of great amusement and surprise for us. In this I think I speak both for myself and for Osofisan. Surely enough, it was something we noted, though we never gave it much thought. I think now that we silently cherished it as an objective, exteriorized manifestation of very deep and sustaining subjective affinities that we felt. Definitely, we knew of distinguishing differences, of individuating peculiarities that each of us had. But these either paled into inconsequence before what we felt we shared, or wonderfully blended as balanced, complementing singularities within a dynamic dyad. This was the light in which we, and others, perceived our friendship until a few months after my return to the country early in 1975 upon the completion of my graduate studies in the United States. This needs a careful elaboration.

*　　*　　*

I came back from that heartland of global capitalism as an avowed Marxist, a veteran of the anti-racist, anti-war and anti-imperialist movements in its elite universities and colleges in the period when I was a graduate student in New York City, the storm centre of these movements. Within a few months of my return, Osofisan and I began to have discussions which more and more widened differences between us, especially in light of the fact that Kole Omotoso, who was also a vigorous participant in these discussions, generally expressed ideas and opinions which were somewhat similar to those expressed by Osofisan. It is perhaps useful to place this development in some broader context.

In 1975, progressive, leftist politics in Nigeria was dominated by the country's campus radicals, teachers and students included. This was a big sea change from the situation in my years as an undergraduate when militants and activists in the trade unions were the most prominent figures in radical, progressive movements in the country. Very few of these figures were genuinely intellectual types, by any definition of the term. On their part, the 'campus radicals' comprised a very small number of individuals generally considered flamboyant oddities in comparison with the bulk of their colleagues. Moreover, these 'campus radicals' were considered, and generally considered themselves, appendages to the 'natural' leadership positions occupied by the militants and activists in the trade unions. By 1975, all of this had changed profoundly. The term 'campus radicals' was now a misnomer for these radicals had forged deep, mutually supportive alliances with working class and other anti-capitalist forces and movements, this without any trace whatsoever of bureaucratic, bankrupt notions of 'natural leadership' of the country's progressive movement. As a consequence of this development, there emerged a creeping encroachment of the postcolonial state, with its security agencies and its apparatus of power, into the workings of the Nigerian university system. This process was then in its infancy and later the time would come when all Nigerian university campuses would be crawling with spies and agent provocateurs from the security agencies posing as legitimate students. But already in 1975, surveillance and intimidation by the Nigerian state was becoming a weighty phenomenon for the 'campus radicals', creating an increasingly oppressive and embattled environment for them. These are by now pretty well known and indeed rather mundane aspects of the historical and social situation of Nigeria's 'campus radicals' in 1975. What remains in the shadows, as an important frame of reference for the subject of the present discussion, is the phenomenon of fierce and often bitter sectarian debates within the circles of the country's radical intelligentsia. The exchanges between Osofisan, Omotoso, and myself, verbal and written, were a composite local and intimate instantiation of the larger, more public fractious debates within the left. In the present context, I can give only those aspects of these exchanges which are salient to the subject under discussion in this essay, this being the emergence of a moment in my friendship with Osofisan when a decidedly revolutionary ethos served to open up very wide differences between us, in the process nearly splintering that 'doubling' which I have earlier identified in this essay as the very basis of the depth and the durability of our friendship.

The exchanges revolved centrally around the question of the form and nature of the class politics needed for the social and political struggles to transform the country, deep into the second decade of its troubled postcolonial history. Specifically, the exchanges focused on the question of the existence or non-existence of a sizeable body within the national intelligentsia that was truly progressive, in a determined and principled way, and what role such a body could play in the social and political movement for deep, long-lasting egalitarian changes. Additionally, Osofisan, myself and Omotoso talked endlessly - and exchanged written memos - on other issues like the nature and structure of the relationship of middle class radical writers, scholars and critics to their own class and to the working poor, the unemployed and the rural communities, all of whom of course constituted the demographic and human majority of the country's population. We exchanged views also on the place of women in the revolutionary process and on how to overcome the inherited divisions of North and South, Christian and Moslem, divisions we considered false and generally prone to opportunistic manipulation by the country's bourgeois political elite. Finally, we of course thought of ourselves as Pan Africanists and internationalists; we looked constantly and carefully at developments in other countries in Africa and the developing world and also in the metropolitan canters of the global order in Europe and North America. This last item was as ideologically driven as it was also a factor of personal or biographical experience since each of us had had all or part of his graduate studies abroad, Osofisan in Paris, Omotoso in Edinburgh, and myself in New York City.

With the advantage of maturer years and hindsight, it is now easy to see that positions and perspectives that seemed in the mid-70's to be very distant, very antithetical are now really a matter of relative, nuanced differences. For instance, it is clear now that for the three of us, class was a crucial, defining basis of radical political subjectivity and activity; consequently, we presumed a division of Nigeria's professional academics into progressive and reactionary camps and that even within that division, we all had a pretty dim view of the revolutionary potential of the progressive camp. But at the time, Osofisan and

Omotoso seemed far less sanguine on this point than I was in my near absolute insistence that except for pockets of individuals here and there, as a fragment of a class, a distinct social category, a truly revolutionary intelligentsia was non-existent in the country. On the basis of this view, I insisted that the important task was to break off completely from the main body of middle class professionals in the country and go over, body and soul, to working class unions and peasant formations in the rural communities, this at the institutional, social and even personal and existential levels.

There were significant differences within the seemingly common ground of Osofisan's and Omotoso's disagreement with me on this issue. Omotoso took the general position that if it is the case that middle class professionals as a whole lacked revolutionary potential, this did not therefore imply that all groups, strata and individuals within the class should be written off; rather what was needed, Omotoso argued, was the development of a consciousness, a program of how to relate to groups and individuals within the class to foster in such identified elements a general preparedness for specific tasks in the revolutionary process. Omotoso even developed a concept of 'politicos' among radical academics and writers, these being those who had the personality and inclination to work closely and consistently with working class and peasant groups. On this last point, he cast me and a few other colleagues at the University of Ibadan like Omafume Onoge and the late Ola Oni and Bade Onimode in the role of such 'politicos'. He declared that he personally was willing to be 'directed' by such 'politicos' as long as it was realized that this did not thereby confer on the 'politicos' any 'natural' or unquestionable leadership roles.

On his part, Osofisan consistently articulated a deep and fervent interrogation of the moral implications and practical ramifications of cutting off ties with middle class professionals as a group, especially in light of the fact that individuals within this group were people you worked and lived with, people you'd been to school with and whose spouses and children your spouse and children knew and related to on often intimate terms. This stand was somewhat ironic because at conferences and symposia, Osofisan often expressed the most scathing disdain, the most withering contempt for individual writers and academics that he deemed confused or irresolute on matters of progressive ideology and practice. Shades of 'Katangese' acting like 'Kutites' and vice versa, of social imaginaries embodied in ironic inversions: at some of these conferences and symposia, I would sometimes in fact play the role of conciliator and bridge-builder between opposing camps while Osofisan battled irresolute, wavering souls! But in the private exchanges between the three of us, his voice was always the most insistent in raising questions about the *human* cost and the moral implications of turning one's back totally on an entire class, especially on *individuals* within the class. I was of course the immediate target of this last point and in one particular written piece, Osofisan bristled with cautionary predictions of an unperceived, unacknowledged movement towards self-righteous messianism and a reckless will-to-power, on my part in particular and, more generally, within the ranks of some formations of the left in the country.

In the profile sketched above of the exchanges between the three of us, the impression may have been given that these were abstractly theoretical and ideological debates, that answers and resolutions were sought purely or even mainly at the level of ideas and rational persuasion. Nothing could be further from this view. For the ideas expressed and the positions maintained in these exchanges were, at least at the time, lived and embodied in everyday practices and experiences. For instance, one area of ground level experience where abstract ideas and views exerted considerable stress for the friendship between the three of us was the fact that my house on campus was often filled with persons and types known and unknown to Osofisan and Omotoso, persons and types who looked at my two friends and were in turn looked at by Osofisan and Omotoso with great reserve if not with suspicion. Of this myriad of strangers or revolutionaries who often showed up in my house or office, those known to Osofisan and Omotoso were invariably students of the university where we taught, students on the extreme left of the country's youth and students' movements. Those unknown were generally militants and activists from trade unions, peasant collectives and diverse intellectual and non-intellectual pressure groups. It is difficult to overemphasize the spoken and unspoken worries and anxieties felt by Osofisan and Omotoso in their encounter with these individuals and types, either in my house or at my office, especially in light of the fact that I was not exactly forthcoming on what was going on between me and these strangers. Indeed, as time passed, I began to spend as much time on off-campus contacts and projects as I did on professional and political work on campus, without being able to share with Osofisan and Omotoso information on what transpired in my off-campus contacts and projects. Osofisan worried greatly that I was moving into very desperate and dangerous waters and he communicated this to me more by pregnant silences than any overt words, silence being, by the way, one of the things we'd always been able to share as an evocative element in our friendship.

These worries and anxieties fed into the debates between the three of us and the debates themselves then fed into virtually everything that each of us wrote at the time on anything concerning the crises in Nigeria and the African continent. A few examples of this point might be useful here. One of Omotoso's staged plays of this period was *Shadows on the Horizon*. The play's subtitle should serve to show how much it was a product of those exchanges between us: 'A Play on the Combustibility of Private Property'. Indeed, Omotoso's third published novel, *To Borrow a Wandering Leaf*, was saturated with aspects of those exchanges, so much so that the protagonist of the novel, Barry Jogunde, is often referred to as 'BJ'; moreover, he directly espouses some of the ideas that I had expressed in the exchanges between the three of us. Similarly, virtually all the essays collected in my second published book, *The Truthful Lie*, bear the imprint of controversies that we had engaged in the exchanges. The following closing sentence of an essay in the book, an essay on *The Road* that I had written and delivered as a seminar paper at the time, resonates with sentiments I had expressed to Osofisan and Omotoso in those exchanges: 'Of the critics who have buried this and others of Soyinka's plays in pretentious, metaphysical non-meaning, the less said the better, most of all the conjurers, the sophists, the casuists, the windbags – the minds of the Right and the Center'.

Osofisan perhaps presents a more comprehensive and intriguing pattern of this refraction of our exchanges in the things we wrote in the period. In the first place, nearly all of his plays and fiction from the period are literally and passionately about, yes, revolution, nothing short of this. Secondly, he brought this grand subject of revolution into his plays through elaborately celebratory and ironic masks and disguises which considerably enriched the subject matter in ways that never compromised the belief in the prospects and necessity of revolution, though this often produced bafflement in the ranks of other progressive writers and critics. This artistic swerve, this technique of engaging a revolutionary ethos of the greatest moment with estranging masks and disguises Osofisan brought to bear on how he inscribed the exchanges between himself, Omotoso and myself in his writings. And he did so in a manner which, indirectly and subliminally, provided a metacommentary on the strain of that revolutionary ethos on our friendship. This point has to be made with as much precision and thoughtfulness as possible. For this reason, in a somewhat deliberately digressive manner, I will use the particular case of one of Osofisan's plays from the period, *The Oriki of a Grasshopper*, to illustrate this point. Of how he refracted the exchanges between the three of us in his writings of the period.

*   *   *

We have great cause to be grateful that it was Abiola Irele who was asked to write the Introduction to the first collection of Osofisan's plays to be published outside Nigeria, *The Oriki of a Grasshopper and Other Plays*. For in this introductory essay to the volume, Irele is in his usual top form when it comes to the capacity to simultaneously account for the broad context while delineating the intricacies of formal and thematic patterns in the playwright's crafting of individual plays. But there is one moment in the essay when Irele's justly celebrated and superb abilities to see both the big forest and the individual trees in literary analysis and cultural criticism somewhat comes up short, perhaps in a manner beyond his control. This is the moment in which, having quite accurately located the production of Osofisan's early plays within the context of his immersion in the circle of radical writers and academics then known as the Ibadan-Ife group, Irele goes on to assert that the character, Imaro, in *The Oriki of a Grasshopper* was modelled 'on a type of individual Osofisan was acquainted with in his own circles'. The simple fact – if 'facts' can ever be simply simple – is that the character Imaro in that play was actually based on a deliberate, canny fusion of aspects of his public persona and mine at that moment in time. More precisely, the mesh of ideas, attitudes and utterances that coalesce in the play as the character Imaro was drawn from those fierce debates between Osofisan, Omotoso and myself. But what are these clusters of ideas, attitudes and utterances? And what exactly does this observation have to do with the title of this essay, 'Friendship - and the Revolutionary Ethos'?

By any reckoning, perhaps the most startling thing about Imaro, the protagonist of *Oriki*, is the fact that as much as he is utterly convinced of the necessity for a fundamental, revolutionary reordering of his underdeveloped, capitalist society in favour of the most oppressed, the most marginalized, he is also a man who loves to drink deeply from the fountains of life's pleasures. He smokes cigars, drinks choice wines and spirits and, for a married man, he has his share of philandering, this with mostly younger women who find his revolutionary subjectivity and activities 'sexy'. And last but not the least, he socializes with the likes of Claudius (the other male character in the play) who are former schoolmates who have successfully, even exultantly, merged into the ranks of the tiny business and administrative elite at the top of the country's pyramidal social structure. To say that these contradictory attitudes in Imaro seem like the very stuff of which a dramaturgic *agon* is made is to say the obvious, but factitious obviousness is far from the moral and psychological punches delivered by Osofisan in this play. The most telling of these punches is that in which, at the climactic moment in the play, Imaro enacts a grotesque ritual of abasement, a savagely sardonic rite of passage from the 'light' of socialist liberation to the 'darkness' of capitalist greed and exploitation. This ritual entails Imaro's impassioned pleas to his friend, Claudius, one of the despised capitalist bosses, to offer him employment at whatever level Claudius deems fit for one like himself who is lacking in the most elementary knowledge of just what makes corruption the driving force of his society. The reversal which comes at the tail end of this rite is equally startling: Claudius in turn implores Imaro not to give up his egalitarian dreams for their country and society, for to do so would be to accept that the cynical, dystopian logic of the dramatic action of Samuel Beckett's *Waiting for Godot* – the play they had gathered to rehearse – has overtaken and subsumed every other aspiration and yearning on the political horizon of their unhappy land. Of course to make this plea, Claudius has to abjure the validity of the system of organization of society and of human lives and needs which he represents. It is perhaps due to the force of this admission that he is made to literally and symbolically walk out of the dramatic action of *Oriki* immediately after uttering this ideological self-negation. Nonetheless, Osofisan sticks to his guns in making Claudius central to the restoration of Imaro's faith in the justness of his cause. Of course this is executed with a deft rhetorical move in which Imaro says that it was not courage in his cause but in *himself* for which Claudius, the incarnation of capitalism, acted as a catalyst. Moreover, it is significant that the play does not end on this note, that in fact no less than about a third of the play's action - the play's effective denouement no less - is given to the working out of this conundrum in which a liberal, reform-minded member of the oppressor class restores the faith of a revolutionary socialist in himself. In this denouement, no resolution is possible, or rather is enforced between Imaro and Moni, his student and lover who is a firebrand radical: he grows stronger, wiser and profoundly sadder; she loses her innocence, but not at the expense of abandoning her sense of the inviolable purity of the revolutionary imperative.

At the heart of Osofisan's dramaturgic construction of roles and identities for the characters of *Oriki* is of course the deliberate triangulation of the play's three characters, Imaro, Moni and Claudius. At the two extreme poles of this structure are Moni and Claudius: Moni is young, and fiercely and uncompromisingly radical; Claudius, on the other hand, is a scion of the business elite and he knows the ropes when it comes to how to manipulate the system of accumulation, how to exert influence in high places. Thus, these two characters live in worlds that are not only far apart, but are also locked into deep, irreconcilable antagonisms (though Claudius tries to reach out in companionable and genuine solicitude to the youthful revolutionary only to be rebuffed by her). Imaro is nothing if not ultimately a deeply enigmatic figure in the ways in which he stands between these two characters and tries to negotiate the conflicting pulls of his attachment or responses to their conflicting worlds. Like Moni, he is utterly convinced of the need for a radical, egalitarian reconstitution of the social order and like her, he is full of withering contempt for the likes of the university's vice chancellor who function as willing minions and tools of the kleptocratic and repressive neocolonial state. Indeed, Imaro is so much a leading figure in the radical movement that at the play's opening scene, he is readying himself for arrest by the agents of the state's security forces as most of the other campus radicals had been arrested and taken away the previous night. But then Claudius arrives and it turns out that it was his intervention that 'spared' Imaro from arrest. After duly railing at his friend for this act, which could only serve to compromise him before Moni and others in the movement, the play then veers into the startling plot twist that has been noted earlier in this essay. This is of course the twist of the inverted ritual passage in which Imaro asks to be admitted into the ranks of the exploiters so as to better understand just how it is that the system can be so effective in wiping out all feelings for equality, for justice and compassion in all who elect to be part of its machinery of corrupt self-enrichment. Again as we have noted earlier, this is merely a cautionary ritual. It is a cautionary ritual because Imaro emerges from it with his revolutionary consciousness not only intact but also strengthened. And this is why what he then has to say about Claudius being a bourgeois who is not only liberal but also profoundly decent as a human being has a ring of truth.

It is impossible to recapture by words alone the great and gutsy courage it took for Osofisan, in 1976 and especially before a conference of radical writers, scholars and critics where the play was first staged, to present this profile of a member of the despised bourgeoisie who is not only liberal and progressive but also decent as a human being. Even this far temporally and emotionally from watching the staging of the play, I recollect now how pleasantly surprised I was in discovering the slyness with which Osofisan executed this bold move. As I explained later to some of those 'strangers' who used to meet at my house and office who did watch the performance, yes, my friend made Claudius a reform-minded bourgeois and a good, personable fellow, but he quickly shunted him off the stage, he did not give the last words, the active work of imagining what is to be done, to him. That he left to Imaro who, after all, remains a dedicated radical socialist. What I didn't tell those 'strangers' confounded by Osofisan's startling inversions in the play - since they didn't pick it up - was that Imaro, the socialist to whom the last words of the play are given, has a split, a doubleness in his radical subjectivity because he embodies a fusion of the ideas and positions taken by Osofisan and myself in those exchanges we were having at the time. These ideas and positions seemed theoretically and ideologically irreconcilable as abstractions but Osofisan merged them concretely and credibly in the character of Imaro in *Oriki*. This of course is an expression of the enormous pressure that a revolutionary ethos exerts on friendship, demanding of it, as on almost every kind of relationship, great realignments of the selves involved in the friendship. In this particular case, the realignment of the selves entailed fusion of aspects of the selves in tension or conflict. But as we have seen earlier in this essay, the friendship - and the 'doubling' of selves that marked its strength and durability - predated the upsurge of the revolutionary ethos and, moreover, survived its collapse. What is left now is to gratefully acknowledge that survival while figuring out how to pick up the fragments left from the ruins of that revolutionary ethos which lasted from about the mid-70's to the early 80's. We need to pick up these ruins for the agenda of the present moment – reconfiguration of new beginnings and fresh starts. But that is the subject of another entirely different essay. For now, it is time to bring this particular essay to a conclusion.

For much of this essay, I have been reminiscing and reflecting on how my friendship with Osofisan survived the stresses placed upon it at a time when both of us became passionately involved in the movement to engage the often terrifying and perplexing contradictions and dilemmas facing our country and our continent. In the course of my reflections in the essay, I speculated that the friendship survived those stresses because it could draw on a peculiar pattern of intimacy and trust established before we both became 'campus radicals' beset by doubts, challenges and risks which destroyed not just other friendships but quite literally many lives. Now, nearly forty years later, I speculate further that it is enough of a challenge for any friendship to survive the common, ordinary and universal fare of small and big trials, defeats and tragedies that make up a large part of human experience. How much more daunting was it then for our friendship to have had to survive the pressures of a revolutionary ethos in which intimations were rife of actual or alleged acts of lack of courage, loss of nerve, opportunistic self-aggrandizement, witting and unwitting self-deception and self-manipulation, and, above all, treacheries and betrayals! Let me put a concrete face to these abstract categories.

In that period of great revolutionary fervour, we drew a line in the sand between our generation and the previous generation of the country's liberal, progressive intelligentsia. We said it was time to move far beyond the *noblesse oblige* that, in our view, had mostly characterized their view of their social and ethical obligations as members of a privileged intellectual elite. We greatly admired the work, the intellectual example of many prominent figures in this formation. Just to limit myself to the University of Ibadan campus when I still taught there, you had figures like Abiola Irele, Michael Echeruo, Dan Izevbaye and Ayo Banjo, all of whom we greatly admired but radically discounted as models for the kind of committed intellectuals we wanted to be. And we were very loud, very clear on this point and they all knew this and of course watched us closely as every generation watches 'upstarts' who arrive on the historical scene to announce the 'irrelevance' of their elders. In our daring, and perhaps our youthful folly also, we went as far as to declare, at the very least, a moratorium on all existing valuations, not only on canonical figures like Chinua Achebe and Wole Soyinka, but on the whole edifice of our country's and our continent's cultural archives in the encounter with global capitalist modernity, in its expressions in our super-exploited, peripheral backwater and abroad in the bloated, over-affluent metropolitan centres. One of the seminal essays from the period in which we called for this moratorium was Omafume Onoge's 'The Crisis of Consciousness in African Literature'; another essay was Osofisan's 'Ritual and the Revolutionary Ethos', the essay from which in fact the title of this essay was derived. And we inspired waves of younger cohorts to look to us for inspiration and direction. I speculate now that it was the double aspect of a quite deliberate *generational* positioning entailed here – drawing a line in the sand with regard to an older generation and looking to serve as a model for a younger generation – that finally brought everything down to earth for us, that immensely broadened what started as a one way street to an egalitarian social and cultural order. In concrete terms, when two sets of generational cohorts are looking at you with the greatest possible scrutiny for consistency and maturity in your declared objectives and perspectives, your declarations matter far less than what you actually manage to achieve. By the mid-80's, the line we drew in the sand had blurred considerably even as we kept tenaciously to the radical perspectives and goals we had set ourselves. I will cite only two instantiations of this development.

There's, first, the creation of the Guardian Newspaper which, by all accounts, changed the intellectual and political substance and tone of journalism in the country forever. In its intellectual perspectives, it was set in motion by a pioneering group which included Stanley Macebuh, Femi Osofisan himself, Onwuchekwa Jemie, Chinweizu, Lade Bonuola, and Tunji Dare. This group straddles the entire ideological spectrum of the country's intelligentsia, this in a manner that casts an ironic commentary on the debates and exchanges Osofisan, Omotoso and myself had had in the mid-70's. In the absence of independent and autonomous bases for progressive and widely influential journalism for the country's leftist writers, artists and activists, this newspaper became a welcoming and beloved home for many of these groups and individuals. And of course it goes without saying that this Guardian project was financed - could only have been financed - by one of the country's biggest family conglomerates, the Ibru group.

On another plane entirely is the phenomenon that is ASUU, the Academic Staff Union of Universities. At the present time, I can only write very sketchily, very sparingly on the phenomenon, reserving a more extended discussion of it for some future essay or memoir. Here I'll have to make a confession: it is difficult for me to write about ASUU at the present time because the energy and hopes that I put into its transformation when I served as its National President beggar what I have put into any other project in my entire adult life, not excluding my professional work as a teacher and mentor of young minds, perhaps the one area of my adult, professional experience that has been the most enriching for me. That kind of sentiment calls for a distance, a detached perspective to the object of recollection and analysis that it is beyond me to achieve at the present time. At any rate, at the height of its institutional authority and influence, ASUU was a big, capacious tent for a great number of patriotic and progressive ideological and political currents which took considerable imaginative inventiveness and practical flexibility not only to hold together but to fashion into a very big player in the determination of the country's present and future prospects. And this was on a scale that was quite unimaginable in the mid-70's when we were having those debates and exchanges.

In conclusion, and in case what I am getting at by invoking the examples of the Guardian Newspaper and ASUU is obscure, let me make the connection clear. The metaphor of crossroads comes to mind here, this as a replacement metaphor for that of the one-way street, the tunnel vision. The conventional meanings derived from crossroads as metaphor emphasize multiplicity of directions, goals and destinies. Here I wish to conjoin with this emphasis on pluralism the indication of intersectionality, which is also powerfully inscribed in the metaphor of crossroads. At crossroads, many roads are open for exploration: some lead to blind alleys, others lead to way stops for reviving flagging spirits and still others take travellers to watered havens. Wherever each road or grouping of roads leads to, one can always come back to the intersection - or networks of intersections - for fresh starts and new beginnings. I think now of those debates and exchanges that Osofisan, Omotoso and myself had in the mid-70's as a nodal point, a space of intersectionality, and a crossroad. But when we had those debates I didn't see them in this light; rather, I saw them as one-way streets. It took phenomena like the Guardian Newspaper and ASUU to make this retrospective reinterpretation possible for me. But this did not come about by mere happenstance. In time, I will be able to acknowledge the two or three other friendships that helped me along the road to making this big, mental and psychic leap. For now, it is of great moment for me to acknowledge in a volume celebrating Osofisan's life and work his friendship as one vast, sustaining source of this insight for me, together with the boon which it brings for confronting many of life's dilemmas and perplexities.

I make this immediately preceding acknowledgement with an acute awareness of a conundrum that pervades Osofisan's plays: they are rife with tropes of the providential boon that may or may not lead to wisdom. And they are also rife with tropes of crossroads wherein one is free, or perhaps *doomed*, to find or lose oneself. In effect, my conversations with my friend are bound to continue: providential boons and metaphoric, heuristic crossroads are aids, not solutions. But having unburdened myself in this essay of debts of friendship owed to Osofisan, I am more than happy to leave exploration of these and other rich lodes of meaning, affect and *jouissance* in his plays and other writings to the other scholars gathered at the feast that is this volume.

I

TRIBUTES

FEMI OSOFISAN: SOME PERSONAL MEMORIES

ALAIN RICARD

I have narrated elsewhere (*Ibadan Mesiogo!*[1]) the story of my first trip to Ibadan. I met with gunfire, Kunle Adepeju died on February 1st, it was a Monday, I believe! But if I remember well, on the previous Sunday, the last Sunday of January 1971, I was taken to the Graduate Hall of Residence by Professor Evans, holder of the Chair of French to meet with a graduate student soon to be going to France, Femi Osofisan.

A few months later, back in France, strolling on the Boulevard St Michel in Paris, I met with him casually: I recognized him. Femi then went to Dakar, sent me a note, went to Ibadan to teach in the Modern Languages Department. And so we started a 30-year long friendship, built on a common love of theatre, respect and admiration for Wole [Soyinka] and also a disrespect of established powers! He is a year younger but I believe we are truly of the same generation!

Femi wrote his dissertation in the early 1970s; at the same time mine was published and he translated it! It took some years for Ife Press to publish it, thanks to Adenike Adeyanju, but it eventually came out in 1983 and I was very proud of this book: my Nigeria was not too far removed from the Nigeria of Nigerians! I would often return to Ibadan (the Harlem of Africa!) and would always try to see Femi; then he went to Benin, to Ife, we kept in touch, corresponded. I followed his journalistic career whenever I came to Lagos: he took me to the offices of the *Guardian*, drove me around the town: I remember him showing me Bar Beach. I remember him bringing to his second floor apartment in Ibadan tanks of water from Lagos in his old 504 Peugeot! He was raising a family and writing an oeuvre at the same time.

In 1984, my friend Jean-Louis Balans, at my request, translated Femi's inaugural lecture 'Do the Humanities Humanize? A Dramatist's Encounter With Anarchy and the Nigerian Intellectual Culture'. We published it in issue 13 of *Politique Africaine*. It is a very accurate and bitter picture of the Nigerian University. It is also an act of faith in the power of the humanities. In 1986 we met at the Jahn symposium in Mainz. We shared a room in the apartment of one of the students, Renata Balzar. Femi was always ready to share, to discuss. In a way we had a common literary vulture: francophone and anglophone. I knew of his satirical wit. He had written devastating little pieces against well-known Ibadan campus figures in concise and acute prose! The college atmosphere could have drained

---

[1] Adelugba, D, R. Raji, O. Segun and B. Olayebi, eds., 2001. *Ìbàdàn Mesiògò: A Celebration of A City, Its History and People* (Ibadan: Bookcraft Ltd).

his creativity: that was not the case. He kept writing for newspapers, being a committed intellectual!

In 1989, I spent a month in Nigeria acting as a literary advisor for a film shot by Bankole Bello, 'Soyinka, a citizen and a poet'. Femi had become the head of the School of Drama in Ibadan. I included an interview with him in the theatre in the film. As always Femi was very articulate and clear and made very perceptive comments.

> He was one of the first people to establish this place, the department of theatre arts. Unfortunately, he didn't stay long before he was imprisoned by the government then, and when he came out he didn't stay long either before leaving on exile. The Gowon government had put him in prison during Nigerian civil war. But the little time he did spend here, he was able to leave some landmarks from which we have benefited, his approach to directing people who normally speak Yoruba for example farmers from the interior and rural areas. How do you put them to the stage of speaking English? To do this and to make it convincing, Soyinka worked out a style which has become the paradigm, has become modal, which we have all since been using. So that's one sense of structure of the place, which we have benefited from; the other also is in the mechanics of music; dance, spectacle of our own folklore; the world of our fables which he has also been able to exploit (Osofisan, interview with Ricard, 1989).

Femi as a theatre director is interested in questions of forms. As a committed writer he is interested in the effects of the form. He is a dialectical thinker: he does not live in a campus ivory tower: his plays are shown everywhere, on tour in Nigeria!

Some years later I had the ability to observe directly Femi the director and Femi the professor, during a workshop I ran with him in Lomé, Togo, in 1997, for actors and writers of the Coast of Benin. The workshop was open to Francophone and Anglophone practitioners. We had to teach in the two languages. I dealt with history and sociology of drama, Femi conducted a writing workshop. But how do you conduct a writing workshop in two languages at the same time? Femi managed convincingly to explain and more than that, to produce experimental texts. He would go back and forth from one language to the other and of course in the background there was his great command of Yoruba. We shared a rented apartment in Edem Kodjo's house, in downtown Lomé, and had many chances to discuss at length the future and the present of literature. He also told me of his years in Paris, of his difficulties: he had no money, his scholarship never materialised in those turbulent post-war years. But he decided to stay and to live a truly Beckettian life: not in a barrel but sleeping outside, like the homeless. He had not told me this when I met him on the boulevard in Paris 25 years before... Femi is now writing poetry, he has another persona, a poetic persona. I have most of his published works: he has always been very generous and I am proud of this little collection.

What I really admired about Femi was that he was always ready to travel and yet chose to be based in Western Nigeria, dealing with practical problems: he was not a cabinet Marxist, he knew the real life, the housing problems, the driving problems. His analysis of social reality was always built on examples. To students he was also a master: showing them how to do things, how to say them. But he also insisted on the need to acquire a literary culture: you cannot be a writer if you do not read, that was his message to the workshop students.

What has been and still is important to me is the fact that we are carrying on our conversation: we discuss places, peoples, works! We share practical life experiences, trips, workshops! We both address reality in pragmatic terms, but Femi has the ability to transform this reality into plays and poems and that is a marvellous gift!

SUBVERTING THE PROSCENIUM: A BRIEF NOTE ON FEMI OSOFISAN'S STAGECRAFT

MARTIN BANHAM

In 1978 the young Femi Osofisan described his aim in writing for the stage as a desire 'to get desperately close to the spectator, to each and every one I have trapped in the darkness or half light, to penetrate very close and intimate, like a knife in the ribs. I want to make that spectator happy but uncomfortable. I want to turn him open, guts and all, spice him, cook him in the filthy, stinking broil of our history. I want him washed inside out, in the naked truth, and then I sew him back again a different man'[1]. Elsewhere Osofisan comments on two formative venues in his experience of the theatre – the simple stage built by Derek Bullock, the legendary theatre-enthusiast headmaster of Osofisan's school, Government College, Ibadan, and the stage of the Arts Theatre in the then University College, Ibadan, where Osofisan went first on school trips, and later as a student himself. Both those stages – like most performance areas built in educational establishments in Nigeria in the 1950s and 1960s - were essentially end-on proscenium arch in form, effectively separating audience from actors, the former sitting usually in darkness, the latter emerging from behind a curtain and illuminated by stage lighting. Osofisan records the magical excitement of theatre in such conditions. Recalling a visit to the Ibadan Arts Theatre to see Wole Soyinka's *Kongi's Harvest*, he writes[2]: '[T]his one was totally mesmerising. I was entranced by the scenic effects, by the costuming, the play of lights and colours, the dancing, the music. I had never seen anything like this', but he continued to say that even in this imported architectural form and technically sophisticated environment, 'the evening was like an initiation into the secrets of what true African theatre should be'.

Osofisan as a student would, of course, have been aware of other kinds of performance arenas. He would possibly have seen Hubert Ogunde performing his great popular plays either in the open air courtyards of hotels or in the huge auditorium of Mapo Hall in Ibadan, where Ogunde confronted his audience directly, breaking through any sense of theatrical illusion with a genuinely shared experience. (In a BBC documentary interview with Ebun Odutola Clark[3] Ogunde famously described the western audiences he had witnessed in Europe, sitting quietly in the dark with their arms folded, in contrast to his own audience, sharing the lighting with the performers, responding to songs, dance, action and

---

1 Ossie Onuora Enekwe, 'Interview with Femi Osofisan, 1978' in *ed.* Muyiwa P.Awodiya *Excursions in Drama and Literature*, Kraft Books, Ibadan, 1993, pp. 18-22.

2 Femi Osofisan, 'Wole Soyinka and a Living Dramatist', in *ed.* Adewale Maja-Pearce, *Wole Soyinka: an Appraisal*, Heinemann, London, 1994, pp. 43-60.

3 BBC 'Monitor' programme, *c.* 1980s

words with their own vigorous vocal and physical contribution.) He may have seen the work of the great Yoruba entertainer Kola Ogunmola, including perhaps the famous mid-1960s production of a version of Amos Tutuola's *The Palm Wine Drinkard*, again in the Ibadan Arts Theatre. Duro Ladipo's performances in the courtyard theatre of Mbari Mbayo at Oshogbo again would have been part of Osofisan's experience – directly or indirectly. He would also have experienced the Mbari Club's open performing space in Ibadan, perhaps seeing Wole Soyinka's production of J. P. Clark's *A Song of a Goat* in the early 1960s.

So how does Osofisan reconcile the desire to 'cook; and 'wash inside out' his audience, with an obvious delight in the technical and scenic abilities of western-style formal theatres, and the fact that, inevitably – as a writer of 'literary' theatre – such will be the venues in which his work will – more often than not – play? Other playwrights and theatre practitioners partially resolved the issue by creating their own performance spaces in what they regarded as a more sympathetic indigenous form. For instance, at Ife Ola Rotimi and colleagues famously created the Ori Olokun arts centre, converting the open courtyard of an old hotel into a performance space. In Ghana, the playwright Efua Sutherland was a prime mover in the design and creation of the Ghana Drama Studio in Accra, inspired, as James Gibbs tells us,[4] 'by the courtyards or compounds that are focal points for much creative activity in Ghana' though, as Gibbs further comments '[r]evealingly, it incorporated a modest proscenium arch stage on one side'. Keeping a discreet foot in both camps, perhaps! Further afield, in Zambia, staff and students of the University of Zambia – specifically Michael Etherton, Andrew Horn, Mapopo Mtonga, Masautso Phiri and others – created the open air Chikwakwa Theatre. Osofisan, however, decided to subvert the proscenium arch by the simple but dynamic device of invading the audience! Osofisan will have recognised and, I suspect, relished, that one factor of the proscenium arch stage and the apparently comfortable separation of actor and audience that the end-on stage offers, is a sense of security for the audience. They sit in formal rows, often in darkness, watching the action essentially from outside. Into this safe and slightly removed world, Osofisan hurls chaos, surprise, and alarm. A prime example of this is the opening of *Morountodun*.[5] The 'safety' of the audience is broken down by a series of escalating actions. Initially the stage direction reads *'Stage opens on the Dressing area'* indicating a curtain drawing back or lights going up on stage action. A character, the Director, enters and starts talking to the other characters on stage. The audience are immediately reassured of the normal relationship between themselves as observers and the actors on stage they have come to 'watch'. Then, in the second action the Director, as the stage direction reads, *'steps out'* of place, and

---

[4] James Gibbs, 'Ghana', in *ed*. Martin Banham *A History of Theatre in Africa*, Cambridge, 2004, p. 165

[5] *Morountodun and Other Plays*, Ikeja, Longman Nigeria, 1982

approaches the audience. The invisible comfort barrier between stage and auditorium has been subtly breached. He begins to talk directly to the audience. As he does so 'noises' begin to be heard from outside the theatre. He becomes increasingly nervous, but continues talking to the audience. The stage directions tell us *'Noises rise again, but subside as attendants are heard talking to the crowd.* Director *takes a handkerchief and wipes his brow'.* The nervousness of the Director is designed to unsettle the audience. From this point on the action in the auditorium and on stage quickens up. *'Noise grows. The actors freeze, anxious. The* Director *fights to continue...........The noise drowns his voice now......He walks quickly towards the main entrance but is soon violently pushed back by a shouting near-hysterical mob, consisting of women bearing placards, and some handbills which they begin to distribute round the auditorium. The are attended by a couple of drummers who are apparently trying to make money out of the occasion......Full lights return, flooding the entire theatre. Most of the actors on stage have quietly sneaked out........A little group...takes over the stage. Leading them is* Titubi, *a pretty, sensual, and obviously self-conscious woman'.* Titubi climbs on the stage and addresses the audience telling them that she's stopping the play. 'And if you're wise' she tells them, 'you'll go and return your tickets now and collect your money back'. The Director protests. The mob who have invaded the auditorium seize him and slap him. Titubi asks him where his actors have disappeared to. Director (*shouting*) 'Gone for the police! The police!' Titubi and the mob continue to parade over the stage and through the auditorium, abusing the Director. Then: *The piercing sound of a police siren, outside. Sounds of car doors banging. Noise of boots. Then a loud blast on the whistle. Enter a* Police Officer...*accompanied by a* Corporal *in full riot gear: shield, tear gas gun and canisters. Among the crowd, a moment of frozen indecision, and then – panic. Everybody runs out, through various exits, in disarray....* From this point onwards the action refocuses on the stage and, by implication, the auditorium lights, flooded on earlier, will dim and the audience will once again be allowed to watch the action on stage – but not before they have been thoroughly alarmed and confused and disoriented! Osofisan has thoroughly broken through the illusion of the proscenium arch without sacrificing any of the technical effects of the theatre that he so enjoys!

If the above is an instance of Osofisan subverting the proscenium at the beginning of stage action, he can have equal impact when concluding it. A fine example is the ending of *Once Upon Four Robbers.*[6] Here is a play about the impact of armed robbers on Nigerian society, and it is no accident that the design on the cover of the published play depicts stakes tied to barrels to which armed robbers were notoriously tied before being shot dead in an atmosphere of public carnival in the macabre Lagos 'Bar Beach Show' in the late 1970s. Despite the awful impact of robbers for ordinary Nigerian people, Osofisan typically does not offer a play that sees any troubles in society in simplistic

---

[6] *Once Upon Four Robbers*, Ibadan, Heinemann, 1991

terms. Nor does he allow the audience the luxury of letting the playwright make moral or social decisions on their behalf. He demands that the audience takes decisions and faces the consequences. So, at the end of *Once Upon Four Robbers*, the 'Epilogue' freezes the stage action at a point where robbers and soldiers are coming into a final confrontation, and the Storyteller (in the character of Aafa – a nice little reference to Soyinka's *Madmen and Specialists*?) in a typical piece of Osofisan stagecraft, moves into the auditorium and speaks directly to the audience. No longer spectators, the audience are now vital participants in what is to occur.

> *Aafa*: A stalemate? How can I end my story on a stalemate? If we sit on the fence,
>
> Life is bound to pass us by, on both sides. No, I need your help.

He engages individual members of the audience in discussion, demanding that they vote either to proceed with the execution of the robbers, or release them. After discussion – and this is genuine, not pre-scripted in any way - a vote is taken in the audience, and alternative endings are offered. If the audience decides to free the robbers the characters on stage break from their freeze and attack first the villagers in the play, stealing 'shirts, bubas, geles, even trousers' and then move into the audience robbing and harassing them! If, on the other hand, the audience vote to carry on with the executions they are graphically carried out in stage action that is designed to be brutal and shocking. For either ending the audience is responsible and complicit. Once again Osofisan has shattered the illusion of security that the proscenium arch or the end-on stage gives. In the programme note to the first production of the play (March 1979 at the Arts Theatre, University of Ibadan), in which Osofisan himself played one of the robbers, the playwright wrote 'I hope this play shocks us into a new awareness'. Throughout his work, through imaginative stagecraft, Osofisan works to turn the audience into 'a different man'.

CELEBRATING OSOFISAN AT SIXTY

MUYIWA AWODIYA

Introduction

When Femi Osofisan turns sixty on June 16, 2006, the day would not be an ordinary day for the scholar and creative writer whose giant intellectual strides have made their marks on the landscape of world literature in terms of his large output of plays, poetry and fiction.

Indeed, Professor Babafemi Adeyemi Osofisan, who by acclaim is the most prolific Nigerian playwright after Wole Soyinka, deserves to be celebrated with pomp and fanfare at sixty. Throughout his over thirty years of scholarship, he has experienced, no doubt, the genuine metamorphosis that must accompany any originality in intellectual pursuit. From being a Wole Soyinka's dramatic disciple, to being an activist in the fight for the creation of the literature of the Alternative Tradition, to an era when he has carved out his own separate theatrical identity, Osofisan has come of age, both literally and metaphorically. Because of his hard-work, coupled with a distinguished career as a playwright, creative artist and a scholar, Osofisan was appointed the General Manager and Chief Executive Officer of the Nigerian National Arts Theatre, Lagos in 2000. He managed the theatre for four years during which he sought to integrate the literary performance culture in Nigeria with that of the traditional practitioners. He returned to his academic base at the University of Ibadan in 2004.

Osofisan's sixtieth birthday celebration is therefore based on his outstanding contribution to the development of the Humanities, especially in the field of dramatic literature, theory and criticism. Osofisan has also worked in journalism, where he was one of the pioneering members of the Editorial Board of *The Guardian Newspaper*, now unarguably Nigeria's most influential newspaper. For many years, he was one of the leading popular columnists in that newspaper. He has also contributed to the *Sunday Times* and the *The Comet*. As a scholar, he has edited a number of academic and literary journals, including *Black Orpheus, Opon Ifa, Positive Review*, and, currently, he is co-editor of the *African Theatre*. Among his prolific output as a writer are 33 published full-length plays for the stage, another 10 Television plays and one for radio, three books of academic essays, a play for juvenile readers, three novelettes and four collections of poetry. In addition, there are at least 10 other full-length plays and two monographs that are yet to be published. His plays are performed in many countries outside Nigeria, including the USA, Britain, Australia, Sri Lanka, South Africa, Ghana and Sierra Leone. Indeed, some of them were originally commissioned and premiered by theatres in these countries. Apart from his profile as playwright, Osofisan also features in numerous drama productions himself, playing various roles, as actor, director, dancer, song writer, drummer and producer. He was Drama Consultant to the 2nd World Black Festival of Arts and Culture (FESTAC '77), to the Nigerian Movement for Mass Mobilisation, Social and Economic Recovery (MAMSER), to the 1992 Olympic Games in Atlanta, and recently to the Creative Task Force, the team responsible for the Opening and Closing ceremonies of the 8th All-African Games (COJA) in Abuja. In 1991, he became the Grand Patron of the Ghana Association of Writers (GAW), and ten years later, was given one of the Distinguished Alumnus Awards of the Faculty of Arts of the University of Ibadan.

Osofisan has repeatedly won the Association of Nigerian Authors (ANA) prizes for his works, both for poetry and drama, and in 1988, he was the African Regional winner of the Commonwealth Literature Prize. In 2000, he was on the final list of nine writers short-listed for the prestigious Neustadt Prize. In recognition of his achievements therefore, Osofisan has enjoyed Fellowships in different countries and institutions, two of the most recent being from the DePauw University in Indiana, USA, where he was appointed the Lee G. Hall Distinguished Playwright-in-Residence in 2003, and the Zentrum fur Litteraturfoschung in Berlin in May 2005.

Osofisan has been President of the Association of Nigerian Authors (ANA) for two consecutive terms, and is currently the President of the Nigerian chapter of the International PEN International. In 2001, Osofisan was conferred with the medal of the National Order of Merit by the French Government, and last year, in 2004, with the Nigerian National Order of Merit in the Humanities.

Dramatic Techniques

Osofisan believes that the theatre should be used as an instrument of change in the society. For this reason, his theatre not only educates but attempts to empower the audience in order to bring about socially and politically responsible change in the society. He believes that if he jolts his audience out of their identification with the actions on stage, he would succeed in spurring them to think about what they see on stage. *Once upon Four Robbers, Another Raft* and *Esu and the Vagabond Minstrels* are examples of these plays. In terms of structure, Osofisan's plays are typically composed of a series of short episodes connected by songs. The purpose is to engage the interest and belief of the audience and then to break the spell on them by urging them to evaluate the meaning and implications of what they see in the episodes. The playwright uses flexible dramatic forms that have great stage adaptability, and in which are embedded traditional African elements of music, dance, songs, drumming, mime and improvisation. His language also consists of a simple and accessible diction – the prose vernacular of every day life. But the beauty of this simplicity is the subtlety that permeates it; and often, the dialogues possess a harsh, condemnatory tone, meant to subvert, thwart and frustrate the hypocritical sentimentality of the bourgeoisie ruling class in Nigeria.

Satire and humour are at the heart of Osofisan's theatre and these are expressed both verbally and visually, such as in *Who's Afraid of Solarin?* and *Midnight Hotel* where the playwright satirises the rampant materialism of the ruling class in Nigeria. Nevertheless, beneath this seething militancy, Osofisan always reveals a genuine artistic talent by transcending the simple emotional possibilities of social drama. His situations and events are credible, and his characters emerge, not as mere ciphers, but as real people, for whom the audience is made to identify with in real life situations. All these factors, together with the fact that the plays are stylistically and technically accessible to professionals and amateurs alike, explain why the audience finds Osofisan's aesthetics captivating and why, today, his plays are the most frequently performed on the Nigerian stage.

The language is simple and accessible in lucid and accessible prose. Osofisan's basic material is the expression of rebellion, an element that recurs overtly or covertly in his work. Discontented with old and static forms, Osofisan finds it impracticable to identify with the existing art forms, government, system, or programmes, or even to ally himself with any leftist revolutionary vanguard. His revolt against human forces of oppression, corruption and injustice is a means of engaging the status quo and agitating for moral, social, artistic, religious and political transformation. His theatre reflects both his sympathy for human suffering and his outrage at human absurdity, alternating between moods of wistful pathos and flashes of ironic humour, which disqualify his plays from being adjudged mere slices of life. All his works share common thematic concerns with virtues of collective struggle and the individual's will-power to fight and survive in a community of struggling beings. From an early play like *The Chattering and The Song* (1977), where he highlighted the need for men to act in concert in order to attain democracy as against autocracy, to the recent *Women of Owu* (2004) where he preaches peace against violence and the meaninglessness of war in our war-torn present days, these concerns are predominant. With vibrant use of song and chants in *Women of Owu*, he has asked us, his audience, always to strive for peace and to seize our destiny in our own hands. We come to know from these plays that as long as we refuse to surrender, as long as we ourselves rise up to confront adversity, that we can never be doomed as individuals, groups or as a nation. We learn from these works that if we wish to live in freedom, we must unmask the fables of superstition and conquer fear. We are also informed that all of us can be heroes against the caprice of fate or circumstance by believing in ourselves and in our capacity to change our environment and show the way out of ignorance and squalor.

Conclusion

51

I therefore pay this tribute to Osofisan at 60 in order to elucidate his laudable contributions and devotion to theatre arts in Nigeria. Osofisan has just begun to enjoy deserved appreciation by his fellow compatriots and the international community for a life devoted to the humanities, scholarship and a creative struggle that seeks to transform society to the ideal.

A TRIBUTE TO FEMI OSOFISAN – THE ALCHEMIST OF COGNITION, AT SIXTY

OLU OBAFEMI

Nothing could delight me much greater than an opportunity to be a part of the celebration of the sixtieth year anniversary of someone, who over the past two-and-a-half decades, has moved from being a bosom friend to a brother. In showing unalloyed gratitude to Sola Adeyemi, who has spear-headed this Anniversary Publication to further the process of celebrating Femi Osofisan, simply Africa's most prolific playwright and multi-talented literary artist, scholar, theatre practitioner, musician, painter, media worker and humanist, I must confess that I do so with an innate feeling of guilt. This derives from the fact that ever since I wrote my first and over-cited essay on Osofisan in 1980, published a year later in 1982 by Eldred Jones in *African Literature Today*, I had conceived a project of writing the first full-length study on the celebrant. A number of factors came in my way to abort – I believe postpone – the materialisation of that pet-intent.

However, the most ironic of the factors arise from the very fact of my intimate friendship with the subject. I happen to be one of the most privileged of his friends, in terms of his writing career and process. This position can be contested, of course by his older friend and radical literary scholar, Biodun Jeyifo, and Muyiwa Awodiya. Each time we sat together, these many years, wondering over what has happened to the dream of the becoming-ideal of this troubled nation, our own frustrations in it and our mediatory effort through literature and culture work, I find that there are so many manuscripts that Femi is working on. I would push forward the idea of publishing a book on a man with such disarming, if not alarming, fertile creative fount. Secretly, I would postpone the idea of bringing out a book, which would be virtually unrepresentative of his indomitable *oeuvre*. This is how a certain burden of selfish vacillation, or is it greedy procrastination, led to an indefinite suspension of one of the writing projects I had held closest to my heart, until some other more positively aggressive scholars – including our mutual friend, Muyiwa Awodiya, who everybody now knows as the Osofisan Scholar and the American-born Osofisan specialist, Sandra Richards – seized the initiative to illuminate the literary world with the creative feat of Femi Osofisan. In the particular case of Awodiya, who showed me every manuscript that he had written on his subject and who put so much pressure on me to become his editor and consultant, it became a question of morality for me to shelve my own project until he had fulfilled, in part, his dream to churn out books on Femi Osofisan, his friend and mentor. Having so publicly exposed myself, I know

now that I shall never feel fulfilled until I have accomplished the plan to write 'The Essential Osofisan'.

This explains why, even though, all these years of our friendship and fraternal affinity, which I consider both an honour and a gift, I have hardly written anything in which Osofisan is not an inspiration and a vicarious guide, the ultimate project of a full-length study on him, has continued to elude me – so far. It is therefore from the standpoint of a mesh of positive envy and profound appreciation, that I grab this platform generously offered by the sponsors of this study to join the celebration of sixty years of a crowded life of creative activism and robust prolificity of the year 2005 winner of the Nigerian National Merit Award for the Humanities, Femi Osofisan. I have used the terms prolific and multi-talented rather frequently already, unsubstantiated, but without trepidation, as many of those who will genuinely celebrate Femi Osofisan must know. How else can one describe a man who has published thirty-three full-length plays, four novels (he would describe them as novelettes, and actually published them under a pseudonym), four books of poetry, three robust works of literary scholarship, numerous edited journals and hundreds of published newspaper columns?

Striding deep into the autumn season of life must be intimidating – both to the personage in question and his associates, especially those of us over whom he is always eager to exercise his 'egbonhood'. In the case of Femi Osofisan, it is a worthy life and living, worth rejoicing about and also reflecting upon. His is a life of tonic and the ever-mellifluous taste of wine. The more he matures, the more profound, the more sage-like he becomes. Judging from the restlessness of his creative spirit – like the restless run of locusts he created and dramatised in 1968, even as the Nigerian Civil War raged – it is a great delight to look forward to his attainment of his master-piece. Femi is the first to let you know that he has not written the play or the novel of his dream. You can see this immediately in the diversity, the innovativeness and the experimental nature of every one of his ever-tumbling creative products. Every new work is an experiment and a fresh way of enlightening and illuminating the world – be it a play, a poem or a story. His compulsive passion to engage society – both the prey and the predator – in the dialogue of change, propels him to seek diverse outlets, mostly creative, but a times stridently polemical, for a troubled and traumatised humanity.

It is difficult to write coherently, and in a very constrained space, about someone who has offered rare friendship and with whom I have shared genuine and cherished comradeship – in the sense of companionship. It would simply have been better just to write about his work publicly and send him an emotional birthday cake and the smoothest bottle of wine that one can afford. Everybody, including those who will merely join in the wining and dining on June 16, 2006, without truly cognising the essence of the celebration, will do that and the point will be sorely missed. Femi Osofisan will prefer a sound and robust discourse on the society of his dream than an endless bout of carousing. He has led us to the awareness that 'birthdays are not for dying'. Every year since he turned fifty, he has given himself a Birthday gift – a harvest of publications, which shower fresh lights on our blighted social landscape. He can (will) then, after nourishing the soul, go ahead to salute the gut and arm the bowel, with cakes and ale.

I have learnt quite a chunk from this peerless oracle of words. One such a lesson is that love rekindles. For him, and he shares it with me, even at moments when it is most difficult to accept, the greatest armoury against betrayal and despondency – at the individual level (of social relationships) and the communal level of bankrupt governance – is to understand that bitterness and despair blur and blunt the edge of vision. A man who offers his friendship when it is most suicidal and unpopular to do so (and I am a grateful beneficiary of this friendship in a risky moment – a friendship that heals a wounded spirit), Osofisan teaches us that love humanises and aids survival and regeneration. Perhaps, because of his inimitable depth of understanding of human nature, human foibles and the intractability of the human character, I have found his friendship most priceless at critical climes of need. Many times, when certain human actions lead one to self-doubt and the abyss of cynicism, Osofisan has gently rekindled the spirit and made the world worth the while. And this to me, is the nerve-centre and forte of his creative vision – a recognition of the burden and ordeal of the artist, to search with the compass of tropes, images and narrative, for the creative and regenerative essence for a society in the throes of obsolescence, decadence and loss. Osofisan's life and works reveal the Herculean business of the artist, who is the arrow-head of sensitivity, compassion and the collective memory; to elucidate and paint the canvass of social pain as well as etch a visionary path towards communal healing and rebirth.

From the passionate anger and impatience of his early works such as *A Restless Run of Locusts* (1969) which denounces, with fiery outburst, the political elite which thrived on the betrayal, political thuggery and violence, which led to the fratricidal carnage that was raging at the time, to the profound materialist dialectics of *Morountodun* (1983) – a play I will always cuddle, as it offers a name to my first and only daughter, even to those plays which rattle the empyrean (fable and mythical) world to reconstruct new tales for the contemporary world, such as *Many Colours Make the Thunde –King* (1997) and *Twingle-Twangle A-Twynning Tale* (1995), Osofisan has consistently enlisted his art in the service of the down-trodden and alienated masses. Dialectics – the art of a consistent inquiry after truth, through (literary) discourse – is the creative weapon of this 'fabulous' aesthete and 'alchemist of cognition' – either in the darkness and half-light of the stage or through the rhythmic verse of performed poetry. The ardent message of his committed art is the urgent need for the 'wretched of the earth' – the mere pawns in the political elite's predatory game of 'hide and steal' – to liberate his/her consciousness, in readiness for the imminent and inexorable struggle for regeneration and social rebirth.

If the message is not new, and it is by all means not, the manner of telling – the rhetorical mechanics in its profound lucidity and lyrical eloquence – is uniquely distinct. In all his writing and of all genres, Osofisan is an instruction in the possibility of creating simply and profoundly. I have said elsewhere that Osofisan's literature is consciously and deliberately engaging, evocative and reachable. I have said that the artistry of Osofisan heads Nigerian literature towards the path that shuns obscurantism and impenetrability, in the manner in which they show us that literature need not be difficult to be high-cultural or elevated. Let me end this tribute by quoting from the *Foreword* which Osofisan privileged me to write for his latest volume of poetry – *Pain Remembers, Love Rekindles* – to restate my persuasion that accessibility, not propaganda or literary pugilism – is the forte of the political art of the artificer that we are celebrating:

> In this volume, we confront the wordsmith (Osofisan) who insists that you need not be archaic to be imagistic. The poet's diction compels the fulfilment of the pivotal requisites of serious poetry; the connotative and the denotative. For in these poems, the literary and the literal, the ordinary and the associative, the exact and the figurative, effortlessly mesh to produce the desired levels of meaning and social message (2000: ix).

As you celebrate a bee-busy and productive life at sixty, the challenges of society in a humbling state of flux, and to which you have devoted your entire life trying to fashion positive and creative and alternative to, are even more daunting and more deplorable. We rejoice in the fact that your creative arsenals are sharper, maturer and more eloquent – even if some think they are less combative. You lead, and must lead, us on to greater promise. Your compassion and genuine friendship is a source of inspiration for me and I believe, to hundreds of acolytes, whom you have adducted to your creative Muse.

Happy birthday, brother and soul-mate.

II

INTERVIEW

TALK WITH FEMI OSOFISAN, 1995*

VICTOR AIRE & KANCHANA UGBABE

AIRE & UGBABE: *Femi Osofisan, we would like, in this interview, to veer a bit from the beaten track and elicit from you information that has so far not received much publicity. Is that acceptable to you?*

OSOFISAN: Fine.

AIRE & UGBABE: *We notice that many of your plays so far have been published in Nigeria. Has this fact had any adverse effect on the fate of the books or on you as a writer?*

OSOFISAN: Yes, obviously. When I began writing seriously in the early nineteen-seventies, I and a couple of other writers, including Kole Omotoso, met in what we called the KOMFESS Artists and wrote a manifesto. One point was that we were not going to bother ourselves about the foreign audience or foreign publishers; that we were going to do our work exclusively in Nigeria. This came out of a number of things. We felt that we wanted to write the kind of literature that would have an impact on the society itself, on what was happening and that if we were thinking of foreign audiences or foreign publishers, we would necessarily be orienting our work toward that audience. And we didn't think that the kind of priorities that the foreign audiences want were the kind that our society needed. We felt that that was going to be a kind of distraction. So, you know, instead of concentrating on the themes that would benefit our own society, then we would be pandering to foreign audiences, whose interests at that time were mainly exotic. So, we took that decision. And the other reason of course was that, when the books were published abroad they were not readily available even in the country itself. They had to be imported and, if you were looking for these books, you had to go abroad to buy them. And we felt, no, this wasn't right. The reason why some of our people, at least those who came before us, were also publishing abroad was that the publishing situation in the country was also underdeveloped at the time. There weren't many publishers. But this was precisely why we felt we should then do our work at home, to help the development of the publishing industry too. You know, we had to provide the manuscripts at home. So, for a number of reasons, we took that decision. And for at least twenty years I kept within that decision and I didn't bother to look for foreign publishers. But of course, that had its effects, some positive, some negative. The thing of course was that, once the situation in the country began to

---

* Interview conducted on 18 June, 1995 at the Metropolitan Hotel in Tel Aviv, Israel, during the Conference on African Literature organized by the University of Tel Aviv, Israel.

deteriorate economically and politically, and so on, the disadvantages became more obvious. For instance, the books are still not available at home. Even if you go to the bookstore you hardly find the books because the publishers themselves have been going through all kinds of problems. I think they are not also adventurous enough. But, in any case, publishing itself has even worsened at home and books are not even available. You get very little in terms of royalties or none at all, anyway. Not many publishers are honest, you know. And then, plus the disadvantage that you are then not known abroad. Until recently when I began to operate abroad, for instance, many people only thought in terms of Soyinka and sometimes [John Pepper] Clark [Bekederemo]. Whereas we had been working for 20 years at home and had developed quite an audience at home. But, all the criticism and so on, you know, was on the older generation writers. Again for sometime, I thought about this. Maybe I am not right. There is also some factor which is a bit unfortunate in the sense that even our own critics at home tend to take their bearings from foreign critics. I mean in the sense that one began to get the impression that, if a foreign critic had not written about an author at home, then our own critics wouldn't think that author was worth writing about. Having done so much work at home and to find that there was very little critical attention being paid... Well, I thought the critics at home should be the ones to take the lead and let the foreign critics follow, at least, as it concerns our writings. But, it's just been the opposite and I can almost say that, until the foreign critics now began to rediscover us, even our own critics didn't think the work was worth writing about. So, you see, in that sense, it's been some kind of loss. And it's kind of made me modify my own stand now. This is why I am becoming more and more active outside the Nigerian environment.

AIRE & UGBABE: *Thank you, Femi. Have you since tried to vary your publishers? That is, reach out in terms of having more of your books published outside than inside?*

OSOFISAN: Well, if you look at the situation inside, you will find that there is hardly any notable publisher I haven't used. I kept moving from publisher to publisher because of this dissatisfaction with the distribution... And, it just didn't seem to improve. Well, so, of course, you know, I then decided to try outside publishers and last month a collection of my plays just came out from Howard University Press[1]. And last year[2], I had one of my prose works published by Heinemann. This was the Junior African Writers' Series, *Ma'ami* which I had done in a series... in *The Guardian*. So, obviously, you know, I am trying to reach out to foreign publishers now. I must say that, it's also a painful period to be doing this because, you see, there seems to be a lack of interest now in

---

[1] 1995. *The Oriki of a Grasshopper and Other Plays (with an introduction by Abiola Irele).* (Washington, D.C.: Howard University Press).

[2] 1994. *Ma'ami* . (Oxford: Heinemann Educational Publishers). [Serialised in *The Guardian*, 1988].

Africa. And the publishers are not... because, you see, they can't sell their books in Africa any more, except maybe in Zimbabwe or South Africa or someplace like that. Just because of the way our economy has been ruined almost virtually. The publishers find it difficult to sell their books in Nigeria or in West African countries. I got a manuscript turned down last year from Macmillan precisely because of this. They wrote that, well, we don't have accessibility to Nigerian markets again and we've decided that any story located in Nigeria now is not worth our while. They were honest enough to write me. I mean, I am sure most of the publishers in U.K. and elsewhere must have taken this kind of decision. So, it's become extremely difficult for unknown or not well-known writers to get onto those foreign publishers' lists now. So, in fact, it's very difficult times to be doing this. I am particularly worried about the younger writers, those who are not even known, they can't get published at home, they can't get published abroad. And so, what is going to happen?

AIRE & UGBABE: *Is there a dwindling interest in Africa in the Western world?*

OSOFISAN: Yes, because, once you have the situation in Russia and other Eastern countries, the interest seems to be moving in that way, you know, investments are moving that way. Then you have South Africa, this is a new market again. So, they are all moving there. West Africa, you know, it's a sad story. Why should we bother? So, they are just losing interest. Since we don't have the means to support ourselves, I don't know what we're going to do about the fate of literature.

AIRE & UGBABE: *You mentioned your prose work Ma'ami and I know you also wrote a prose text many years ago, Kolera Kolej. You also have Cordelia. What other prose works have you published?*

OSOFISAN: Not much really... You know I was trying to do an experiment with the newspapers. I felt that since the situation in publishing was deteriorating so much, maybe something yet could be done. So, we had to look for new ways of reasoning and I was thinking that, well, if the public will not come to literature, maybe literature should go to the public. And, since I had my column with *The Guardian*, I thought maybe I could try this out. For many years, I fought to have a fiction column in *The Guardian*. I couldn't, I didn't win this war. So, I just decided that, OK, I will turn my own column into a fiction column and see what will happen. This was what I did. Then I began the *Tales the Country told me* series and, starting with such short stories, I then thought, well, we could try a long story and *Ma'ami* was the first one which ran for seven weeks and it's an interesting story because, while it was running, there was no feedback at all. And I kept wondering, 'was this thing succeeding or wasn't it succeeding?' I didn't even know whether people were really reading the story... And there was the editor who kept telling me 'Look, when are you going to end this *Ma'ami*-Miami thing?' Apparently, he didn't even read it. And I thought, maybe he was reading it and he didn't like it. It was getting to the end of the year, anyway. So, I just said, well, OK, last week of the year, I will just end it, which was what I did. And it was then that the reactions came in. There was an avalanche of reactions from all over the place. I mean, it was quite astonishing, the response. So, I just said, Ok, maybe I should try this experiment again. So, the next one was *Cordelia*, which is now published by Malthouse. Then, I decided to become a bit more ambitious. I wanted to see how far we could go with this kind of serial in the newspaper. So, I decided to try *Wuraola for Ever*. And my plan was just to run for as many weeks as possible, to see when people would get tired of it. In fact, the response to this was even more rapid. Many people had now discovered my pen name, that I was the one writing the thing. So, I used to get prizes all over... and it was interesting, particularly in Lagos, people were discussing this woman as if she was real. And, you know, it went on for 27 weeks. I ended it abruptly because I was leaving *The Guardian* then. This was when we had problems with *The Guardian* and we all had to leave. But, it went on for 27 weeks. And then, you know, again, responses. Why did you stop this? People were not happy. So, anyway, when we moved to *The Times*, the editor said: 'Why don't you bring this thing back?' This was when we had some other problems with my column from the security agents and so on. Anyway, we decided to bring back the fiction thing. This was the time I tried the other story *Abigail* as a real experiment, taking a full page. So far, up till that time, it was a half page. This time, I said, OK, let's expand it and see what people would say. These were all, for me, experiments, to test how the public would react to it. And *Abigail*, you remember, ran for 35 weeks. Again, it ended when I had to leave *The Times* organisation. But it had a full page, running into 35 weeks. I learned from that also. In the end, it occurred to me that that was too long. Some people still followed the story passionately. But, I found that the audience gradually dwindled... So, if you ask me now, I would say it's better to do a half-page story and, maybe run it for some twenty weeks. That would probably make for a good story. So, these are the kinds of experiments I have done to see how we can get from journals and newspapers to literature.

AIRE & UGBABE: *Femi, coming to poetry, you once edited a journal at the University of Ibadan called Opon Ifa. And, in 1987, your collection of poetry, published under a pen name, won the Association of Nigerian Authors first prize for literature. Do you still write much poetry?*

OSOFISAN: Well, I still write poetry. My second collection was – is it last year or the year before? – called *Dream Seeker on Divining Chain*. But, poetry has been for me more or less a secondary thing. I don't really write much poetry. So, that first collection was more like a fluke. I didn't even think that I would ever publish that kind of poetry. It came by accident. Incidentally, it was because of Iowa. We were going to Iowa on this graduate programme and they asked us to bring anything to read. And I was thinking, how are you going to read plays if you don't have a cast? So, I began to hunt for all these small bits and pieces that I had been writing over the years and I put them together and had this collection *Minted Coins*. And it was while reading these poems in Iowa and in the USA generally that I came to find that people were interested in them. That was what encouraged me to send the thing in for publication. I was quite startled when the collection won the prize; it was quite surprising. And I did immediately try to write another one, of course, I couldn't. It's taken a number of years for me to do a second collection, which is now out. But, I don't think it's got much publicity really. With *Opon Ifa*, we couldn't continue it in the old format when we used to type the thing out ourselves, roll it out. It was too much energy. I mean, it had to stop. What I decided to do is to revive it in a now printed format and to expand it. It became *Opon Ifa Review* rather than just *Opon Ifa*. And it now includes short stories, plays, excerpts and the occasional essay. I felt very strongly about it because all these journals that used to publish creative writing are almost all dead. *Nigeria Magazine*, for instance, is gone. I felt that we needed at least a forum. So, we raised the money to publish at least the first number. Unfortunately, I have not been able to publish the second number, which has been ready for almost a year now. It has an interesting interview with Amos Tutuola[3] in Part II. But, you know, to raise money is the problem to support this journal. Because I paid for the whole issue myself; that was N17,800 then. And we haven't even sold three quarters of it. That is the problem with creative writing at the moment in the country, an enormous one.

AIRE & UGBABE: *Within the last few years, many of your fellow writers have left the country for greener pastures abroad. People like Kole Omotoso, Biodun Jeyifo, Isidore Okpewho, just to mention a few. What has kept you from joining this unfortunate exodus?*

OSOFISAN: Well, first of all, I have never felt totally comfortable outside the country. It's not that the pressure hasn't been there, a tremendous amount of pressure for us to relocate. As I said, if you look at the problem with publishing, what is the point in writing if you don't have an outlet for people to even read it? The cost of production is enormous. So, there is a lot of pressure to go out. However, as a creative artist, I am not quite sure how I can live outside the country, being away from the material which you are writing about. So, that's been a problem for me. I don't want to seem unduly heroic about this. It's been a deeper kind of response from me. I can quite appreciate the decision of those who have left. I mean, I can sympathise... So, I don't want to criticise that. What I have tried to do is to find a mid-way, wherein I can go abroad for a couple of months, do some work, earn some money and then come back and use that to support the family, because, as you know, the salaries we are being paid are so ridiculous, you can't support any family on that. I go abroad, do some work for a couple of months, come back, then I can renew my acquaintance with the realities on the ground with my primary material, with my primary audience. So, I can refresh myself when I come back. I guess that is a half-way solution I am going to follow as long as I am able to. I've always regarded exile as a last

---

3 Amos Tutuola died on 8 June, 1997 at the age of 77.

option which I am going to resist as much as possible. But, I'm not a martyr in any sense, and it's becoming increasingly difficult to educate the children. Not just in terms of money but even to get them a good education and, you know, when you look at their contemporaries, the kind of education they are getting and the kind that your children are getting... You know that you are not giving them a fair chance at all. So, you want to take them to places where they can have some better education. Then, you've got to be able to pay for them and to pay for it, you have to go and get a better job which means that you may have to relocate. So, these pressures are there. I haven't quite resolved these questions at all. But, so far, you know, I'm still one way in, one way out. I hope that can last me a while.

AIRE & UGBABE: *A number of critics have often referred to you as the foremost disciple of Wole Soyinka. Do you think that your career as a playwright may have been affected by Soyinka's shadow looming over yours?*

OSOFISAN: Well, I don't necessarily see his shadow looming over mine. He was a pioneer in Nigerian writing (in general) and, therefore, his example was there for us to follow. Yes, definitely, I have been influenced by him and I have been inspired by his work and I continue to be inspired by such works as his. The question of being overshadowed – I personally don't see it that way. Somebody begins, other people follow and... it's like the sky, it is large enough for many birds to fly without colliding. I take it that it is only the most dim-witted critics who would be trying to make unnecessary fuss out of... somebody's there, therefore other people can't come in because... (laughter). So, it's a vast landscape. I think we were fortunate to have somebody like Soyinka in our cultural life and to have had the kind of influence that he continues to exert. But, I have moved beyond that; I started under his influence, under his inspiration, and I think I have developed my own voice. However, I am not at all worried about his overshadowing me at all.

AIRE & UGBABE: *Thank you very much. Now, like Wole Soyinka, you write with a profound knowledge of Yoruba culture and literature. Can you throw some light on the role that myth, in general, plays in your drama?*

OSOFISAN: Well, the thing is that, you know, I think that this is a way of rooting yourself within your own particular environment. If you take just the simple fact that we write in English. English has become a universal language. How do you then distinguish between a story that is located somewhere in England, in some remote village in England, or somewhere in America and so on, you know. I take it that, one way to really define the characters is to root them within the particular culture that we are dealing with. I mean, when we talk of Ogun or Obatala or Sango, it is obvious who we are, who the characters are. You know they are not Englishmen. So, I am sure, for me that's a very important aspect of things. The other thing of course is that our culture, the Yoruba culture has been one of the most resilient. Usually, when you go to the diaspora, I find it fascinating, to explore this, explore parts of it. Of course, this is a problem for me because I am essentially a materialist. So, my own approach to this culture has no religious basis at all. It is purely ideological in terms of defining identities, not more than that. The gods and goddesses for me are just like basic metaphors, not any kind of superstitious hold or anything. It's a way of anchoring myself within the tradition, within the tradition of my people, redefining our own identities but, without any slavish or metaphysical attachment to this.

AIRE & UGBABE: *Does this have something to do with your own personal rootedness in your own culture, as a child, drawing from that?*

OSOFISAN: Again, you see, one doesn't want to emphasise this too much. Obviously, we grew up in an environment where these things were still very much alive. Ogun worship in my own grandfather's compound, our going out with the masquerades, running around, all kinds of things like that were still very much part of our own reality. Even take the question of moonlit night where we told fairy tales and so on. Now, all that has disappeared. Take my children now, who are growing up on the campus, they are completely alienated from this. And one regrets it. One regrets how you have the satellite and television age. People have lost this background to their own culture. But, again, you must think that we were always the generation that went to school and went to Christian schools and many of these things also vanished. By the time we really began to grow up into our really important years, we were already within the Christian perspective. So, we were also the ones losing these things and being alienated from them. So, it has been a conscious return for me and I really have to re-educate myself. It's not simply that it comes from knowledge that I already have, but that I have to explore, I have to do research. And some of it has been very, very fascinating for me, just rediscovering this thing. I have separated myself from Soyinka's own Ogun in his own central image, the Ogun god, for specific reasons. I take it that, even his own Ogun is a dual character, representing creativity and destructiveness, the warrior and the poet. It's mainly the warrior aspect that is emphasised and, for me, I think the warrior image has had too much run in African history. We were always emphasising the role of warriors, the warrior-leader. And I think, in a sense, this is what has made for the career of some of the dictators that we have in our present world. That martial image and so on has dominated our politics and wrecked it. These soldiers who are seizing power all the time. Whereas, I take it that the really positive contributors in any culture are not the warriors who are destroyers. We have doctors, engineers, pharmacologists and so on. And I think we haven't paid much attention to this in our own history. We are always searching for warriors. We have our local medicine, the herbs and the leaves to cure several diseases and we haven't paid much attention to that. And it pains me, because what then seems to happen is that we say that science technology, these are all foreign things, that they are not African. I mean, it's very annoying to me, because, who were those who discovered those herbs, how did they discover them? They must have gone through experiments and so on. But, if you read the Ifa corpus, it begins to give you an idea of what our people used to do. Because the knowledge of pharmacology, for instance, is in Ifa from the start and all kinds of things. I take Ifa like an encyclopaedia, where all that knowledge is stored. People were very superstitious through oral history, they had to memorise these things. But, if you read these things, you find a lot of details of scientific knowledge. And so, you know, science is not alien to us. It was just that it wasn't available to everybody. It's just like in the West too. The monasteries and so on were the ones who were doing all these things. It wasn't available to everybody. It was a certain period that knowledge was made general and so on and many people had access to it. This was what was prevented here by the coming of the colonialists. The democratisation of knowledge had not taken place. But that is different from saying that our people didn't carry out experiments, they didn't even know... They built these houses with these architectural roofs, with these conical roofs, which, as you know, are so appropriate to these windy areas. When the storm comes, it doesn't carry off the roof; it just goes round it. Now, we just build these flat roofs, the wind comes and carries the thing away. Or, for example beans, we had all kinds of ways of preserving food. When we ground beans to make *akara* when I was growing up, you just take a piece of charcoal and you put it there and that would preserve the thing from getting spoilt. I mean, who discovered it? How did they find it? And it's a very cheap thing, you don't have to go and buy a fridge or anything. So, all kinds of knowledge available in our own traditional set-up which came through, you know, testing, experimentation and so on. It wasn't called science then. It was called something else. This is why I have made Ifa a more central principle in my own works. That we should begin to find a way from warriors and political leaders. We opened a newspaper, this was something we were trying to do in *The Guardian*, trying to shift the focus away from just the political and military leaders into the more positive areas where people are making contributions in medicine, in architecture, in literature in things like that. And I believe that Ifa corpus represents that as the central image. That's what I have shifted to in my own work.

AIRE & UGBABE: *But you agree that there should be a complementarity between the martial aspect and the creative aspect, right?*

OSOFISAN: Yes, but you find something... You find that, on the divining tray, you always have Esu there. There is a complementarity already implied in Ifa. Because the Esu principle is there. That is the Esu thing, that is the spirit of destruction, the spirit of questioning, of challenging and so on, you know, the trickster image. So, there is always, already, embodied in that Ifa thing, that other aspect of overturning tradition, of questioning orthodoxy, of tricking and so on, you know, signifying upon. So, you see, it's already there. The thing is that it's got a different emphasis in the Ogun image. That emphasis, of course, Ogun is part of the old pantheon and you can't ignore him. But you have to remember that Esu is there at the entrance of every shrine. Esu is always there. And the complementarity is Orunmila, he is always there too. It's not that you just have Orunmila. So, the question of disruption, constant questioning, revolution – Esu is a revolutionary principle, he is already there. But, after that, it's not just overturning for its own sake, of killing just for the sake of power. But here, it's for knowledge. The thing is you question and all the rest, but then you learn from it and then you come out with a certain knowledge, with something that is useful, that is positive for the progress of the community.

AIRE & UGBABE: *Could you elaborate a bit more on the dangers of subordinating the creative to the martial for too long, if we can now come closer home?*

OSOFISAN: It's not a question of subordination. This is not what I mean. What I mean is this. You see, the pantheon draws up quite a number of icons, different gods and each one is necessary to the life of the overall community. There is none that is not necessary. The Yorubas have 401 deities. Every day of the year, a different god is celebrated and there is none that is not important, that you can just ignore. Each one represents a certain value in the community. But the point is that you mustn't give too much precedence to a particular one. So, it's not that in any community, you can ignore political leaders, ignore military leaders. You know, you haven't even begun to understand politics if you think you can ignore all these people. But, how much attention do you pay to them? How do you now make them supreme? You are a somebody just because you can shoot guns, assume leadership of the community without any brains, no knowledge, nothing. Just because he controls the trigger, therefore he can now dictate to people who are older and who are more experienced and who have had knowledge. You create them into a certain myth that then encourages them into seizing power and all that.

AIRE & UGBABE: *Continuing with what you were saying concerning myths, you have drawn generously on the Yoruba myths and the resources of female power in Morountodun. We haven't seen a strong woman in your plays since then. How do you reconcile myths with modern reality? What are your views on that?*

OSOFISAN: Well, I don't know.... In fact, I have just finished an adaptation of *Antigone*, which I call *Tegonni*, which was done in Emory last October [1994], where the central character is female. And also, the play which was commissioned by the Guthrie theatre in Minneapolis[4]. Although that's on Sango, but you have Oya and Osun who are two strong characters there. So, it depends, I have different types of strong women. It depends on the play. In fact, it is not correct that I haven't had strong women since *Morountodun*. But, what was the question you asked about?

AIRE & UGBABE: *How do you reconcile the mythic cult of strong women with modern reality?*

---

[4] 2003. *Many Colours Make the Thunder-King*. (Ibadan: Opon Ifa Readers).

OSOFISAN: O.K. You know, the thing is that... Look at our society and... I am some kind of feminist, I mean, I believe that a lot of our culture is weighted against the women. But that doesn't mean that all of it is... but, a lot of cultures is weighted against women and I, looking at the Yoruba culture, I find it a strange thing, because there have always been very strong women in Yoruba culture. At the same time, I know there is a bias against strong women, because they are easily demonised. They are the ones who are referred to as witches. The thing is, once they begin to challenge certain powers in the community, I guess.... But, you see, my feeling is that that is not necessarily just a female thing. I just take it that once the contest for power began, people who're, who we now referred to as rebels, people who have a different vision from the orthodox vision and all the rest.... it was a useful way of dealing with them, by just saying that they were witches and wizards and... If somebody discovered electricity for example; we are used to electricity so much now, but if somebody, if you look at somebody discovering that in an age where, you know, people.... You know, they will get frightened about this person and they would say he must be a witch or a wizard. But, I just think that, at a certain period, women began to have the worst of this, and that some of it has survived till now, that women get discriminated against in many, many areas. And to the point where some of the women have even come to accept it, to accept their own inferiority as normal. And this is not what they should be doing and anybody who does it is not even a woman because they themselves, because the women themselves have accepted this and defend it. So, what I decided to do in creating my own women is to provide a different model and then inserting these things within the tradition, just to show that this is not something new. The argument – there is always a strong argument – that when you are trying to change things, they say this is not African, this is something from abroad. You are being a traitor to your own tradition and all the rest of it. But, you see, then, I take these mythical figures who themselves are representatives of the culture and who have challenged orthodoxies and fought for their own freedom and so on, you know... So, for me, they become a model for the kinds of women in the new society, the kind of attitude that I think some women should take. So, that is the sense where I create these figures or recreate them or take a different reading of mythologies that were inherited. I think I was just saying how I conceived my own adaptation of figures in Yemoja who becomes the real mother-principle, the original essence... She is the one who sends out her daughters from time to time. This is why you have many Antigones. Each Antigone at a specific time in history, where there is oppression, injustice or tyranny. She then sends out one of her daughters who becomes the opposing principle, who now then confronts that dictator and leads to his fall. So, this is what really happens. So, this is why you have many Antigones in history, one after the other. At least this is how I saw it. So, there is this woman Tegonni during the colonial period of British colonialism in the early years of colonialism, in 1895. She confronts the Governor. So, again, you see that strong woman in there.

AIRE & UGBABE: *Thank you. One of your plays is called Who's afraid of Solarin? What was your relationship with the late activist and what did you set out to do in the play?*

OSOFISAN: Well, you know that Solarin was regarded in many circles as a morally upright, courageous and outspoken individual. Not that he didn't have his failings, but that sense of an outspoken moralist who also had his positive views about the direction society should take. He was appointed the Public Complaints Commissioner of the Western State... And even though the whole thing was meant to be a charade, he took it very seriously and he began to hunt down all these corrupt officials. Of course, he didn't last long. He was manipulated out. He had stood for that kind of anti-corruption crusade. And when I was adapting Gogol's *Inspector Kol*, it seemed appropriate to name the play after him, particularly at that period when he was embattled, when he was being made to resign his job. And I wanted to call attention to that and so I used his name as a moral principle in this local government. Of course, the local government was just merely representative of the whole military government then in the country. In fact, when we first did the play, we were going to have problems, because it was felt that it was the State Governor that I had targeted. I found it funny then that if he felt targeted, maybe he was doing some of the things... So, this is why I named the play after him at least as a remembrance of that fight that he carried out once, and a kind of cleansing principle for our society. And, of course, I had a very cordial relationship with him before he died. At least to some extent. That is why I gave it that title. But it also has an alternative title of course – *Waiting for the Commissioner*. I had been thinking of reworking the last title just because of the international audiences who may not be familiar with Solarin.

AIRE & UGBABE: *You are generally considered as a committed writer. What have you done in this capacity to affect the lives of your fellow Nigerians, particularly given the current climate, given the economic situation? What have you done to invigorate other writers?*

OSOFISAN: This is a very big question and it is not one that you can easily answer in any categorical sense. How has one influenced or impacted on other people? Well, you know, it's not the writer himself who can answer this. I guess it's the people who have been influenced who can say so and say, well, you have influenced this way or the other. What one has done... Obviously if you put a play on stage, people are coming to watch and you get reactions from them. So, in a sense, by doing these plays around, this is the intention to have a certain impact on society. How has that impact been, I don't know. But, what I can say is that, at least for a number of years now, there is no month, absolutely, when a play of mine is not being done in that country. In fact, in any month at all, more than two or three are being done in some places. And I find that completely pleasing. Many of the times, I don't even know. I just arrive and they say 'Oh, we've just done this play or we are doing this play'. I have just seen an announcement coming here now that there is a play being done at the Maison de

France in Lagos. They don't even tell me. But on all campuses and Television Stations and Cultural Centres, these plays are being done. That means that they must have some kind of influence or some impact on some people. So, in that sense, maybe you can draw from that and say 'yes, there has been some effect or consequence.' Then, one would like to point out that you can't achieve everything on the stage. If you have a kind of concern, of course, the stage can only reach a certain limited number of people. If you have to come and watch the play, it depends on how the play is done and all kinds of things. It is precisely because of this that one is active in other fields. For instance, if you write in the newspapers, you are hoping to reach a wider set of people. You write novels, you teach in the classroom, you give lectures around. So, it's not just one activity, it's a series of combinations. So, it's not as if you hope that you write one play, and then you are going to get a revolution right from that. You are active on that front, you take other fronts. Other people are active on other fronts. And, for me, it's a combination of all these things that will finally lead to a desired change. This is why I am not particularly bothered when people come and say, 'you've written this play, what have you achieved, which legislation have you changed, what revolution have you caused and all that.' It's a question of sowing ideas. When you do this, through various means, sometimes it's a poem you write, sometimes, it's a novel, sometimes, it's a short story. But, behind it all is a governing ideal, a certain vision that you have and that you are just trying to share. I have also taken the trouble to promote the works of other writers, particularly younger writers. This is why I created *Opon Ifa*, for instance. This is why I edit journals. It is partly why I went to the newspapers. When we went to start *The Guardian*, it was because I was already worried, I was concerned already about the lack of outlet for creative works and other activities when I went to the newspaper. And you will see that we did give a lot of attention to creative works and to criticism in *The Guardian* which we then also took to the *Daily Times*. And, you do that and then you see how the thing spreads. Not just what you do, but what you encourage others to do, or what others learn from you and begin to do. So that, at least now, the quality will not be very high, but there is hardly any newspaper that doesn't publish poetry, give at least some space to poetry or has an arts review page. The quality may be uneven and all that, but at least we've got that side going, so that the thing just doesn't die. We used to give front page space to news about the arts, just to raise the importance and to encourage people to think about this area, the valid area. So, in various ways, one has made his contributions here and there, to give importance to this area and make an impact on society. But, as I said, it's others who can now come and give a feedback and say 'yes, you have succeeded in this or that.'

AIRE & UGBABE: *Thank you. In fact, I think the next question links up with that, what you just said. You may choose not to respond. What are your personal thoughts on the present situation in Nigeria?*

OSOFISAN: I can respond. All I say is that I am just as confused as anybody. Which is partly why I have not resumed my journalistic work for sometime. There have been so many editors who have wanted me to come and resume my column and I haven't. I can say that I don't feel enlightened at all about the present situation. You can see what we have and it's not just the fact of a military government in this age and time. It's an unenlightened military government that we have which is just interested in power. Now, the fact is that I am not... my anger is not against the military government so much as the people who make this possible. It's not as if this military government just came from the blues. This came as a result of the political situation. We've got a ruling class composed of politicians, intellectuals, soldiers and so and so forth. It's this ruling class that baffles me. The way I read the present situation, the military was in complete retreat. The military had been defeated. Even to the point where they themselves were saying that military government cannot rule any more, we don't want military government. Even the military were saying it. And at the point of defeat when the military itself was in rout, that's when you have some of the progressive leadership, people who had confronted [General Ibrahim] Babangida, who had even put their lives at stake, who could not be bribed, suddenly decided to team up and give power to the military. [Lateef] Jakande, [Olu] Onagoruwa, [Ebenezer] Babatope... [Baba Gana] Kingibe himself. These were the people who had stood up and defended a civilian government, who had defended the right of a civil society to take over power from the military. And these were the people who now went and virtually surrendered at a time when it was just not necessary. So, how does one interpret it? If it was money they wanted, Babangida was ready to give them money. If it was power, he was ready to share power with them, but they said no, and fought Babangida to the point where he could no longer stay. He had to go. But, at the same time, all these people now went and threw themselves at the feet of [General Sani] Abacha. Now, how do you explain it? Was it a question of just the personality? Was it just Babangida's personality that they didn't like or what was it? I take it that it wasn't that, but that they thought that they could manipulate Abacha and went to team up with him, which means that they themselves were just power mongers. And so, of course, the man outplayed them. But, in the process of outplaying them, it is the civil society that loses and that has lost. And, when you say people are now not protesting... it's because people are confused. Who could they now trust, who are they supposed to team up with? So, what I mean is that, what we have is a current state of paralysis and I don't really see us getting out of this, because we've got to create a new leadership entirely. And it's so difficult when there are so many people who have made such loud noises who have been trusted and have let the people down. There's a search now... people are confused and I'm just as confused. That is why I have not written anything, because to write something, it means that you need to say something that at least will have some sense, that will shed some new light on the situation. I don't have anything new, I am just looking... you just don't know who to trust anymore. And so, because the personalities themselves represent these ideals, these ideals themselves have failed. People now have to fight for themselves. What can you get out of this? There is so much cynicism. So, it's going to take a while before we can get beyond this. And this is why the military government is going to endure. It's not just the military; it's all the people who are collaborating with them. There is a lot of collaboration, because people now say, well that is the order of the day, just make your own and get out of the place, that's all. It's a terrible stage for any nation to be going through.

AIRE & UGBABE: *Thank you. This question concerns the Association of Nigerian Authors. At the Makurdi 1988 Convention of the Association of Nigerian Authors, you were elected the President of the Association. Another playwright was elected the secretary. It seemed like a match made in heaven and we all expected a lot from your executive. But things didn't seem to have worked out. What happened?*

OSOFISAN: Well, I don't know. When you say things haven't worked out, it's relative. I can count the achievements we made. For instance, the *ANA Review* which we raised to 40 pages with substantial news about the Association and other people's works and which we gave out free of charge. The thing of course is that ANA itself has a lot of problems. We have no funding whatsoever to run it. You have to remember that we want one association for writers, there is no money to run it, there is no subvention from anybody. The writers themselves don't have much money to contribute. So, you are running around searching for help here and there. And this is further limited by the fact that the places where you can even get money from are few. Most of the people who have money are the kind that ANA will not like to associate with, because you know where they got this money from. So, how do you then run an association without money? I was particularly concerned about the younger people who don't have money. You can jerk up the association's fees, the membership fees and say, okay, each person must pay N5,000 so that you can have money to run the association. Immediately you do that, you throw out so many of the younger people. In any case, the older writers who even can pay this thing, how many are they? So, ANA has a lot of problems with financing. We don't have any kind of support from whosoever. But, we tried our best. The whole ANA story ended, of course, quite unhappily. Some allegations were being made... You keep sacrificing so much of your time and energy and then you get the unfortunate case of some people who are not happy and would now want to destroy your name and all that. But, by and by, I am satisfied with what I did in ANA and what I tried to achieve for the association.

AIRE & UGBABE: *What is the Association doing about the fate of Ken Saro-Wiwa, a former president?*

OSOFISAN: I personally don't know. I must say that I don't really know much about what is going on nowadays. You know that Ken's case is particularly difficult to do anything about other than insisting that the trial be done, which is now being done. If it was when he was detained and you didn't know what was happening, you could write protests and so on. And ANA has tried to solicit outside help from various associations who have kept writing in and so on... You see, again, if ANA had money, it would try to support the trial. ANA doesn't have money. So, this is our problem. I think that, beyond just keeping up the public awareness, keeping up public attention on the case, I don't see much else that ANA can do[5].

AIRE & UGBABE: *You once did a stint at the University of Benin as a Professor of drama. There seems to have been a slight controversy about your stay in Benin City. What is the truth of the matter?*

OSOFISAN: The truth is simply that I don't think that I really want to discuss it anymore. This issue seems to me to have been slightly overflogged. I accept it's normal that when you try to bring change or effect progress in any place, you must have opposition. So, I had the usual opposition and I did my best to confront that opposition.

AIRE & UGBABE: *Now, taking you back to your school days. I know that you attended Government College, Ibadan. Did your years there play a role in preparing you for your career as a writer?*

OSOFISAN: Yes, certainly, I think so. At the Government College, our Principal, Derek Bullock, was very much interested in drama and organised these annual shows which he did with girls schools, Saint Theresa's College, Ibadan and then Yejide Girls Grammar School, at Ede [Queen's College, Ede]. And then Saint Anne's [Molete, Ibadan]. So, there were a lot of dramatic activities by Derek Bullock and then there were the activities at the University itself and then at the Mbari Club. So, a lot of things happening in Ibadan which I think generated my own interest in these areas. But, it wasn't that I was particularly focused on drama at the time. It was after I had reached the University, particularly when I began to orientate my own research on drama that I began to focus more and more on drama. In fact, the first work that I published was a novel, a short novel called *Kolera Kolej*.

AIRE & UGBABE: *Femi, you hold a B.A. and a doctorate degree in French literature. How can you reconcile that background and training with your career as a playwright writing in English and a professor of drama or as a writer in general.*

OSOFISAN: French... no big deal about it. French is just a language and what you use the language for is what is important. I owe a lot to French authors like Jean-Paul Sartre and so on. The atmosphere of literary activities in France, in Paris, the artistic atmosphere is very strong and very invigorating, very inspiring. You go round the town and you see statues of writers, painters and artists; you see their houses preserved. There is so much given in French life to culture, so much attention that it really inspires you. But, you see, what will be

---

5 Ken Saro-Wiwa was hanged, along with eight other Ogoni activists, on 10 November, 1995.

the point living in Nigeria and writing in French? So, I began to write more and more in English. I decided in fact not to write in French at all. Obviously, conflicts began to mount about my own professional life and the kind of literary activity I wanted to engage in. So, I began to feel slightly alienated from the French Department. And the biggest problem I had was the orientation of the Department. I felt that if we had a French Department in Nigeria, anywhere in Nigeria, its great emphasis should be on the French-speaking countries surrounding us. And I felt that if something were to happen in Mali, for example and somebody said that, okay there is something happening and he wants to find out, where would he go? I felt that the first place he should come to should be the French Department to say, 'oh, this thing is happening in Mali, tell me more about it. This something in Senegal, what is it?' The establishment did not see this. I tried to struggle for this, that we should begin to change the emphasis of the Department, to put more emphasis on the countries surrounding us, speaking French, not on France. Of course, this wasn't a popular idea particularly as the funding was coming more and more from France. Nowadays, I think the situation has changed because France itself has distanced itself; she doesn't have any money to pay anymore, so the country is having to find its own money. But, you see, this issue, I felt very strong about it and I just felt that it was an issue I couldn't win and it increased my alienation from the French Department. So, when I had an invitation to come to the Theatre Department... Actually, all along, from the beginning of my teaching career at the University of Ibadan, I was teaching in three different Departments. Not just French, I taught in French, but I also taught in English and I taught in Theatre Department. So, for six, seven years, I was teaching in three Departments and only getting paid in one. But, I was enjoying it until I then began to concentrate more on my own work and I felt more and more alienated from the French Department. And the two Departments, English and Theatre, then invited me to come over and I simply made a choice. I decided to go to Drama instead of English. I suppose I could have chosen English too. That is what really happened. But, I still keep my interest in French Literature and in French cultural life and that is very important.

AIRE & UGBABE: *So, your interest has been wide-ranging from what we've heard. Now, is the real Osofisan, the actor, the writer, or the theatre director?*

OSOFISAN: Well, I don't know which is the real Osofisan. I think Osofisan is all of this. It's an interesting thing about my work in theatre. I would rather just be a writer. The work on the stage is extremely interesting. The rapport with actors and so on. But, really, I am first and foremost just a writer. What takes me to the stage is just the nature of plays. You know, a play is not really a play until it has been done on stage. You could write all the words down and they may look beautiful, but when you get on the stage, they may not work at all and you have to remove all those beautiful words and rewrite, or sometimes even change the dialogue to music, write songs. So, for me, the directing is simply a part of writing. I take a play on stage. I direct all my plays myself, I direct the first production. But, that's because that's part of the writing process. So, I would rather just stand back and write and not do any other thing. This is just the way that I complete my own scripts. That's why as an actor, when you do that, you are obliged to also form a company. In our country, you have to do everything, you have to do the producing, you have to look for the funding, you have to recruit the team – you are everything. It's unfortunate. This is part of the advantage of working abroad, because you can leave the other parts to the other people to do their own work. You can just write the script and watch. But, one is ambivalent about that because, again, as I said, the life with actors is something very, very interesting, that whole aspect. So, I guess I will continue to do everything. But, I would rather just write scripts.

AIRE & UGBABE: *You see the work from its conception, giving birth to it.*

OSOFISAN: Yes.

AIRE & UGBABE: *Finally, Femi. We are all here in Tel Aviv, Israel, for a historic conference. Do you have any thoughts on the conference that you want to share with us: expectations impact...?*

OSOFISAN: The world is changing all the time. Being in Israel, I take it is a very important thing in itself. That African literature is being taken seriously in Tel Aviv is an important thing. We too are, I am hoping also to discover Israeli literature and Israeli theatre. This is something you just do not know. We are so Eurocentric, inevitably, I suppose, because of our colonial history. We know what is going on in Europe, at least what we are told is going on. We have now discovered America. But most often, other places, Asia, the Far East, the Mediterranean... So, coming to Israel is very, very important, I am excited by it. I hope that I will be able to learn much about what is going on at the same time they too will know what we are doing. The more we share knowledge about ourselves, obviously, the better the world will be.

OSOFISAN: *We thank you very much, Femi Osofisan, for giving us your time and responding with honesty and vigour to our questions. We wish you more power to your elbow and we hope that we shall continue to have the opportunity of meeting you and talking to you. Thank you very much.*

OSOFISAN: Thank you.

III

ESSAYS

ANTIGONE AND AFTER *ANTIGONE*: SOME ISSUES RAISED BY FEMI OSOFISAN'S DRAMATURGY IN *TEGONNI*

JAMES GIBBS

Over the years, Femi Osofisan has found himself being asked to write plays by friends, students, or theatre companies. In looking for inspiration to satisfy this demand, he has often matched himself with or against those who have preceded him in the theatre. He feels that he has the right to 'steal' ideas and plots, and demonstrates the ability to transform what he purloins. Relationships between him and his 'sources' have sometimes been quite simple, but on occasions the assured, creative artist has shown great originality in manipulating material[1]. This quality is on display in *Tegonni: an African Antigone* in which he uses a complex dramaturgical approach to take unawares his campus-based target audience and provoke a response.

Over the creative decades Osofisan the playwright has taken ideas from the theatres of different ages and continents. The list of those he has 'robbed' includes Gogol (*Who's Afraid of Tai Solarin?*, with a glance in choosing the title at Edward Albee, 1978), Feydeau (*Midnight Hotel*, 1982), Soyinka (*No More the Wasted Breed*, 1983), Clark-Bekederemo (*Another Raft*, 1987), Chekhov (*The Engagement*, 1991), Dickens (*One Legend, Many Seasons*, 2001), Shakespeare (versions of *Hamlet* and *Coriolanus*), and Euripides (*The Women of Owu*)[2]. From his writing it is clear that, on the level of dramaturgy, his engagement with Bertolt Brecht has been extensive, and he has also defined himself in relation to Augusto Boal and Antonin Artaud. Osofisan's use of Sophocles and the classical tradition is particularly subtle and complex in *Tegonni*, his *African Antigone*, a play that takes to a new level the interaction between contemporary Nigerian playwrights and the classic texts.[3] As a playwright, his most characteristic and individualistic strategy is that of the ambush: over and over again, he shocks and surprises his audience.

In linking up with a classical source, Osofisan placed himself in a distinguished tradition of those working in the Nigerian theatre who have responded to the power of classical texts. He also put himself in the tradition of political writers who have drawn on the Greeks. Geoffrey Axworthy produced of a double-bill of

---

[1] Osofisan has described how he wrote *A Restless Run of Locusts* 'on demand', see foreword to that play. He described himself as 'an incorrigible plagiarist' and spoke about writers stealing when being interviewed by Biodun Jeyifo. Osofisan, 2001: 230.

[2] For lists of Osofisan's plays see Adesola Adeyemi, and collections of Osofisan's plays from Opon Ifa.

[3] This paper should be seen as a sequel to the paper on 'Antigone's African Sisters' that I presented at a conference on the Classics in Post-Colonial Worlds, Birmingham, May 2004. In that I considered productions and adaptations of *Antigone* in the Gold Coast / Ghana, 1932-2004.

Antigones (Sophocles and Anouilth) at University College, Ibadan. Among those who attended was John Pepper Clark (Bekederemo) whose work has sometimes been seen as reflecting Classical influence or reflecting cultural coincidences between the Mediterranean and West Africa (Clark 1964). Axworthy is reported to have said that 'there is no doubt that (the productions) may have influenced some of his plays... I think (Clark) was aware of and attracted by the starkness and power of Greek Tragedy.' (Yerimah 1984: 42.) The Anouilth version, written for performance in Paris during the German occupation, showed other dramatists what could be done by transferring the Greek original into a different context. It provided an example for those interested in adaptations and in using the theatre to challenge their contemporaries. The image of German officers sitting through Anouilth's play as a celebration of French / Classical culture while the Parisian audience behind them revelled in the attack on Nazism embodied in the play is one that, I suspect, Osofisan would relish.

There is acknowledged influence from the classics in *Aikin Mata*, the translation and adaptation of *Lysistrata* that Tony Harrison and James Simmons wrote as Nigeria slithered towards Civil War. And there are political comments on various levels in Ola Rotimi's response to *Oedipus Rex* (*The Gods are not to Blame*), and in Wole Soyinka's *Bacchae of Euripides* (1973) and *Oyedipo at Kholoni*. Despite this evidence of creative interaction and political commentary with the classics, voices have been raised that have deplored the influence of Greek drama on West Africa. 'The Tragic Influence of Shakespeare and the Greeks' was the title of a conference paper delivered at the University of Ife in 1975 by Ime Ikiddeh. From extracts quoted by Kofi Agovi, it seems Ikiddeh argued that during the colonial period the British employed the theatre, including the plays of Sophocles, as part of an 'organised policy of cultural dissemination' in order to subvert and divert genuine cultural nationalist movements. (Agovi 1990). The reference to the 'tragic influence' summed up the perception. The Ikiddeh/ Agovi argument would seem to be for cultural isolationism, in line with that taken by Chinweizu and the Neo-Tarzanists. The strongest riposte to this myopic point of view is provided by the plays just mentioned and by *Tegonni*: they show abundant evidence of the power unleashed by the interaction of two traditions.

Inevitably, scholars have followed in the footsteps of the creative writers, and several studies have been written that investigate why and how the classics have been used by African dramatists. In the van among the published critics in this field are Martin Owusu and Kevin Wetmore, and the latter has devoted some space to *Tegonni.*

In this paper, I look briefly at some of the issues raised in the play that I see as illustrating Osofisan's independence of thought and characteristic dramaturgy. I direct particular attention to the benefits he draws from engaging with

Sophocles' play and with Shelley's 'Ozymandias'. I suggest that in *Tegonni*,[4] Osofisan incorporates *Antigone* parallels in a complex dramaturgy with confidence and authority. He creates a situation characterised by the 'approximate duplicates' that allows him to present a wide-ranging discussion about tyranny, the relative merits of decrees, and the response expected by those with principles. Antigone is presented as the twin revolutionary sister of Tegonni. They are united across continents and ages in defiance of tyranny; one in a Shelleyan confidence that oppression will be overthrown.

The 'complex dramaturgy' referred to includes a witty, deliberately confusing historical context designed to deny the audience the comfort of knowing precisely when the play is set. Various, sometimes conflicting items of evidence concerning the date are produced. For example, the British raise a toast to Queen Victoria so, using that evidence and reading the play as a conventional drama, it *must* be set during her reign. (62). That is to say between 1837 and 1901. However, we also gather that the action takes place after the punitive campaign against Benin, that is to say some time after 1897. This reference is found in the central exchange between the Governor and Tegonni and is worth quoting. The Governor says: 'You're young, but I'm sure you've heard about what happened to the great Benin City.' (116) Put this way it must be taken to suggest that the punitive campaign happened several years 'ago'. Yet there was no time for this, there were only four years between the raid and the end of Victoria's reign!

To reinforce this sense of temporal confusion, we learn that Governor Carter-Ross had earned the nick-name 'Slap-My-Face' in the railway construction camps (86). If this refers to construction camps for the Lagos-Ibadan line then it can only be dated to between 1898 and 1901. That is to say, to near the very end of Victoria's reign. These and other points of historical reference set the brain racing to no avail except to expose the unsatisfactory nature of this plodding investigation. As readers or members of an audience, we have two options: we can convict Osofisan of being a careless historian and an incompetent stage craftsman. Or, and this is the option I take, recognise that he is evoking circumstances rather than chronicling events. He scatters references in order to suggest, and he is not afraid to disconcert. Osofisan's desire in establishing these circumstances is to subvert precise expectations. He does this in order to generate discussion about the experience of oppression as a result of British colonial activities. Quintessentially, the activities referred to took place while the Queen who was also Empress of India was on the throne, and typically they included pacification campaigns and laying down railways. All these reference

---

[4] Wetmore works from the version of *Tegonni* used for the premier in Atlanta (1994). I have had access to only the script that was used for the Ibadan production of some four years later (November 1998) and was published by Opon Ifa in 1999. All references are to that text. It is not clear how greatly the texts differ, but the optional Prologue might have been an addition, prompted by the scarcity or absence of white actors in Nigeria. 'Jones' seems, from an interview with Osofisan, to have had the 'more Sophoclean' name 'Herman' in the earlier version. (Osofisan, 2001: 216.) The same source refers to a more substantial alteration: the 'elimination of the racist theme' f.n. 221.

points are established in *Tegonni* and point to it being set *in the colonial period* – that is the point.

Osofisan shows that he wants to provoke and engage his audience by other means as well. These include the names of the some of the characters. He handles these to prompt intellectual engagement, to challenge, test and demand a response from his target audiences. The names found in the list of characters include 'Lt. Gen. Carter-Ross' who is described as the 'British governor of the colony of Nigeria'. For those familiar with Western Nigerian colonial history, this double-barrelled name brings together that of Sir Gilbert *Carter,* with that of Capt. W. A. *Ross* The former was a hard-line Governor of Lagos, who was responsible for despatching the military expedition that defeated the Ijebu in 1892, and is immortalised (more positively) in the name of a bridge. The latter was posted to Oyo in 1902, and remained there for his entire career, rising to be Resident. (Atanda 1973). He had a reputation for being very close to and for indulging the Alafin of Oyo. For example, he arranged for him to buy a Rolls Royce and supported his wish to present a pair of elephant tusks to a member of the British royal family. The linking of these men in the brisk, even brusque, name 'Carter-Ross' sends out deliberately contradictory signals that Osofisan expects us to think about. The 'double-barrelled' name suggests the many faceted quality of British imperialism; it fights against easy judgements and reminds that there were phases in the colonial period. For example, punitive raids might be followed by close alliances with traditional leaders; both were part of the colonial period.

The name, and the life story and conduct of the Rev' Bayo Campbell are disconcerting in a somewhat similar way: they surprise and disconcert, upset and deliberately thwart those who want to over simplify. First of all, the name: 'Campbell' might be taken to neatly indicate Scottish heritage or ancestry. However, Nigerians with a sense of the past and a knowledge of their community will recognise that 'Campbell', no less than 'Macaulay', is a name that has been carried by distinguished Nigerians. Nigerian music lovers of Osofisan's generation and a bit older would easily make the link between Bayo Campbell, and the Nigerian musician Ambrose Adekoya Campbell who led the West African Rhythm Brothers the 1940s, 1950s and 1960s. (Osofisan, personal communication 15 May 2004, and http//:members.lycos.co.uk/dudcitizen /ambrose.html? – accessed 23 June 2004)

Campbell's life story and position also prompts thought. He is said to have been sold to slave traders and transported to America where he came under the influence of the Southern American Baptist Church (107 and 61). He is described as a Missionary of that Church, yet despite this he is prepared to pour a libation, an action that was long regarded as anathema by West African Christians (56). His language is often untypical: for example, he refers to his followers as women 'from the parish' (55) – a term associated with established churches not Baptists. Furthermore, he describes himself as 'a poor colonial priest' (56). I think one can confidently say that a Baptist *minister* as fluent in

English as Campbell would not use the word 'priest' of himself or herself. Once again, the options are either to condemn Osofisan for ignorance of particular usages or to see the portrait, with its many liminal qualities, as very deliberately drawn to surprise and to prompt thought. This is the option I go for.

Like several of Osofisan's other works, *Tegonni* delights in playful theatricality that nudges and jostles members of the audience, keeping them constantly alert to the complexity of their experience in his theatre. For example, not only may we have the disconcerting Prologue in which black stands for white, but members of Antigone's retinue keep changing roles. The playwright enjoys their versatility, insisting on the obviousness of doubling or trebling of parts (83). Osofisan has, it seems, invited us into his theatre and says: 'You have come to see actors perform. Good, now watch as these actors take several roles. Aren't they proficient? Don't they change roles with style and impersonate with conviction? You have come to the theatre for pretence, artifice, versatility and uncertainty. Look your fill and watch out for twists, turns and surprises.'

Tegonni herself is an extraordinary character and provokes to assessment and reassessment. Her name obviously has links with Antigone and these can be stretched to suggest that it includes the Greek term 'agon', or contest with links to 'protagonist' and 'antagonist'. So far so good, and useful for those who approach unfamiliar with the Yoruba resonances. But much more emerges from the dissection of the name by Yoruba speakers Biodun Jeyifo and Osofisan in a discussion about the play recoded at the time of the first production and published in *Insidious Treasons*. It seems that the Yoruba echoes include a link with 'egon' or 'egan' that can relate the name to 'spite' or 'spitefulness', and through this Tegonni can be associated with a saying that Osofisan translates as 'it is because of spite that they won't appreciate us'. This the playwright links with pride, and the pride that comes before, or leads, to a fall (2001: 230-1).

Having said so much about the name, what can be said about the character who bears the name? She may be a traditionalist in that she feels very acutely the obligation to bury her brother, but in other respects she is reshaping her community, she is a groundbreaker and glass ceiling smasher. She has embarked on a truly astonishing career and has already realised her ambition to become a carver and a brass caster. In the course of the play, she shows her willingness to venture into other areas regarded as the preserve of men. For example, we see her and her female companions dressed as *Egungun* masquerades, and she has contracted a barrier breaking marriage with Captain Allan Jones.

This marriage provoked a lot of discussion and deserves closer examination. (20) In assessing the implications of the relationship between the 'native girl' and Jones, it is, once again, very helpful to listen to the exchange between Osofisan and Jeyifo. Jeyifo recalls that 'many, though not all, of the initial critical remarks' about the working script found the use of marriage 'a radical departure from the actualities of historical colonialism' and 'a recycling of "the good colonizer" whose "sincerity" goes beyond the invidious self-exoticization of colonizers who "went native".' This suggests a rejection of the position of Tegonni because audiences could not accept that there ever was intermarriage between coloniser and colonised. ('A radical departure...' should be taken to mean 'Such things did not happen.') In a wide-ranging response to a multi-faceted observation, reproduced only in part here, Osofisan argued that

> Most of [the colonial officers] ranging from M.C. Atkinson to Sir Alex Raven to the forester Philip Allison, kept African mistresses, and acknowledged it, as accounts from various colonial servants confirm, despite a conspiracy of total reticence, none of them ever daring to talk about it openly, even in their drinking clubs.

The playwright, who has obviously done some research, goes on to consider the relationship from other angles, including that of the women. He writes:

> For some of them surely and oral history is evidence here, these liaisons with white men were an insidious strategy of hitching themselves up (to) the saddle of power, of enhancing their own social status, and, by implication, that of their families (2001: 217-218.)

Having cited instances but not convinced on all counts, he moves on to contrast the perception of marriages involving partners of different 'races' in Nigeria and the United States, and implies that the version presented in Atlanta addressed that issue in particular. My response may be clouded because of amendments to the Atlanta version with regard to the Tegonni-Jones relationship, but Osofisan emerges as well prepared to argue his case. He has names and in some cases occupations of those involved with local women. However, the issue of *marriage* remains unresolved. I am intrigued, incidentally, by the use of the word 'insidious', used in the passage just quoted with 'strategies'. The word is also found in the title of a collection of Osofisan's essays etc. where it is linked with 'treasons', and again intrigues. I suggest that Osofisan's approach to the stage incorporates the sense of an *ambush* that lies behind the word 'insidious'. The playwright lies in wait for his audience, gives them a false sense of security, sets traps, springs surprises, takes unawares.

Some who find the marriage issue a distraction and continue to object on historical grounds may miss some of the ideas about 'progress' and 'change' that are introduced for consideration through Antigone. The determination that she shows, and the robust positions she adopts as a powerful woman, have unchallenged historical precedents. These are embodied in the courageous Amazon warriors from Dahomey, and in the roles played by Nigerian women in, for example, the Aba Riots (1929) and the tax boycott in Abeokuta (1948-9). The phrase 'Women's power' is used in several contexts so that the possibility or practicality of the various steps Tegonni has taken and takes prompt thought. This is just what Osofisan wants. The audience is asked to consider whether Tegonni could really have become a brass-carver, could actually perform as a masquerader, could in reality become the wife of a District Officer, or could 'historically' defy the Governor of the Colony? The implied follow up question, the 'ambush', is 'if not, why not?'

The rich mixture of performance conventions that Osofisan stirs into *Tegonni* is an additional method of making the play challenging and surprising. After the optional Prologue that addresses production constraints and raises identity issues, the play 'proper' begins with a spectacular and melodious 'Opening Number': the arrival of the Yoruba Water Goddess, Yemoja. This will raise questions in the audience's mind, such as 'Yemoja, in a play like this by Osofisan? What am I supposed to think about her? Certainly, I am not supposed to *believe* in her as, say the daughter of Obatala and Oduduwa, or as the mother of Ogun. Let me think: does she symbolise or represent something or someone? Guided once more by Osofisan, it is note-worthy that he has described her as a 'symbol of this eternal resistance to "colonialism", mother of all Antigones'. (2001: 226.) If this is not apparent (and it may well not be given the range of roles played by Yemoja), the artifice that rubs our noses in the theatricality of the occasion certainly is. For if this is Yemoja, she is 'only a stage Yemoja'. She offers us a spectacular Opening Number, almost an opening glee. And her dramatic qualities at the end of the play, discussed below, add further insight into her function.

In the course of the play, Osofisan introduces a panoply of cultural performances. These include Oriki poetry (23), Ifa divination verses (24), a bridal procession with music, dancing and more poetry, (34-40), a funeral rite with dirges and keening (49-50), a Pentecostal composition such as, he tells us disingenuously, is used 'nowadays' (63). Other 'performance elements' include the sound of a bull-roarer (108) and the appearance of bronze-faced Egungun masquerades (110). The bold, popular appeal of full-blooded confrontations is exploited (67-8), and 'interludes' allow the inclusion of 'the Story of the Tiger and the Frog' (94-101 and the recitation of Shelley's 'Ozymandias' (128-9). Time and again these outrage any lingering sense of Aristotelian restraint or Attic decorum. However, a catholic approach would appreciate that they are part of the Nigerian dramatist's dialogue with the Greek convention. They say 'Yes, I can both refer to the classical tradition and fill the stage with diverse action. I can quote from the Attic theatre and move from place to place; refer to the distant past and mix different genres'. He enriches the performance and contributes to the working out of the theme by, for example, the use of Antigone and 'Ozymandias'.

The thematic and metatheatrical elements that have been noted from time to time often cluster around Antigone. Antigone is the quintessential protestor, the human rights activist, the theatrical embodiment of principled conduct. Her very presence recalls her story, and this story is well known – certainly familiar to Osofisan's campus audiences. Her first words (suitably disconcerting) in this script are 'Greetings. Has the play started?' (25). She soon finds that her story is known and she then explains the (conveniently) accomplished manner in which she and her entourage perform in a Yoruba context. She says: 'We've had long rehearsals about your customs' (27). From time to time throughout the play, particularly when Antigone is on stage, we are reminded of the theatrical conventions we have accepted by sitting down in the theatre. For example, Antigone, behaving like a concerned stage-manager, provides members of her retinue with helpful props when they have to impersonate soldiers (30). The soldiers in turn, 'surprise us' by stepping out to complain to her (perhaps now company manager) that impersonating soldiers is 'no fun at all!' (74) They go on to list the tasks given to them as soldiers, including carrying corpses, building execution platforms, terrorising people, burning and plundering houses and collecting bribes. It is easy to appreciate the recognition this would trigger in Nigerian audiences for these are all activities that have been undertaken by soldiers in Nigeria. I think I can safely say that everyone in the audience for the Ibadan premier would have been quick to recognise that Osofisan was using the 'Athenian' soldiers to comment on the state of the nation. The audience would have appreciated why the retinue (of decent men) wanted a change and in all probability would have shown their recognition (75) .

The introduction of 'Ozymandias' is a particularly resonant example of the metatheatrical, and of subtle intertextual wit. The poem, written by a romantic revolutionary with a seething loathing for the arrogance of power, is used after Antigone has tested Tegonni by pretending to believe 'Freedom is a myth which human beings invent as a torch to kindle their egos'. (126). When Tegonni passes the test by challenging this easy cynicism, the two women stand, hands linked, reciting Shelley's poem. Their laughter at Ozymandias' overweening confidence, and their repetition of key ideas provides a shared commentary that is the more powerful for being delivered in an isolated spotlight. This passage seals their common confidence that 'oppression can never last' (127), and stiffens Tegonni's resolve to undertake the confrontations that remain. (There is solidarity and a sense of achievement, but no resting on laurels: *la luta continua*.) In the conversation with Jeyifo that forms such an enlightening companion to the text, Osofisan says that he used the poem 'to further expose this mask of fraudulence', to extend the discussion far beyond that of colonial oppression (so clearly established by the historical background) to include 'all hegemonies imposed by force of fiat, ruling over people by coercion and cunning.' (2001:225). The fact that it is a well-known poem and that it welds its perceptions on to a compelling image adds to its impact.

In an Epilogue, the profound sisterhood of Antigone and Tegonni is insisted on in a dumb show that involves them kneeling before Yemoja, being rewarded with gifts, and taking their places among those rowing and singing. The rightness of Tegonni's action is confirmed by this mime, and the playwright's approval of her courage is confirmed through the kinship established with the quintessential activist from classical antiquity. The fact that the theatrical manner has shifted to a fusion of opera and dance cues the audience to relish the theatricality of this ending! Like the opening scene, it is outrageously stagy and so, like so much else in the play, prompts consideration. It encourages members of the audience, who are predisposed to expect a 'moral' or lesson from the dramatist at this point, to ask, as they have been forced to ask so many times already: 'What do I take from this experience?'

Conclusion

Time and again, it is through Antigone and through his 'dialogue' with Greece that Osofisan broadens and deepens the debate he has opened up in *Tegonni*. It is appropriate to note that this journey with Antigone has taken us a long way, and part of that journey has been a suitably circuitous route from, say, Axworthy's double-bill of *Antigones* in Ibadan through the performance of *Tegonni* in Atlanta, and back once more to Ibadan. Osofisan's confident handling of Sophocles' play shows how right Axworthy was to throw down a challenge, to put on the two plays, saying, in effect, saying 'Look here on this Sophoclean original and now on this mid-Twentieth Century politicised version.' The end of the century, some thirty-five years after independence, saw the follow up. *Tegonni* is the work of a Nigerian playwright, who with supreme confidence, has raided the store-house associated with the former colonial power and stolen what he wants, and he has used history, names, theatrical conventions, and goddesses to surprise, disconcert and stimulate. Ikeddeh may talk about the influence of Sophocles as 'tragic'; *Tegonni,* profoundly indebted to Sophocles, achieves its aim of provoking to thought about contemporary issues with wit, and with *insidious* theatrical panache.

Bibliography

Adeyemi, A. *Femi Osofisan: A Chronology*, http://www.scholars.nus.edu.sg/landow/post/nigeria/osofisan/fechron.html (22/06/2004)

Agovi, K.E. 1990. 'The Origin of Literary Theatre in Colonial Ghana, 1920-1957.' *Research Review (*Legon), 6, 1 pp. 1-23.

Atanda, J. A. 1973. *The New Oyo Empire* (London: Longman).

Axworthy. G. 1984. *Geoffrey Axworthy in Interview with Ahmed Yerimah* (Ibadan: LACE Occasional Publications, 1, 9).

Clark, J.P. 1964. *America, Their America* (London: Deutsch).

Echeruo, M.J.C. 1981. 'The Dramatic Limits of Igbo History', in Ogunbiyi, Y., ed. *Drama and Theatre in Nigeria: A Critical Source Book* (Lagos: Nigeria Magazine, pp. 136-148).

Enekwe, O. 1981. 'Myth, ritual and Drama in Igboland' in Ogunbiyi, Y., ed. *Drama and Theatre in Nigeria: A Critical Source Book* (Lagos: Nigeria Magazine, pp. 149-163).

Gibbs, J. May 2004. 'Antigone's African Sisters.' Unpublished paper, presented Birmingham, UK.

Harrison, T. W. and J. Simmons. 1966. *Akin Mata* (Ibadan: Oxford University Press).

Ikiddeh, I. 1975. 'The Tragic Influence of Shakespeare and the Greeks', unpublished conference paper delivered at the University of Ife.

Osofisan, F. 1999. *Recent Outings (Tegonni* and *Many Colours make the Thunder King)* (Ibadan: Opon Ifa Readers).

Osofisan, F. 2001. *Insidious Treasons: Drama in a Postcolonial State [essays]* (Ibadan: Opon Ifa Readers). (Includes Interview by Biodun Jeyifo, 202-256.)

Owusu, M. 1983. *Drama and the Gods: A Study of Seven African Plays* (Roxbury, Mass: Omen Ana).

Rotimi, O. 1971. *The Gods Are Not to Blame* (London: Oxford University Press).

Soyinka, W. 1973. *The Bacchae of Euripides* (London: Methuen).

Soyinka, W. *Oyedipo at Kholoni*, unpublished.

Wetmore, K. J. 2002. *The Athenian Sun in an African Sky: Modern African Adaptations of Classical Greek Tragedy* (Jefferson, NC: MacFarland).

Yerimah, A., See Axworthy, above

TROJAN WOMEN IN YORUBALAND: FEMI OSOFISAN'S *WOMEN OF OWU**

FELIX BUDELMANN

This chapter is devoted to one of Femi Osofisan's most recent plays, *Women of Owu*, an adaptation of Euripides' *Trojan Women*, in a production by the American-Nigerian director Chuck Mike. The play premiered in Chipping Norton in rural Oxfordshire in February 2004, and then toured across England and Scotland, including London's Oval House Theatre.[1] Since then, Osofisan himself appears to have produced and directed it in a semi-staged student performance in Ibadan.[2] This chapter looks at *Women of Owu* from a classicist's perspective. In this respect, it is the latest of a number of Greek tragedy-inspired plays by writers from postcolonial states, or more specifically, writers from West Africa. Such plays have become subject of increased interest especially among classicists, but also within drama and postcolonial studies. Kevin J. Wetmore's *The Athenian Sun in an African Sky* (2002) and *Black Dionysus* (2003) are book-length accounts of Greek tragedy in Africa and in the African American theatre. Greek tragedy in African drama is also the focus of several pieces in Lorna Hardwick and Carol Gillespie's edited volume *Classics in Post-Colonial Worlds* (2004), of a monograph currently prepared by Barbara Goff and Michael Simpson, and of an earlier article of mine (Budemann 2004). Greek tragedy-related work by Irish dramatists (a rather different sort of postcolonial situation) has recently been the subject of a volume edited by Marianne McDonald and Michael Walton (2002), as well as several individual articles by

---

* A very slightly different version of this chapter appears in Hardwick & Gillespie, eds. 2007, the proceedings of a 2004 conference at the Open University in Birmingham (UK), supported by the British Academy. I am grateful to the editors for the permission to publish the chapter here as well, and to Pantelis Michelakis, as well as the anonymous readers and the editors of the Oxford volume for helpful comments on earlier versions.

[1] I saw the play twice, on 4th February in Chipping Norton and on 6th March at the Oval House Theatre. A video recording of one of the Oval House performances is deposited in the Theatre Museum in London. At the time of writing this chapter, Osofisan is still in the process of preparing the text for publication. I am grateful to him for showing me a working script and letting me quote from it, and to the good services of Sola Adeyemi in this. There may be discrepancies from the eventually published text. In the absence of verse and page numbers, I quote by scene numbers (I-V). In addition, I draw on the programme notes, as well as an email response from Femi Osofisan (7th July 2004) and notes from a conversation with Chuck Mike (London, 13th May 2004). I would like to record my thanks to both of them for being generous with their time.

[2] According to a review in the Nigerian *Daily Sun* of 23rd March 2005, at http://www.sunnewsonline.com/webpages/features/arts/2005/Mar/23/arts-23-03-2005-003.htm (last accessed December 2005). I have not been able to find further information on this production.

various scholars.[3] Most wide-ranging, perhaps, is Lorna Hardwick's article on 'decolonising Classics' which traces the complex interaction between Greek drama and anti-colonialism in various regions (Hardwick 2004). This is a selection of just a few recent publications, none of them earlier than 2002, but probably enough to give an impression of the surge in work on this topic.

In the context of this volume, Femi Osofisan hardly needs introducing, but it may be worth pointing out that *Women of Owu* is not his first venture into adapting a Greek tragedy. In 1994 he wrote *Tegonni*, using material from Sophocles' *Antigone*, commissioned in the United States. Chuck Mike was born in New York but has lived in Nigeria for much of the time since 1976. His troupe in this production, *Collective Artistes*, was made up almost entirely of actors with strong Nigerian affiliation, half of them having lived in Nigeria for considerable periods. Osofisan and Mike have worked together before, including on a 2002 production of *Tegonni* in New York. Their collaboration is close enough for Mike to be able to change the play-text in the course of the rehearsals. As with many new plays, it is impossible, therefore, to separate play and first performance completely, and I will draw on both. Future performances and the eventual publication of a text will inevitably change perspectives.

The play is set outside the burning city, not of Troy as in Euripides, but of Owu in Yorubaland, part of what is now Nigeria. The wider historical backdrop is the fighting between rival groups in Yorubaland in the first half of the nineteenth century, in the course of which large groups of people were displaced and enslaved. Owu was destroyed in the 1820s after a siege of many years.[4] Each of Osofisan's characters corresponds to one of Euripides' characters, and his play follows the plot structure of *Trojan Women* closely, with just a few significant deviations.[5] Owu has been destroyed. The men have been killed or enslaved. The women, including the former queen, are camping near the burning ruins. The play focuses on the group of women lamenting what has happened to them. As in Euripides' play, there is relatively little action. The emotional highpoint is reached when one of the soldiers of the victorious army takes away the child of one of the women to kill it. In the end, the women go into slavery, each to a different master. It is immediately clear, then, that Osofisan sets up a three-way

---

[3] Several essays in Dillon & Wilmer, eds. 2005 are devoted to Irish versions of Greek tragedies, as is Taplin 2004 and Wilmer's piece in Hardwick & Gillespie, eds. 2007.

[4] On the Owu war, seeMabogunje & Omer Cooper 1971 and Law 1977.

[5] In my view, the three most substantial deviations in structure are: (a) Osofisan moves the discussion between the two gods from the beginning to after the first interaction between chorus and queen. Instead, *Women of Owu* opens with a dialogue between the despondent women of the chorus and just one of the two gods, the city's protecting deity Anlugbua. (I discuss the gods below). (b) *Women of Owu* ends with the queen and chorus performing a 'ritual valediction to the dead', eventually bringing Anlugbua back on stage. (c) The choral songs are not all in the same places as in Euripides. They are in Yoruba rather than English, and their text does not closely follow the themes of Euripides' songs. (I discuss the chorus, but not the detail of the songs, and very briefly, later in this essay).

relationship: ancient Greece, nineteenth-century Yorubaland, and any present-day war relevant to the spectators, whether in the United Kingdom, in Africa, or elsewhere. This relationship, which Osofisan had exploited in a different way already in *Tegonni*, is at the heart of this chapter.

I will first discuss four notable features of the play, all related to the blend of Greek, nineteenth-century Yoruba and contemporary European/American and indeed African elements: (1) its presentation of an aggressive war and its consequences, (2) its emphasis on communality rather than individuality, (3) its treatment of gender, and (4) its form and tone. On the basis of this discussion, I will then (section 5) think more generally about the way different audiences might respond to this blend of different traditions, characteristic of *Women of Owu* as indeed of many other postcolonial plays. Finally, I will finish off with a section (6) on the more abstract audiences constituted by different scholarly disciplines, and place this chapter in the interdisciplinary discourse of Classics and postcolonial studies.

1 War, slavery and responsibility

Women of Owu is a play about the sufferings imposed by war. Its main mode is empathy and pity for the victims of war, mostly women. Owu is in ruins. Its former inhabitants are constantly threatened by rape, displacement, slavery, degradation and death. Even the victors are affected, as war changes their behaviour: Okunade, the Mayé or war leader of the aggressors, corresponding to Menelaus in Euripides, was once a peaceful artist but has turned into a ruthless killer. Gesinde, a herald of the allied army and based on Euripides' Talthybius, has worked out that only opportunism will bring survival. Repeatedly, he stresses that he only executes orders, against his will. In Mike's production, the perversion of normal human relations is epitomised by the scene in which the baby boy of the Andromache character Adumaadan is taken away to be killed: although he is about to smash the child's head against a tree, Gesinde handles him with great care. The irony is powerful.

Despite the nineteenth-century setting, Osofisan and Mike give the war present-day resonances, as two examples will show. First, the slavery theme that runs through Euripides' play is made even more prominent in *Women of Owu*. An aim, or at least an inevitable by-product, of the war seems to be the enslavement of the female population of Owu. Throughout, the women voice their fear of slavery, aware of their imminent departure for their new fates. In the final speech of the play, Anlugbua, the ancestral and now deified founder of Owu based on Euripides' Poseidon, says: 'Owu will rise again! Not here, / Not as a single city again, but in little communities / Within other cities of Yorubaland. Those now going / Into slavery, shall form new kingdoms in those places.' (V). This and other statements about slavery open out perspectives, well beyond Yorubaland, onto the black Diaspora across the centuries. Secondly, the play quite obviously alludes to the 2003 invasion of Iraq, in which the US along with some other nations, including the UK, deposed ruler Saddam Hussein. The besieging army is called the 'Allied Forces' (of Ijebu and Ife), as was the US-led coalition. It claims to have come to liberate Owu rather than to act out of any material greed, but the women repeatedly pour scorn over this assertion (e.g. 'They do not want our market at all— / They are not interested in such petty things / As profit— Only in such lofty ideas as freedom', divided between three speakers, II), evoking intense and prolonged debates over the complex motivations for invading Iraq. At one point, in Mike's production,[6] they even turn to face the audience and shout something like 'you say you came to liberate us'. The programme note mentions Iraq in the first sentence, and also refers to Kuwait, Bosnia, Rwanda, Algeria, Liberia and Sierra Leone. Although set in a colonial context, *Women of Owu* has clear postcolonial and neo-colonial overtones. It is about the consequences of military aggression any time, anywhere: in nineteenth- and twentieth-century Africa, in the Middle East, and wherever audiences care to make connections.

Against the backdrop of this stark account and indictment of the brutality and lies of war, one of the most interesting aspects of the play is its subtlety in treating responsibility and causation. The immediate cause of the women's misery is the sack of their city, but why was the city sacked? Partly no doubt because of greed, as the women suggest, but that is not all. As in Euripides, there is also the complex issue of Iyunloye (Helen in Euripides), who caused her husband to take up arms as the leader of the Allied Forces as she left him, voluntarily or otherwise, to live with the youngest prince of Owu (V). In addition, Osofisan introduces a further element, taken from the history of the Owu war. The goddess Lawumi, grandmother of Anlugbua, wants the Owus punished because they enslaved other Yoruba in the past, and behaved arrogantly against Ife Ife, the most renowned cradle of the Yoruba race (III). Osofisan likes using gods, calling them in an interview 'metaphors of some of the enduring qualities of society', but presents them (like other aspects of society) rarely as beyond criticism (Awodiya 1993: 48; similarly p. 80). In this play, he develops Euripides' gods, making it even more difficult to disentangle individual shares of responsibility. Anlugbua comes too late to save his city and is angrily scolded for this by the women (I); Lawumi does not just seek the destruction of Owu but also talks Anlugbua into unleashing a storm on the attackers on the way home to make them pay for their religious impropriety, yet appears anything other than dignified as she makes her, rather personal, case against both the warring parties. (III). Scenes I and III show that the gods have a role in the human suffering, yet in the end (V), Anlugbua puts the blame squarely on humans, leaving it to the spectators to draw their own conclusions: 'You human beings, always thirsty for blood, / Always eager to devour one another! I hope / History will teach you'. Osofisan's gods, like Euripides', are

---

[6] Based on my performance notes (n. 1); not in the draft play text.

influential and moral, yet pettish, elusive and the target of human attacks. Finally, in this complex web of responsibilities, the role of the European colonisers is handled subtly, too. The whites are there: they have provided firearms and they are slave-traders, but they are in the background. They do not appear on stage, they did not take part in the siege, they are not the only slave-traders, and they are not the only brutal oppressors. Osofisan has protested repeatedly against the notion that all postcolonial drama focuses on protest against the 'centre' (much as such protest matters to him), and has stressed the importance of engagement also with the challenges of present-day Africa in his work.[7] The open-endedness of his treatment of responsibility should probably be seen in this context. Nobody is innocent in this play, and nobody is the sole guilty party.

2 Communality

Perhaps more than any Greek tragedy, *Trojan Women* dramatises the story of a group; the chorus and the individual women all face similar struggles. What Mike and Osofisan have done is to further increase the emphasis on communal suffering that is already present in Euripides. As one would expect, the chorus dance dances and sing songs. But there is more. Throughout the performance, different combinations of two or three actors form mini-choruses chanting together. In some scenes the chorus provide a vocal audience to the interaction of other characters, whether with words or just exclamations. Moreover, Mike stresses the emphasis on ensemble work and the avoidance of star cult in his rehearsal work. He calls the rehearsal process a 'sociology'. Actors were allocated their roles only a good week into the rehearsal process; and many of the clearest expressions of communality were the result of improvisation in rehearsals rather than original scripting. As a result of all this, the production achieves an unusually powerful solution to the notorious problems posed by Greek choruses. As in fifth-century BCE Athens, the chorus here is not an embarrassing interruption of a good plot, but central to the play, and as in Athens participating in the chorus is conceived as a social act.

However, and I think this is important, the play does not portray the women's enforced community as bliss, or choral song and dance as a panacea for all woes. The women quarrel; most of the dances seem to be cut short as members of the army arrive on the scene; a soldier even urinates during one of the dances; and (again as in Greek tragedy) there is the concept of the perverse song: the deranged seer Orisaye (Cassandra in Euripides) keeps asking for a song to celebrate her imminent forced marriage with one of the victors, but the chorus refuse this kind of song (IV). Osofisan and Mike force spectators to reflect upon what they see at the same time as submitting to its power.

---

[7] In particular: Osofisan 2001: 153-173. On Osofisan's general concern with present-day Africa, see also below.

Moreover, there are lines of demarcation between communality on stage and in the auditorium. The choral songs are in Yoruba, a language few members of the mostly white Chipping Norton audience are likely to have understood. Moreover, Chipping Norton theatre – with a raised stage and a proscenium arch – sets obvious limits to the degree the audience will feel part of any dances on stage. Unsurprisingly, audience reaction was more vocal in London's Oval House, a more informal and integrated performance space, with a predominantly Afro-Caribbean audience including people with Nigerian connections. Communality set in nineteenth-century Yorubaland can extend into twenty-first century Britain, but only to a degree.

3 Gender

It hardly needs pointing out that *Women of Owu* is, among other things, a play about relations between men and women: women suffer at the hands of men. As Osofisan puts it:

> women, and children, are the ones who suffer most from the effects of war - brutalized, raped, disfigured - and are then left alive to face the consequences... In a way therefore it is easier for the men, they are gone from the scene and so beyond pain. But think of the widows and orphans, the mutilated women left with their wounds and memories... Euripides must have chosen to concentrate on these victims in order to further highlight the horror and brutality of war. A message which is particularly pertinent today, with Iraq, Afghanistan, Sudan, etc.[8]

But as in Euripides, the women's suffering and powerlessness is poised against their resilience and resistance. The male characters are not just a minority, they are also rather weak. Especially, the Mayé is brutal and uncaring, altogether lacking the women's stature. The women tend to have the better of the arguments, repeatedly exposing the senselessness and cowardliness of the war propaganda, and maintain their dignity throughout. In performance terms, their actions as a group create a sense of organised resistance. The women sing together, they dance together, they curse together; at one point in Mike's production they all bare their breasts as a weapon of last resort, an ill-omened act in many African cultures.

Interestingly, this dramatisation of the women's powerlessness and resistance is juxtaposed with a rather different treatment of gender in *Women of Owu's* version of Euripides' Helen scene (V). The Mayé comes to punish his wife Iyunloye, undecided whether to take her back home or have her die straightaway. A scene of debate ensues between Iyunloye and Erelu (Hecuba in Euripides). Iyunloye portrays herself as a victim of circumstances, always

---

[8] By email (n. 1).

missing her husband, while Erelu tries to persuade the Mayé to kill her for lightly abandoning him for her rich and handsome youngest soñ. Osofisan's and Mike's scene resembles Euripides' in many ways, but deviates in a vital point. It further increases the erotic charge that is already present in Euripides. Quite explicitly, Iyunloye tries to seduce the Mayé. Threatened with execution, Iyunloye, dressed in bright red with long plaited hair and set off against the other women in sombre blue and with shaved heads, pulls all the stops to make herself desirable to him, both physically and rhetorically. The scene ends without final decision, but as we hear later from Gesinde, Iyunloye eventually succeeds. The Mayé succumbs to her allure.

It is not easy to say what messages to take away here about gender. Iyunloye is perhaps the conceptually most daring and most problematic character in the play. Even more than Gesinde or the Mayé, she shows how extreme situations can force people into certain roles. She makes herself a sexual object and succeeds. Powerlessness or power? Legitimisation of patriarchal authority or female subversion? The ambivalence increases further if we bring in statements characters make about male-female relationships. 'I know as a woman how it feels / To be chosen as the favourite of such a man' (V), Erelu says to Iyunloye, referring to the physical attraction and status of her son. And Adumaadan, having learned that she has been selected to live with a particularly loathed member of the victorious army, worries that she will respond to him sexually despite her hatred: 'For I am only a woman, with a woman's familiar / Weaknesses. Our flesh too often, and in spite of itself, / Quickens to a man's touch, / And a night of loving is all it takes, they say, to tame / The most unwilling among us.' (V, cf. *Trojan Women* 665-6). Sexual attraction and the inability to resist it are a major aspect of gender relations in this play. 'Talk', Erelu says, 'is the only weapon I have left for mourning' (II), but Iyunloye has understood that her only weapon of consequence is sexual seduction. Slavery is not for her. Erelu again: 'Women like her are dangerous, / Especially to their lovers. Once they catch you, you're hooked / For ever: They have such powers of enchantment, eyes / That will set cities ablaze.' (V).

For a number of years now, productions and adaptations of Greek tragedy have extensively exploited the gender themes inherent in the ancient plays. Helene Foley has recently discussed how such work does not just point to female suffering but is often just as interested in powerful and outrageous women (2004: 77-111).[9] Osofisan's and Mike's Iyunloye can no doubt be seen in this context, but what about the West African context? As Foley points out in passing, gender themes are generally less prominent in African than in American, Japanese or Irish versions of Greek tragedies – no doubt reflecting differences in local discourses. This is not true, however, for Osofisan. As one would expect, he explores gender themes also in the *Antigone*-play *Tegonni*, but

---

[9] The comment on Africa is on p. 77.

he does so extensively elsewhere, too. *Morountodun*,[10] *Yungba Yungba and the Dance Contest* (none of them based closely on western plays) and *Midnight Hotel* are obvious examples. 'The female question', as Muyiwa Awodiya puts it, 'is one of the themes that Osofisan is most preoccupied with.' (Awodiya 1995: 88-89).[11] In a West African context, the prominence Osofisan gives to women is perhaps noteworthy (if by no means unique), and one might be tempted to detect influences from outside the African tradition here.

Yet that is too simple a conclusion. Women as powerful seducers as well as women unable to resist seduction are Greek themes, written into the Helen myth from early on, but are not perhaps themes that are currently exploited in American or European theatre as much as the violent power of Medea or Clytemnestra. Much of what Osofisan does with Euripides' gender themes is remarkably close to the ancient play, and not so close to recent European or American discourses. Emblematically, the second half of Adumaadan's lines about responding sexually to her new master, quoted above, are almost a close translation of *Trojan Women* 665-6, and at the same time (to me) the uneasiest lines in the entire play. Arguably, in fact, they become even more shocking and even more problematic as they are brought to life in an African context. Nineteenth-century Africa may feel distant to many UK audiences, but less distant probably than fifth-century BCE Greece. In other words, using an African past, Osofisan has found a thought-provoking way of translating some of the most problematic aspects of ancient Greek gender relations for today. Different audiences, and indeed different spectators, with different cultural and personal experiences and expectations, are bound to disagree over whether the result is shocking or not, whether it confirms or challenges gender stereotypes, and whether the distance created by a nineteenth-century Yoruba setting moderates any discomfort. But there can be no doubt about the effectiveness with which *Women of Owu* stages a new version of the gender issues in Euripides' play.

4 Form and tone

As pointed out above, *Women of Owu* follows the plot structure of *Trojan Women* for the most part quite closely. This section discusses how Osofisan and Mike adopt and adapt also the *form* and *tone* of Euripides' play. Perhaps the most obvious characteristic of *Trojan Women* is its sombre tone. In this respect, there is little to choose between the two plays: *Women of Owu*, too, is a

---

[10] Of all Osofisan's plays, *Morountodun* is probably closest to *Women of Owu* in its treatment of gender. See the discussion by Ajayi 1996.

[11] In 1987, when asked why he chooses women and common men as the main heroines and heroes, Osofisan replied: 'I don't really deliberately privilege women in my works. As I see it, women are part of the whole struggle. I've written plays in which women are the heroines and I've written plays in which women have been demons.' (Awodiya 1993: 79).

predominantly sombre play in which suffering never ends. This similarity goes beyond the subject matter and owes much to formal characteristics. Osofisan and Mike keep the formal feature that contributes more than any to the sombre effect of *Trojan Women*: the almost never-ending lament by all the women, especially the chorus. A way of throwing Osofisan's and Mike's choices into relief is by comparison with Sartre. When Sartre influentially adapted *Trojan Women* in 1965 as a play of protest against European and American imperialism, in the aftermath of the Algerian war of independence and during the Vietnam War, he politicised and psychologised Euripides' play in many ways.[12] His conception of a political play did not leave room for choruses and extensive lament, prompting him to break up or cut most of the sustained choral passages and to tone down all lament. His unease is summed up in his description of *Trojan Women* as an 'oratorio' and not a 'tragedy'.[13] As Nicole Loraux complained recently, what Sartre did is effectively silence what she regards as one of the main features of Greek tragedy overall: the mourning voice (2002: 1-13). Osofisan's and Mike's decision not to go this way is remarkable not least because Osofisan, an admirer of Sartre, used Sartre's version as one of his base texts for writing *Women of Owu*.[14]

Clearly, however, as it sends forth its mourning voice, *Women of Owu* departs from Euripides in form and tone in other respects. Most important, the lament is punctured repeatedly by comic elements. *Women of Owu* is less homogenous in tone than *Trojan Women*. In both performances that I saw, Gesinde's intimations to the audience of his thoughts on his superiors were repeatedly rewarded with laughter. Other characters, too, are sometimes (involuntarily) funny. In particular, the Mayé's smugness and lack of self-awareness is rather comical, and even the divine dialogue has its funny moments. No doubt there are different ways of producing *Women of Owu*. In Mike's version, comic elements, carefully spaced, were one of the most intriguing features.

Closely connected to these elements of humour are a number of abrupt changes in register. Overall the play is composed in an uncluttered and accessible but not informal idiom, yet at times it stoops consciously to the everyday: 'Just think of having to clean their toilets' (II), one of the women says. Elsewhere, they see themselves as 'stinking in our underwear' (V). Osofisan uses the sustained pathos for regular moments of bathos. Finally, the occasional direct confrontation of the audience in Mike's production is a further compelling

---

[12] *Les Troyennes*. English translation by Ronald Duncan in Sartre's *Three Plays* (1969) first performed at the Edinburgh Festival in 1966.

[13] In his essay about his adaptation; English trans.: Sartre 1969: 285-290, 'oratorio' on p. 288.

[14] Confirmed by email (n. 1). Several aspects of Sartre's adaptation, highlighted in his essay (previous notes), can be traced in *Women of Owu*, e.g., the humorous effect of the Gesinde's wisdom, the Mayé's more explicit yielding to Iyunloye, and the addition of a divine epilogue. More broadly, Osofisan, like Sartre and others inspired by Sartre, uses *Trojan Women* to criticise events in his own country.

deviation from what we know of ancient productions of *Trojan Women*. When the women bear their breast and when they shout 'you say you came to liberate us', they frontally face the audience. Audience address and explicit present-day reference come together here in a way that classicists associate with Old Comedy rather than tragedy.

Such persistent efforts to manipulate the smooth surface of the play can be looked at in various ways. First of all, they may throw the horror into even greater relief, repeatedly varying the mode in which spectators engage with the relentless onslaught. Next they can be put in the context of trends in recent Greek tragedy performances and adaptations. Like Sartre's *Les Troyennes*, many productions deviate from the ancient plays in both tone and form. A systematic study of this phenomenon is not yet available, but compared to, e.g., John Barton's, Peter Hall's and Edward Hall's *Tantalus*, *Women of Owu* is most conservative in this respect. Or, to take another *Trojan Women* adaptation, Charles Mee's and Tina Landau's 1996 *The Trojan Women: A Love Story* uses collage of stories, humour, music, an unusual performance space, and other means to create what Sarah Bryant-Bertail (2000) calls 'postmodern tragedy'. At least one dominant strand in current western theatre aesthetics is deeply wary of unbroken and unselfconscious lament. The reasons are complex, including factors as different as 'emotion fatigue' resulting from constant bombardment with news of immeasurable suffering, the rarity of public lament in most western cultures, the rare use of choruses, vague notions of the 'death of tragedy' and the high prestige of Shakespeare's tragicomedies. Osofisan's and Mike's subtle play with form and tone is by no means unusual.

Apart from this perhaps mostly European or American context, there is also a distinctly African side to these characteristics of *Women of Owu*, so much so in fact that spectators at ease with certain African traditions may not even find Osofisan's and Mike's manipulations remarkable. Duro Ladipo's *Oba-Kòso* (1970), for instance, perhaps the best-known Yoruba folk opera, easily blends what in a European context would be high tragedy and comedy, and so do to a lesser degree several African plays using Greek tragedies. A recent London production of Ola Rotimi's *Oedipus Rex*-inspired *The Gods Are Not To Blame*, for instance, had its audience laugh in several scenes, giving the performance an attractive lightness that sat quite comfortably with the dark themes it explored.[15] The strict separation of tragedy and comedy, with their different canons of content, form and tone, that is maintained by European theorists of various periods is probably less influential in African drama.[16]

---

[15] Arcola Theatre London, directed by Femi Elufowoju, July 2005.

[16] Which is not to say that African drama has no discourse of tragedy and comedy. Especially in the seventies and eighties there was a lively debate over what shape tragedy would take in Africa: see Soyinka 1976: 46-49, Ohaeto 1982 and Agovi 1985: 133-134.

The issue is complicated further by Osofisan's personal dramaturgic preferences. The self-conscious character of much of his theatre is pointed out by all critics. He says himself that 'the area of form constitutes the most visible site of the epistemological break I have made with the [Nigerian] playwrights of the first generation' (1997: 32),[17] such as Soyinka. *Women of Owu* is in fact by no means the formally most adventurous of his plays. Throughout his output, narrators, plays within plays, audience address, and similar devices abound. 'These ways,' he explains, 'I establish the contingent nature of all experience, and hopefully, reveal through the process the fact that we are *not* programmed by any supernatural force for failure, or defeat; that society is always determined by the interventions we bring to it; that our present sorry predicament is not permanent or incapable of emendation' (Jeyifo 2002: 617, Osofisan 2001: 142).[18] Again and again, he has stressed that his play with form serves to provoke debate and self-consciousness among his spectators. Unsurprisingly, many critics have discovered western influences here. Osofisan frequently attracts the epithet 'Brechtian'. However, more recently, critics have begun to point out that – once again – African and European influences are hard to separate.[19] What may look Brechtian to a European or American may be indigenous to a Nigerian. The complex threads tying together Greek, African and European are impossible to disentangle.

5 Greece, Africa and the UK

The subtitle Osofisan has given his play, *An African Re-reading of Euripides' The Trojan Women for the Chipping Norton Theatre, UK*, nicely sums up the blend of African, Greek and modern European elements. Such blending is, of course, a hallmark of much postcolonial literature, making 'hybridity' one of the most debated terms in postcolonial theory,[20] and from their own perspective, theatre studies, too, have taken an intense interest in the topic for a while now, using the label of 'intercultural performance'.[21] In this section, I shall try to pull

---

[17] See also Osofisan 2001: 139.

[18] Similar concerns have prompted Osofisan repeatedly to distance himself from what he regards as the tragic world view of Soyinka and his generation, e.g. Awodiya 1993: 29-30, Osofisan 1996: 16-17, and Osofisan 2001: 128-129.

[19] See Richards 1996: 70-73, Ukala 2001: 29-41.

[20] Bhabha 2004 and Young 1995 are particularly influential. Smith 2004 provides a helpful discussion of the various positions, including recent criticism of an overenthusiastic use of the concept.

[21] Pavis ed. 1996 is still a good starting point. The best known critic of the culturally and politically less attractive sides of intercultural performance is Bharucha 1993 and 2000. The work of one of Bharucha's main targets, Eugenio Barba, has recently been explored in Watson 2002. Richards 1996: 163-193 and Ukaegbu 2001 debate issues of intercultural performance, respectively drawing on a recent US and UK production of plays by Osofisan.

together some threads that have run through the chapter so far by looking at how *Women of Owu* blends different cultural influences and in particular by asking how this blend opens up different kind of opportunities for different audiences. Of course many of the issues are well rehearsed, but what distinguishes *Women of Owu* from most postcolonial plays (and indeed versions of Greek tragedy) is the *three*-way, as opposed to *two*-way relationship, ancient Greek – modern European – African (itself a blend of nineteenth-century and current aspects).

Osofisan is highly conscious of the audiences he addresses. He has stressed again and again that he writes in the first place for all people in Nigeria. He sees his literature as helping to bring about necessary social and political change at home. At the same time, he is aware that by writing in English he does not reach everyone (as indeed, he points out, he would not be able to in any one indigenous language), and has defended any resulting coincidental elite focus as beneficial at least in so far as the elite plays a vital role in any project of large-scale change. Finally, he has lived abroad and especially in recent years has directed his own and other African plays in the West and discussed the implications of this, and he has come to consider publishing no longer exclusively at home, partly to make his work more widely available.[22] These complexities help to situate the genesis of *Women of Owu* as a play by a Nigerian playwright, adapting a Greek tragedy, set in Africa and commissioned and first performed in Europe. In addition they are worth keeping in mind when thinking about the way this particular play addresses its various audiences.

A couple of comments Osofisan has made on writing *Women of Owu* will provide a starting point.[23] In reply to the question of which audience he had in mind he notes:

> ... strange as it may sound, a Nigerian audience, that is, the audience I am familiar with. If I was thinking otherwise, that is, of a British audience or any other audience I am not familiar with, I wouldn't I'm sure have been able to write the play. After all Euripides was writing for his own audience and not thinking of us! You see, as I have said elsewhere, the more 'local' an author is, the more universal, paradoxically, he becomes.

And in answer to the question of why he wrote a version of a Greek play:

> I was commissioned to write this play, so in a sense it wasn't my own decision to do it. Nevertheless, in spite of my initial misgivings, I did enjoy doing it in the end. I was hesitant to do it, not for the story, but because it seems to lack dramatic action, is just a pure lament, if you know what I mean. But then that became the challenge for me as a

---

[22] Nigerian audience, writing in English, and potential elite focus: Awodiya ed. 1993: 24-25, 58-60; Osofisan 1996 especially pp. 16-17. Directing abroad: Osofisan 2001: 174-234. Publishing abroad: Awodiya 1993.

[23] Both responses by email (n. 1).

dramatist... Generally however, the world of the Greeks, as you must know, is very close to the Yoruba one – in for instance, the belief in multiple gods, and the need to link with them through ritual. Of course there is a great difference in the attributes we give to our gods, and to the way therefore that we relate to them, but such differences do not really present obstacles when you are thinking of adaptations. It follows therefore that our own conception of theatre is close to the Greeks', rather than to the contemporary West's. Add to this the fact that the subjects that the Greeks treat are those which concern us all as human beings living in a social space we are never in full control of, nor fully comprehend, and having to constantly negotiate our way with the mystery of death and regeneration, – themes said to be 'universal' – you can see easily why the Greek plays would appeal to a Yoruba dramatist.

Women of Owu originated not in Osofisan's choice to adapt a Greek play but in an approach from Chipping Norton theatre.[24] Mike even goes as far as to say that in directing the play the Greek source text did not matter to him: he simply put on a new play, a play in its own right. Such statements are a healthy lesson for classicists, who are perhaps inclined sometimes to overestimate just how much stake theatre professionals and indeed audiences put by any Greek aspects of new plays. More important, though, they go together with Osofisan's emphasis on writing with Nigerians, including presumably non-elite Nigerians, in mind, audiences that are likely to be much less concerned with Greek tragedy than classicists. I am in no position to draw out the present-day Nigerian resonances in any detail, but it is clear that the play reflects Osofisan's concern with Nigeria. Setting, religious and social universe, and themes such as mass killings and dispossessions, or exposure to the whim of armies without effective protection from the law will all resonate in Nigeria, and more generally Africa, in ways they probably do not in Chipping Norton, and the same is true even more emphatically for the choice of Yoruba for the songs. By contrast, specifically Greek elements that might be alien in a Nigerian context, such as names or gods, are all translated into the Yoruba setting. Apart from the subtitle, *Women of Owu* contains hardly any pointers to its source text.[25]

Still, Osofisan accepted the commission for UK performances, and wrote a play that was by no means incomprehensible to its first audiences. What is more, references to the Iraq war, with its contentious UK participation, made the play topical for British spectators, and more generally the sufferings caused by war,

---

[24] As producer Tamara Malcolm sets out in the programme note she first had the idea of commissioning the production after a 2001 Mike production of Lorca's *Yerma* in Chipping Norton, because of its choral work. Osofisan was approached after Mike's 2002 *Tegonni* production. By contrast, the idea to write an *Antigone* play had been Osofisan's. See Osofisan 2001: 203.

[25] Mike stresses that he approached the play as a new play, rather than a version of a Greek play, and Osofisan's statement in the second quote that he merely responded to the Chipping Norton commission may be seen in the same light.

for women or men, are not an issue confined to Africa. More interesting perhaps, the unfamiliar is attractive in its own ways. One does not have to speak Yoruba to be able to engage with the choral songs. There still is the music and the dance, and – just as powerful – the vague sense of being put in touch with another culture, mediated by a composer, a writer and performers who are themselves familiar with that culture. Something similar is true for the elements of Yoruba religion in *Women of Owu*, and Osofisan's portrayal of gender relations, I suggested tentatively, could not be as provocative and as effective as it is without the nineteenth-century African setting. Distance can open up room for the imagination. This is a principal aspect of the paradox that Osofisan points to, between local grounding – so crucial for giving the play its coherence and moral force – and universality.

But what about Euripides? His play is there too, somewhere, and most spectators will know that, if only from the programme note. Those who are familiar with *Trojan Women* will see its influence throughout. At the most basic level, their knowledge will help them follow and (more or less precisely) predict the action of a play that is not structured around a strong narrative. More fundamentally, similarities and differences between the two plays are likely to shape and reshape their views of both *Trojan Women* and *Women of Owu*. Despite the absence of intertextual pointers, some audiences will look at Osofisan and Mike in the light of Euripides, and vice versa. Comparisons, if not necessarily sophisticated, between the new and the old, appeared in most of the reviews of the UK performances. What is more, the Greek elements can help those less familiar with West African theatre respond to the play. In a recent article, Osofisan discusses the difficulty of producing Nigerian drama on the Euro-American stage (Osofisan 2001: 174-201). Differences in the skills of actors, the circumstances of performances and the cultural knowledge and expectations of audiences all present hurdles, many of which (such as the lack of audience response) are very difficult to overcome. Arguably, the use of song and dance in *Women of Owu*, characteristic of many Yoruba plays, may be easier to accommodate for many UK spectators as an engagement with what they may know from or about Greek plays than as a variety of theatre they do not know at all. The Greek source gives them a further entry point.

For many spectators, however, in Europe, America or Africa, the fact *that* there is a Greek source text is likely to be at least as important as *how* that text shapes *Women of Owu*. The idea of Greek tragedy evokes numerous associations, more or less related to the actual plays themselves. In this context, critics frequently point out that ancient plays can provide a particularly suitable platform for mounting anti-colonial protest. Postcolonial writers use Greek tragedy as a high-profile European genre to express their protest against European colonial or neo-colonial actions (Gilbert & Tompkins 1996: 38-43). Or they use Greek tragedy as a European genre that is less closely linked to the colonisers than for instance Shakespeare, and perhaps itself marginalised, to express their protest against the European colonisers (Wetmore 2002, Hardwick 2004 and Budelmann 2004).

Either way, while it would be reductive to see *Women of Owu* as simply taking a core European genre to the UK and stage it as a critique of UK politics, some such reading is certainly possible.

Interestingly, Osofisan in the responses quoted above does not say anything about protest against European politics, but makes two other points about the meaning of Greek tragedy to him. One (as he says) is well known, but no less true for it: the similarities between Greek and Yoruba drama.[26] Gods, choruses, song, dance, ritual elements, open-door performance spaces – Greek tragedy provides points of contact that Shakespeare and much other early modern or modern western drama does not provide. The success of the choral work and the portrayal of the gods in *Women of Owu* owe much to such affinities between the two theatre traditions.

Osofisan's other point is more difficult. The themes of Greek tragedy, he suggests, 'said to be "universal"', are those that 'concern us all as human beings living in a social space we are never in full control of, nor fully comprehend.' This raises the perennial question of the universality of Greek tragedy: to what degree is Greek tragedy's widespread appeal related to something genuinely universal in the plays themselves such as their subject matter; to what degree is it the reflection of Greek tragedy's accumulated reputation, including its reputation for universality; and to what degree does it depend on particular circumstances in particular places and periods, such as points of contact with African drama or a heightened sense of exposure and powerlessness? Yes, on the one hand Greek tragedy obviously survived for 2,500 years, but on the other hand there has been an explosion in performances in the last thirty to forty years (Hall, Macintosh & Wrigley eds. 2004),[27] with the once mostly western genre becoming popular across the world, and with *Trojan Women*, a once unfancied play, becoming increasingly attractive, especially in contexts of sympathy with victims of military aggression.[28] The appeal of *Trojan Women* as a Greek play to an African playwright and audience is (of course) a cocktail with several ingredients. What matters most in the present context is that spectators unfamiliar with Greek tragedy are, none the less, in more than one way able to engage with both the idea and the detail of a play inspired by a Greek source

---

[26] E.g., Asgill 1980: 175, Gilbert & Tompkins 1996: 38, and Budelmann 2004: 15-20. Osofisan's thesis (which I have not seen) was a comparison between African and European forms of theatre.

[27] See especially Hall's introduction for a discussion of possible reasons.

[28] Victims of aggression: e.g., Sartre's 1965 adaptation; Holk Freitag's 1983 Tel Aviv production of Sartre's adaptation, in the context of the Lebanon War (Levy & Yaari 1998); a Canadian CBC radio play on slavery with black actors (Hall 2005: 25); Courttia Newland's 1999 Edinburgh (UK) *Women of Troy 2099*, in which the Greeks, committing atrocities, were repeatedly referred to as 'English', and the Trojans were dressed in traditional African costumes. Other high profile productions include those by Andrei Serban in 1974, Tadashi Suzuki in 1977, and by Dharmasiri Bandranayaka in 1999 (detailed review at www.wsws.org/articles/2000/apr2000/tro-a03_prn.shtml, last accessed August 2004). Brief general discussion of the reception of *Trojan Women* in Taplin 1989: 261-263.

text. As in the case of European spectators with no experience of African theatre traditions, unfamiliarity need not lead to alienation, hostility or disregard, but can add a range of extra dimensions to the play.

All this, of course, is too schematic. After all, as the London audience of the initial *Women of Owu* tour illustrates, there is a degree (if only a degree) of convergence between Nigerian and UK audiences, or African and western audiences. Similarly, the contrast between audiences familiar and unfamiliar with African or with Greek drama is a sliding scale rather than a clear-cut distinction. But this does not affect the basic conclusion I would like to draw from the discussion in this section. The considerable variation in what Greek tragedy may mean to different spectators suggests strongly that speaking (as I have done) of 'source texts' or of modern plays 'translating', 'adapting' or 'interpreting' ancient Greek plays does not do justice to how spectators make sense of many plays, certainly plays like *Women of Owu* which set up three-way relationships. Such terms are both useful and justifiable, but also limiting. Not only do we need the widest possible understanding of 'translation' to accommodate the fact that the *idea* of Greek or African is as significant as the ancient or modern *text*, and that the associations that 'Greek' or 'African' evokes with spectators and indeed theatre professionals often shape the reception of a play just as much as any interest in the way the new play uses the old. More important, we have to realise that traffic is more than one way. On the one hand, Osofisan and Mike translate a Greek play into an African context, but on the other hand awareness of the Greek play may help some European spectators bring an African play into their own world, while some African spectators may feel that the Greek play itself is theirs in the fist place as much as it is European. Depending on a spectator's position, the Greek side of *Women of Owu* may be familiar or unfamiliar; close to home or foreign; crucial or insignificant; and the source or the catalyst. Some of this is true of all 'hybrid' plays and intercultural performances, but I think *Women of Owu*, both the play itself and Osofisan's comments about it, helps to illustrate that Greek tragedy can be a distinctive element to go into the melting pot.

6 Conclusion: Classics and postcolonial studies

Just as there are different audiences watching *Women of Owu*, there will also be different scholarly communities reading the play: experts in African literatures, in drama, in postcolonial studies and in Classics, to name just the most obvious. Like different audiences, they overlap. At the same time, however, just as Osofisan stresses the local grounding of plays as a prerequisite for their universal appeal, scholars crossing disciplines are – inevitably – shaped by the discipline they come from, with its particular assumptions, interests and methods. I want to end by placing my discussion of *Women of Owu* in the more general context of interaction between Classics and postcolonial studies, and more specifically, between classical and postcolonial literary studies. As the essays collected in Goff's *Classics and Colonialism* (2005) and Hardwick and Gillespie's *Classics in Post-Colonial Worlds* (2004) show, interdisciplinary work between these areas is currently burgeoning.

For classicists the dominant context of this work is of course 'reception studies'. The growing interest on part of classicists in postcolonial literature is one particular aspect of their growing interest in the modern reception of ancient literature.[29] Yet beyond this general place within Classics, several more specific factors come into play. First of all, as I have tried to bring out in the case of *Women of Owu* and as others have done for other works, the blend of Greek or Roman and various African, South American or otherwise postcolonial literary traditions can hold its own fascination for classicists and pose its own challenges. Next, Classics as a discipline comes with heavy colonialist baggage. As Lorna Hardwick has pointed out, studying postcolonial responses to Greek tragedies is one way of confronting this baggage (2004). Yet, thirdly, there is further motivation for classicists to look at such texts that I think should not be ignored. Over the last ten to twenty years, postcolonial studies have been a success story more than Classics has. Postcolonial studies are attacked for their political opinion-making (what stronger testimony could there be to their perceived strength?), while Classics fights a battle against charges of being outdated and quite simply superfluous. One (by no means, of course, the only one) of the attractions of reception studies in general is that they allow classicists to get a share of the vibrancy of subjects such as theatre or twentieth-century literature. Surely, postcolonial studies are particularly attractive in this respect.

There is, I hasten to add, nothing wrong with that. On the contrary, Classics has been so long-lived a subject not least because of its Proteus-like ability to change its shape, and this latest extension of its boundaries is exciting, perhaps even liberating. However, as a classicist, the question that I find difficult to avoid at this point is what Classics has to offer to postcolonial studies or, in the case of *Women of Owu*, to postcolonial literary studies, in return. In concrete terms: why should anybody interested in postcolonial literary studies read this chapter? One-way relationships can be good, but dialogue is better. The use of anthropological methods and themes borrowed from anthropology, gender studies or social history have transformed the study of ancient Greece and Rome over the last thirty years or so, but the other way round Classics has made little impact on anthropology, gender studies or the study of social history.

To put it strongly, from the perspective of postcolonial literary studies, Greek tragedy is simply one of many western texts that postcolonial writing engages

---

[29] Rush Rehm, *Radical Theatre: Greek Tragedy and the Modern World* (2003); Hall, Macintosh and Wrigley, eds., *Dionysus since 69: Greek Tragedy at the Dawn of the Third Millennium* (2004); Dillon and Wilmer, eds., *Rebel Women: Staging Ancient Greek Drama Today* (2005); and Hall and Macintosh, *Greek Tragedy and the British Theatre 1660-1914* (2005) are four rather different publications, in different ways representative of recent work in this area.

with, along with those drawn from English, French or Spanish literature. Like anthropology, postcolonial studies own the overarching theoretical models and methodologies, which can be exported to Classics rather than vice versa. This makes it difficult to see what the study of classical literature will be able to bring to postcolonial studies. Perhaps indeed there is little potential for dialogue, and what we will see over the next few years is classical literary studies learning from postcolonial literary studies without being able to give much back. Classicists interested in interdisciplinary work in this area should I think be conscious of this possibility. Their excitement may not be shared as widely on the other side.

Yet I would like to believe that, within limits, there are also more upbeat points to be made. First, exactly because it is a nervous subject, a subject under pressure, and because it is prepared to question its boundaries and even purpose to such a high degree, Classics is genuinely interested in dialogue, and under the right circumstances that might be attractive to other subjects, including postcolonial studies. Secondly, classicists *qua* classicists will inevitably offer a new perspective. As they start from a different base – their understanding of classical literature and its reception history – they make different connections and see different things. They have a partial angle on postcolonial studies and as has became clear their interest in classical literature may contrast with the interests of some audiences, writers and directors, but as long as it comes without claims to a privileged access to the plays in question, this specific viewpoint should lead to specific insights and contributions, some of which may be of interest also to experts in other disciplines. Thirdly, and most problematically, Classics has its own characteristic methods. It is not by accident that this chapter has concentrated on a single play. Classicists have traditionally been empiricist in their approach to texts, and often study them in enormous detail. The elaborate commentaries written on ancient texts are a good expression of this. Perhaps few subjects apart from theology have channelled as much effort into writing commentaries as Classics. It is obvious why these tendencies are often criticised, but I think it would be a mistake to neglect what is valuable about them. They represent one particular way of trying to appreciate individual creativity as broadly as possible, and this, if done self-consciously, is a worthwhile project with all literary texts.

Classicists know that they will not be able simply to fall back on what they have always done, but I think they should still remember where they come from. They will always remain classicists and will be looked at as such, classicists who live in a period rife with postcolonial concerns and may therefore be *interested*, personally and professionally, in postcolonial studies, but who will only rarely become card-carrying *specialists* in postcolonial studies. What interests me in this respect is that some trends in postcolonial studies may well create opportunities for classicists *qua* classicists to make valid contributions to a field that is not theirs. First, authors and theorists in former colonies point out that 'postcolonialism' is a western concept and that 'postcolonial studies' are an invention of western academia. In an interview about *Tegonni*, Osofisan speaks of the 'merely intellectual discourses of "postcoloniality" which are currently fashionable because they serve scholars so well in the western academic circuit, but which are so remote from the concrete concerns of the people on our continent' (2001: 206)[30] Related to that, I think, is the longstanding concern about lack of specificity in postcolonial literary criticism. The 'postcolonial' (a little like 'the tragic') is a concept that goes beyond particular spaces, moments and situations. There has been increasing dissatisfaction with the blandness of some postcolonial literary criticism that is not sufficiently attuned to the specifics of cultures, literatures and texts. One recent trend, therefore, has been not so much to develop postcolonial literary theory in general as to focus on reading individual texts, and rely on those readings to make their contribution to develop theory more widely.[31] In this context, classical literary studies perhaps *do* have something to offer, as well as so much to gain. They can offer the local position of one of the elements that go into the characteristic postcolonial blend – Greek tragedy in the case of *Women of Owu*; and from this position they can offer their own response to the individual creative work, a different response from that privileging matters postcolonial. This kind of contribution will probably always be modest, but that is perhaps as it should be.

References:

Agovi, K. 1985. 'Is There an African Vision of Tragedy in Contemporary African Theatre?' *Présence Africaine* 133-34, pp. 55-74.

Ajayi, O. 1996. 'Gender and the Revolutionary Ethos of Class in *Morountodun'*. In Awodiya, M. P. ed., *Femi Osofisan: Interpretative Essays*. (Lagos: Centre for Black and African Arts and Civilization, pp. 88-104).

Asgill, E. J. 1980. 'African Adaptations of Greek Tragedies', *African Literature Today 11* pp. 175-89.

Awodiya, M. P. 1995. *The Drama of Femi Osofisan: A Critical Perspective.* (Ibadan: Kraft Books).

Awodiya, M. P., ed. 1993. *Excursions in Drama and Literature: Interviews with Femi Osofisan.* (Ibadan: Kraft Books).

Bhabha, H. K. 2004. *The Location of Culture.* 2nd ed. (London: Routledge).

---

[30]A similar point, in a different tone, is made by Trivedi 1999 in response to the question: 'who is the postcolonial?': 'On the basis of the evidence available so far, a postcolonial is an English-speaking theoretically inclined Westward-looking writer or academic of (or more likely *from*) a former colony which "gained independence" from Britain during the last half-century....' (p. 269)

[31] The complexities of the need for specificity in postcolonial criticism are analysed at length in Hallward 2001, including detailed references to earlier work. Most recently, Spivak 2003 called for more specificity, careful readings and awareness of local cultures in comparative studies.

Bharucha, R. 2000. *The Politics of Cultural Practice: Thinking through Theatre in an Age of Globalization*. (London: Athlone Press).

Bharucha, R. 1993. *Theatre and the World: Performance and the Politics of Culture*. (London and New York: Routledge).

Bryant-Bertail, S. 2000. 'The Trojan Women a Love Story: A Postmodern Semiotics of the Tragic'. *Theatre Research International 25*, pp. 40-52.

Budelmann, F. 2004. 'Greek Tragedies in West African Adaptations'. *Proceedings of the Cambridge Philological Society 50*, pp. 1-28.

Dillon, J. and S. E. Wilmer, eds. 2005. *Rebel Women: Staging Ancient Greek Drama Today*. (London: Methuen).

Foley, H. 2004. 'Bad Women: Gender Politics in Late Twentieth-Century Performance and Revision of Greek Tragedy'. In Hall, E., F. Macintosh and A. Wrigley eds., *Dionysus since 69: Greek Tragedy at the Dawn of the Third Millennium*. (Oxford: Oxford University Press, pp. 77-111).

Gilbert, H. and J. Tompkins. 1996. *Post-Colonial Drama: Theory, Practice, Politics*. (London and New York: Routledge).

Goff, B. ed. 2005. *Classics and Colonialism*. (London: Duckworth Publishers).

Goff, B. and M. Simpson. *Crossroads in the Black Aegean* (in preparation).

Hall, E. 2004. 'Introduction: Why Greek Tragedy in the Late Twentieth Century?' In Hall, E., F. Macintosh and A. Wrigley eds., *Dionysus in 69: Greek Tragedy at the Dawn of the Third Millennium*. (Oxford: Oxford University Press, pp. 1-46).

Hall, E. and F. Macintosh. 2005. *Greek Tragedy and the British Theatre 1660-1914*. (Oxford: Oxford University Press).

Hall, E., F. Macintosh, and A. Wrigley eds. 2004. *Dionysus since 69: Greek Tragedy at the Dawn of the Third Millennium*. (Oxford and New York: Oxford University Press).

Hallward, P. 2001. *Absolutely Postcolonial: Writing between the Singular and the Specific*. (Manchester and New York: Manchester University Press).

Hardwick, L. 2004. 'Greek Drama and Anti-Colonialism: Decolonizing Classics'. In Hall, E., F. Macintosh and A. Wrigley eds., *Dionysus since 69: Greek Tragedy at the Dawn of the Third Millennium*. (Oxford: Oxford University Press, pp. 219-42).

Hardwick, L. and C. Gillespie eds. (2007). *Classics in Post-Colonial Worlds*. (forthcoming) Oxford: Oxford University Press)).

Jeyifo, B. ed. 2002. *Modern African Drama*. (New York and London: W. W. Norton & Company, Inc.).

Law, R. 1977. *The Oyo Empire C.1600-C.1836: A West African Imperialism in the Era of the Atlantic Slave Trade*. (Oxford: Clarendon Press).

Levy, S. and N. Yaari. 1998. 'Theatrical Responses to Political Events: The Trojan War on the Israeli Stage During the Lebanon War, 1982-1984'. *Journal of Theatre and Drama 4*, pp. 99-123.

Loraux, N. 2002. *The Mourning Voice: An Essay on Greek Tragedy*. Trans. Elizabeth Trapnell Rawlings. (Ithaca, NY, and London: Cornell University Press).

Mabogunje, A. L. and J. D. Omer Cooper. 1971. *Owu in Yoruba History*. (Ibadan: Ibadan University Press).

McDonald, M. and J. M. Walton eds. 2002. *Amid Our Troubles: Irish Versions of Greek Tragedy*. (London: Methuen).

Ohaeto, E. 1982. 'The Nature of Tragedy in Modern African Drama'. *Literary Half-Yearly 23.2*, pp. 3-17.

Osofisan, F. 1996. 'Warriors of a Failed Utopia? – West African Writers since the '70s'. *Leeds African Studies Bulletin 61*, pp. 11-36.

Osofisan, F. 1997. *Playing Dangerously: Drama at the Frontier of Terror in a 'Postcolonial' State*. (Ibadan: University of Ibadan Press).

Osofisan, F. 2001. *Insidious Treasons: Drama in a Postcolonial State*. (Ibadan: Opon Ifa Publishers).

Pavis, P. ed. 1996. *The Intercultural Performance Reader*. (London and New York: Routledge).

Rehm, R. 2003. *Radical Theatre: Greek Tragedy and the Modern World*. (London: Duckworth Publishers).

Richards, S. L. 1996. *Ancient Songs Set Ablaze: The Theatre of Femi Osofisan*. (Washington, D. C.: Howard University Press).

Sartre, J. 1969. *Three Plays: Kean, Nekrassov, the Trojan Women*. (Harmondswoth: Penguin Books).

Smith, A. 2004. 'Migrancy, Hybridity, and Postcolonial Literary Studies'. *The Cambridge Companion to Postcolonial Literary Studies*. Ed. Neil Lazarus. (Cambridge: Cambridge University Press, pp. 241-61).

Soyinka, W. 1976. *Myth, Literature and the African World*. (Cambridge: Cambridge University Press).

Spivak, G. C. 2003. *Death of a Discipline*. (New York and Chichester: Columbia University Press).

Taplin, O. 1989. *Greek Fire*. (London: Jonathan Cape).

Taplin, O. 2004. 'Sophocles' Philoctetes, Seamus Heaney's, and Some Other Recent Half-Rhymes'. In Hall, E., F. Macintosh and A. Wrigley eds., *Dionysus since 69: Greek Tragedy at the Dawn of the Third Millennium*. Oxford: Oxford University Press, pp. 145-67.

Trivedi, H. 1999. 'The Postcolonial or the Transcolonial? Location and Language', *Interventions 1.2*, pp. 269-72.

Ukaegbu, V. 2001. 'Femi Osofisan's *Once Upon Four Robbers*: Continuing the Intercultural Debate', *African Theatre: Playwrights and Politics*. Banham, M., J. Gibbs and F. Osofisan eds. (Oxford: James Currey, 2001, pp. 42-56).

Ukala, S. 2001. 'Politics of Aesthetics'. *African Theatre: Playwrights and Politics*. Banham, M., J. Gibbs and F. Osofisan eds. (Oxford: James Currey, pp. 29-41).

Watson, I. (and colleagues). 2002. *Negotiating Cultures: Eugenio Barba and the Intercultural Debate*. (Manchester and New York: Manchester University Press).

Wetmore, K. J. 2002. *The Athenian Sun in an African Sky: Modern African Adaptations of Classical Greek Tragedy*. (Jefferson, N. C., and London: McFarland).

Wetmore, K. J. 2003. *Black Dionysus: Greek Tragedy and African American Theatre*. (Jefferson, N.C., and London: McFarland).

Young, R. 1995. *Colonial Desire: Hybridity in Theory, Culture and Race*. (London: Routledge).

ANTIGONE'S BOAT: THE COLONIAL AND THE POSTCOLONIAL IN *TEGONNI: AN AFTICAN ANTIGONE* BY FEMI OSOFISAN

BARBARA GOFF

Adaptations of classical drama by writers of African descent are increasingly important to students of classics and the humanities generally, not least because classical drama has been integral to the notion of the western tradition, and African adaptations raise questions about what it means to claim a 'western' tradition in the wake of colonialism. Such adaptations also struggle with the fact that the very presence of Greek and Roman classics within African culture, however fruitful for creative endeavour, testifies to the disruption of African history by decades of colonial exploitation. Most such adaptations address more or less explicitly the ways in which the conditions of their possibility can also undermine their project.[1]

Within African rewritings, the story of Antigone has proved very popular, and the reasons for this presumably include the fact that the story involves a confrontation with overweening power.[2] In western rewritings a play based on *Antigone* often figures resistance against an arrogant state, as with Anouilh and Brecht. In African *Antigones*, one might expect Creon to be identified with the colonial occupiers, but in fact, this is rarely the case in any straightforward way.[3] This muddying of the political waters is linked to an aspect of the character Antigone that makes it difficult to recuperate her simply as a figure for African resistance: since she is part and parcel of the cultural equipment that the colonisers drew on to explain the success of their inroads into other cultures, she presumably only comes to Africa by way of colonial Europe.

The most recent adaptation of *Antigone* is *Tegonni: an African Antigone* by Femi Osofisan, first produced in 1994.[4] This play centres on a young Yoruba woman's resistance to British imperialism. Princess Tegonni buries the body of her brother, exposed on the day of her wedding to the British District Officer,

---

[1] For general introductions to the topic of African adaptations see e.g. Etherton 102-142 and Gilbert and Tompkins 38-43. Wetmore is a much more comprehensive survey and very relevant. Classicists who have addressed this issue include Budelmann, Hardwick, Macintosh, and McDonald.

[2] See e.g. Gibbs.

[3] Thus, in *The Island* by Fugard, Kani and Ntshona it is clearly the white apartheid system that throws up its Creons, but there is also a power struggle in the cell, between Winston and John. In *Odale's Choice* by E. K. Brathwaite, it is not clear from the text whether the Creon figure is to be understood as a white coloniser or as a home-grown African tyrant.

[4] Published in Osofisan *Recent Outings I*. The published text derives from a later production. All references to the play are taken from this edition.

Barbara Goff

Allan Jones. The brother was killed in a civil conflict in which the British assisted the other side. Tegonni acts in defiance of the colonial Governor, who has ordered that the body of the rebel be left unburied, and she eventually suffers the penalty of death. The play directly dramatises the nineteenth-century colonial encounter, and in this it is unlike other African Antigone-dramas, but also unlike the majority of Osofisan's plays, which are best known for their probing analyses of *post*colonial, especially post-civil war, Nigeria.[5] I propose to explore here the ways in which the play coordinates the colonial and postcolonial perspectives, and I shall investigate in particular the figure of Antigone herself, who as a character in the play arrives to share the stage with the nineteenth-century heroine Tegonni, but who also announces that she comes from Greek mythology (26). Because this Antigone thus brings with her the weight of her mythical and theatrical tradition, she also becomes the focus for the play's metatheatrical dimension.[6] Through the figure of Antigone the play is enabled to make complex arguments about the relations between colonial and postcolonial, and between British and Yoruba – and it is also enabled to escape from these complexities.

The colonial aspects of the play's politics centre on the man who can be understood as the Creon-figure, 'Lt-General Carter-Ross, who is the governor of the southern colony of Nigeria' (28), otherwise known as 'de big white man, "Slap-My-Face" the big Oyinbo from Lagos' (47). We do not meet him until the play is a third of the way through, so that he cannot make the kind of bid for our sympathy that the Sophoclean Creon makes as leader of a community only recently released from the fear of destruction. Instead, he immediately acquaints us with his racist understanding of the relations between coloniser and colonised. He sees the Empire in simple terms of dominance and submission: 'It is time to take a firm control here, I see, and show who is in charge! The Empire will assert its power!... Fear! That's what these niggers respect!' (65). If firmness is for a moment relaxed, then: 'Chaos! Rebellion! All my work undone! And before we know it, they'll begin to eat each other again!' (114). He does offer a pious discourse about the white man's burden and the civilising mission of the British (131), but this is quickly undermined by his latent violence. His relations with all of the Yoruba characters are characterised by a swift resort to physical force, and he eventually engages in a violent struggle with his own District Officer as well.

---

[5] Jeyifo 121 also discusses this apparent paradox.

[6] Osofisan's theatre almost always coordinates its politics with a persistent and demanding metatheatricality, and this play is no exception. See on this feature of Osofisan's dramaturgy e.g. Dunton 67, Richards 63 and 83, Wetmore 181-182, and Jeyifo 129. Osofisan's aesthetics are often labelled 'Brechtian'; see e.g. Crow, 30, and Olaniyan, 74, who writes of a 'consummate dramaturgic sophistication and openness that takes us a few steps beyond Bertolt Brecht'. Richards 71 makes the point that these aesthetics derive at least as much from traditional African performance styles as from Brecht.

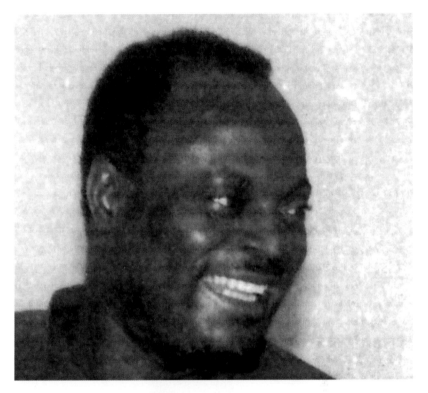

Femi Osofisan at Ibadan 1991   *Photo: Sola Adeyemi*

Esu and the Vagabond Minstrels at Ife, 1986   *Photo: Olu Elufowoju*

Òsofisan rehearsing *The Engagement* with musician Tunji Oyelana and
Yinka Ige for the Five-College tour of the USA in 1992

Photo: Opon Ifa Readers

An evening of poetry, Lake Forest, Chicago, USA, 1992

Photo: Opon Ifa Readers

The bridal dance for Tegonni in *Tegonni, An African Antigone* at Emory, Atlanta, USA, 1994

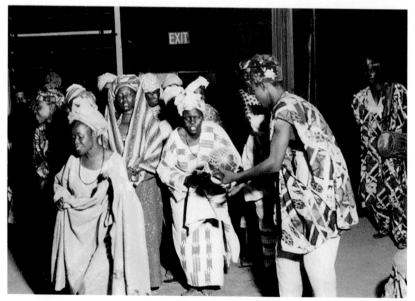

The bridal dance in *Tegonni, An African Antigone* at The Arts Theatre, University of Ibadan, Nigeria, 2002

Women of Owu, directed by Chuck Mike
Performed by Collective Artistes, United Kingdom, 2004

Photo: © Chuck Mike / Collective Artistes

Rehearsing *Nkrumah-Ni!...Africa-Ni!* in Colombo, Sri Lanka, 1995
Photo: Opon Ifa Readers

Nkrumah-Ni!... Africa-Ni! at the National Theatre, Accra, Ghana, 1994
Photo: Eckhard Breitinger

Nkrumah-Ni!... Africa-Ni! at the National Theatre, Accra, Ghana, 1994
Photo: Eckhard Breitinger

Femi Osofisan at Bayreuth University, June 2005

Photo: Katja Breitinger

Femi Osofisan at Bayreuth University, June 2005

Photo: Katja Breitinger

A straightforward physical violence is not the end of the account of Carter-Ross, however. Even though he is a man of brute force, he has a fine sense of occasion and of drama. For instance, some of the characters conclude that he orders the exposure of the corpse of Tegonni's brother not in order to drive home the political lessons of loyalty, but to afford a deliberate provocation that will disrupt the planned wedding between Tegonni and the District Officer (e.g. 121). The exposure of the corpse is thus an action with a staged, theatrical dimension as well as a political charge. It is also metatheatrical in that the part of the corpse is played by one of the soldiers who accompany the character Antigone on to the stage (29), so that on one level there is no 'real' corpse in the play at all. Others of Carter-Ross's gestures as Governor are also conditioned by theatricality. Thus, when he plans to execute Tegonni and her women friends, he has them watch while the scaffolds are erected, so that they will be the more frightened. This theatrical plan actually backfires, since they remain unmoved (72).

Despite his colonial attitudes, Carter-Ross is also brought on two separate occasions, once by the District Officer (122-23) and once by the joint efforts of the Yoruba elders, to countenance a pardon for Tegonni. The Yoruba elders in fact use the theatricality of colonial power against Carter-Ross, because they offer to stage a scene in which Tegonni is to make a humiliating public apology, in return for a pardon (87-88). The possibility that Tegonni may be pardoned, and live, sets Carter-Ross apart from the Greek Creon, who never wavers in his determination to execute his niece.[7] These offers of pardon by Carter-Ross may also be seen to constitute a kind of metatheatrical crisis: will the new play save the Antigone-figure, the Yoruba princess Tegonni, or will it save the Antigone-plot in which the protagonists have to die? Such questions, about the possibilities of different endings and of escape from tradition, can also be understood as questions about the weight of the colonial past, and so bear here a special urgency.

In this connection we should look at Antigone herself, who is the most obviously metatheatrical figure in the play; she enters the stage with the words 'Greetings. Has the play started?' (25) and she constantly draws attention to the fictional, theatrical quality of the proceedings. But we should note that the drive behind her metatheatrical utterances is almost exactly the opposite of that which impels the other characters, many of whom are striving to spare Tegonni. Whereas much of the play is invested in *not* being like the Greek *Antigone*, so that the heroine can survive, the character Antigone frequently tries to ensure that this drama repeats the traditional plot, and thus plays out exactly as did her own. When she arrives, she is convinced that this drama *is* in fact her own: 'I heard you were acting my story. And I was so excited I decided to come and

---

[7] Other Creons, such as those of Anouilh and Brathwaite, offer to overlook Antigone's deed, but this is usually done on the grounds of family relationship, which is not applicable here, and is usually done in secret.

participate' (25). She reinforces this attitude in her next scene, when she is preparing the soldiers who have accompanied her to take up their new theatrical roles as African mercenaries: 'A story goes on, no matter when one arrives in it'; 'It's just history about to repeat itself again'; 'You know what to do, you've been well rehearsed'; 'The script is the story we rehearsed, as it's happened at other times, in other places' (28-29). Throughout this scene, then, she insists on the inevitability of the story that they will enact.

This stance on the part of Antigone is intriguing for a number of reasons. If we do think of an Antigone as necessarily a figure of resistance, we should acknowledge that here she is almost the opposite, and as we shall see, other characters take it upon themselves to resist her, as well as there being the underlying drive in the play to rescue Tegonni and thus defeat the ancient Greek plot imperative. There is only one scene where Antigone also seems to try to rescue Tegonni, and thus to overcome the weight of her own legacy, and as we shall see, this scene has its own difficulties. Overall, there seems to be an identification of Antigone with a form of coercion, and in this respect she may indeed remind us of the coercive dimension of the colonialism that makes her story available to the Nigerian author in the first place. To see her simply as a figure of opposition to the colonial power may be insufficient.

So, there are at least two versions of colonialism at work in this drama. Carter-Ross offers almost a caricature of violent racist attitudes, but also allows us to read his power as merely theatrical. The character Antigone may also be seen to offer a version of colonial coercion, despite her usual identification with resistance. There are also, on the reading that I shall offer here, at least two versions of the *post*colonial in *Tegonni*. These may be broadly characterised as negative and positive. One version concentrates on the internal conflicts within Nigerian society and lays the blame for Nigeria's problems not only at the feet of the colonisers, but of the indigenous people. The second version, centring on the figure of the boat on which Antigone arrives and later departs, suggests even more forcefully that the colonisers may be irrelevant. These aspects of the play are postcolonial not only in a broadly temporal sense but also in that they subvert the ideologies of colonialism by training their focus on relations among Africans rather than on relations between Africans and the occupying British.[8]

Although the play is shaped by the obvious overriding conflict between the Yoruba and the British, there are also several ways in which the African society in the play is shown to be divided against itself. We are invited to see that these divisions characterise a pre-colonial period, and that they extend in significance

---

[8] In this essay I am using the terms *colonial* and *postcolonial* in a way that has become fairly received, so that *colonial* refers to the actual historical period of occupation while *postcolonial* is temporally later but also refers to various kinds of critical thought about and dissent from the ideologies that accompanied occupation. See, e.g. Boehmer 2; Gilbert and Tompkins 2; Quayson 2. Osofisan's version of postcolonialism also resists the neo-colonialism which puts corrupt indigenous elites in place of corrupt colonialists. To an extent he rejects the label; see e.g. 'Theatre' and Jeyifo 122.

to the postcolonial period. There is the civil dispute which kills Tegonni's brothers, but also a persistent state of hostility with the neighbouring peoples (22), and references to war with the Dahomi and the Nupe (84). Within the town of Oke-Osun, where Tegonni lives, it is made clear that male and female are often antagonistic to each other, sometimes violently so,[9] and that there is also conflict between the representatives of the traditional ways and those of a more progressive tendency (e.g. 21). On a larger scale, the play suggests that discord among Africans aided and abetted the colonisers in their project. Chief Isokun speaks of black participation in the slave trade (107-8):

> Take reverend here! When I look at him, for instance – I ask, Who were the people who came and captured him, and sold him to the ship that took him to slavery in America? Was it not our own people, of the same colour of skin as you and me? … Tell me, what cruelties have we not inflicted on ourselves, we black people, as agents in the service of others!

The colonial occupiers do not present the only examples of oppression in the play.

The soldiers who accompany Antigone in her entry on to the stage, and who are then assigned the roles of African mercenaries in the Hausa constabulary, constitute the play's most striking illustration of Chief Isokun's claim about the propensity for conflict and exploitation among black Africans. They are acting Africans who readily enlist under the white coloniser in order to carry out military actions against other Africans – in this case they are deployed by the British against the forces headed by Tegonni's brother. The soldiers' attitude to their task is alarmingly pragmatic; they are working for the British because the British pay more than the Africans' home communities could (32-33). There is few signs that Africans can readily make common cause against the colonial occupier, for as Antigone says 'here the soldiers obey their white commanders blindly, and ask no questions' (29). The soldiers in the play cannot even make common cause among themselves, because one of the leitmotifs of all their appearances is their constant quarrelling.

This depressing scenario, however, does not run for ever, and the soldiers, even though divided, find a way to mount some resistance. As we have seen, Antigone introduces the scenes with the soldiers by impressing on them the inevitability of their participation and the inevitability of the story that they will enact: 'It's just history about to repeat itself again' (28). What is significant is that the soldiers immediately undermine her assumptions. For instance, when she delegates one of them to play the corpse of Tegonni's brother, he

---

[9] In the play, Tegonni precipitates much of the expression of this hostility by her desire to become a bronze caster and sculptor, something that no woman has done before. The town is united in its disapproval of her move, even though she is its princess, and she is variously threatened with torture (130) and death (78). It is Allan Jones, the white British D.O., who saves her from the latter.

immediately protests: 'Me! But I just woke up, fresh from the grave!' (29). In the next scene, when the other three are drinking over his body, he jumps up and demands his share (30):

4TH SOL: Give me, make I drink!

2ND SOL: Gerrout ! You supposed to be dead.

4TH SOL: (*Standing up*) - If I no drink my own, I no dey die again!

2ND SOL: (*Giving him*) - Take am! World don spoil finish! When dead person begin to drink!

When we recall that Antigone introduces this scene with much emphasis on its pre-ordained quality, we can see that what the soldier who is playing the corpse does is refuse to follow the script.

This resistance, the force of which is here almost entirely comic, is played out again on a larger and more serious scale, when the soldiers decide against building the scaffolds that they have been ordered to construct for Tegonni and her friends. While they at first congratulate themselves on their craftsmanship – 'See? Solid! Even the Queen of England go want to die here!' (71) – they subsequently start to rebel against their task; they become disgusted with their jobs as oppressors and confront Antigone to demand new roles. When Antigone arrives, they describe all the horrible things they have to do while in character (74):

1ST SOL: Demoralised. All we do is carry corpses.

2ND SOL: Or build execution platforms –

1ST SOL: Or terrorise people –

2ND SOL: Burn and plunder houses –

4TH SOL: Collect bribes!

She again tries to sway them with a metatheatrical necessity and claims that they cannot acquire new roles so late in the day: 'before the play ends? You must be joking!... You can't quit before the play ends'. This provokes from them an answering threat to derail the play itself: 'when we quit, the play will end' (75). Antigone is forced, by this brief power struggle, to find them new roles as part of the delegation of elders who will plead with the Governor for Tegonni's life. Far from finding the metatheatrical dimension constricting, as Antigone earlier on seems to want it to be, the soldiers use it to afford themselves a measure of resistance and even a kind of freedom of action. They convert the role of the oppressors into that of people who are working to save Tegonni.

Their resistance does not encompass only Antigone and the colonial power, however. At the end of their complaints about their roles, they sum up: 'We're so ashamed! Is this all that soldiers do in this country?' and Antigone replies 'it's the times we've come into, my friend' (74-75). The temporal and geographical vagueness in the exchange allows it to be read as an indictment of contemporary

Nigeria, rather than only of the colonial power,[10] and this possibility becomes increasingly insistent as Antigone continues: 'It just so happens that the soldiers here are trained to look upon their own people as enemies. As fair game to practice their weapons on' (75). Given the history of the military's involvement in the politics of post-independence Nigeria, the reference to their oppressive role in their country is hard to avoid.[11]

The soldiers' dramatic identity as Africans who are fighting other Africans, coordinated with their metatheatrical resistance to that identity, clarifies the play's postcolonial critique. Africans are culpable – they were complicit with the predation of the colonisers, and they bear much of the responsibility for the contemporary failures of the postcolonial period. But if Africans are part of the problem then by definition they can be part of the solution. The possibility of the soldiers' resistance to the inevitability of the story, as described by Antigone, opens the possibility of resistance against what Osofisan has elsewhere called 'Afropessimism', a state of mind that consigns the continent to the inevitability of its noxious history.[12]

The metatheatrical dimension of this version of the drama *Antigone*, then, affords the vehicle for some of its trenchant criticisms of both colonial and postcolonial oppression, but it also works to imagine a way out. The struggle between these two dynamics is seen very clearly in the important scene towards the end of the play between Antigone and Tegonni. Antigone gives up the pretence of being just a character alongside other characters and appears as 'a metaphor. From the past', and Tegonni accuses her of being 'a relic in the memory of poets' (125). At the beginning of this scene the two women are in a position of antagonism, because while Tegonni is determined to defy the colonial power, even to the point of death, Antigone counsels quiescence, and survival. She has, she claims, given up the practice of freedom, because (126)

I've learnt from history, and I have grown wise. Freedom is a myth... Go and look down the ages, my dear. Human beings throw off their yokes, only for themselves to turn into oppressors. They struggle valiantly for freedom, and in the process acquire the terrible knowledge of how to deny it to others.

This history from which she has learnt has also, she claims, 'contaminated' her so that she is no longer the Antigone that Tegonni knows, 'the hero men remember' (125). To this extent her discourse here is consistent with her urgings to the soldiers, in that she appears as a figure tamed by her knowledge of colonial and postcolonial history into a refusal of resistance and an acceptance

---

10 The 'Programme Notes' to *Tegonni* similarly target the horrors of contemporary Nigeria rather than its colonial past. See also Osofisan 'Theatre', in which he argues that a focus on the colonial, or even the postcolonial, detracts from the pressing business of freedom and justice in present-day Nigeria.

11 On this point see also Wetmore 188-90.

12 See Jeyifo 129.

of the inevitable. As such, Tegonni violently rejects her – 'Leave my story' – and proclaims her devotion to the 'undying faith' of freedom (126-27). At this point Antigone changes tack, announces that 'I was testing you' and joins forces with Tegonni, sure that for all the tyrants who arise, 'furious to inscribe their nightmares and their horrors on the patient face of history... as many times will others come up who will challenge them and chase them away into oblivion' (127). The two women jubilantly celebrate their solidarity and newfound determination.

One interpretation of this scene sees it as straightforwardly celebrating the courage of freedom fighters throughout history, and thus as shifting the play's centre of gravity to a point where it can proclaim its faith in an ultimate liberation. But when Antigone speaks of the way in which freedom fighters turn into oppressors, her arguments cannot simply be dismissed, because she is describing the lived history of many contemporary states.[13] That she is adopting a pessimistic persona to test Tegonni – that she is acting, in fact – does not mean that she is not speaking the truth. The fact that she reveals her theatrical act also means that it becomes possible to question at what other points she was acting, and thus to query her integrity throughout. In this respect she is like numerous other characters in dramas by Osofisan who suddenly reveal themselves to be quite different from how they seemed, with alarming consequences for the audience's faith in its own perceptions.[14] Moreover, when she performs her volte-face and encourages Tegonni to resist, the upshot of the scene is that Tegonni does indeed die, replicating the plot of the Greek tragedy. The story is saved instead of the woman. When Antigone claims that she has been contaminated, she may in fact be correct; we have seen already that she speaks for the inevitability of the Antigone-story with its freight of death, and perhaps she has indeed been made into an oppressor by the weight of history.

These questions about the significance and indeed identity of the Antigone-figure are posed emphatically at the beginning and end of the play, but receive there what I suggest are much more positive answers. Both her arrival and her departure are marked as spectacular and mysterious. She arrives, the stage directions tell us, in the retinue of a goddess, on a beautiful boat: 'On a platform, the Water Goddess, Yemoja, in full, resplendent regalia, is rowed in,

[13] Wetmore 191 comments on Antigone's words here: 'Antigone offers an explanation as to why cycles of oppression continue: once power is achieved, it is always abused and then the freedom fighters are more concerned about holding on to power than about achieving true freedom. Power corrupts. In Osofisan's view, this is a false argument, as the history of class struggle is not cyclical but linear. Struggle is a process rooted in the idea of progress. Once the bonds of oppression are truly broken for all, argues Marxism at its most basic, then they will not reform, they will dissolve for ever'. As will be clear, I think this account is over-simplified.

[14] On this feature of Osofisan's dramaturgy see e.g. Dunton 69 and 71, and Crow 48. Richards 4 comments on the use of 'authorial manipulation' in early dramas.

in a much–decorated boat' (17).[15] On the boat Yemoja, her boatmen, and her attendants, who include Antigone and Antigone's soldiers, are singing a song that is at first inaudible, and perhaps not quite clear to the sight: 'just a spectacle of dazzling colours and fluid, synchronised movements, all silent, as if observed through transparent glass' (17). Overall, the arrival partakes of the nature of a dream sequence. At the end of the play, when the action is over and the principals are all dead, the boat appears again in an epilogue (141):

Lights come up on the boat of Yemoja, the figures frozen on it, as we saw them last. Their song gradually becomes audible again, as the figures come alive, rowing around the Goddess.

Antigone then approaches Tegonni, who has been killed in the previous scene of riot, rouses her, and takes her on to the boat, where they are welcomed: 'There is immediate, visible joy on the boat, with perhaps a few crackers'. The women are further rewarded: 'Antigone and Tegonni kneel before the Goddess, and are each rewarded with a crystal fan and a dazzling blue necklace' (141). The boat opens and closes the play, and thus invites us to speculate on its significance. I suggest that the boat makes Antigone less a figure of colonial coercion and more a figure that upholds the independence of African culture, rendering the colonisers almost irrelevant.

Wetmore, who is commenting on a performance rather than on the published text, identifies the boat as a slave ship, and suggests that its movement across the stage recalls that of the Middle Passage (2002: 183). While I cannot completely agree with this interpretation, Antigone's boat does ask to be situated in relation to the various forms of mobility, forced or voluntary, that have characterised the colonial and postcolonial periods, and that include the trajectory of the dramatist Osofisan himself, who went from Nigeria to Atlanta in order to direct the first performance of *Tegonni*. At the same time, however, the boat clearly refuses to be confined to the historical dimension, and takes on a mythical or symbolic aspect. At the end, for instance, when Antigone takes Tegonni on to the boat, the boat may be understood as moving through space and time as a kind of spiritual haven for, and commemoration of, all those who have resisted the many manifestations of tyranny, and have paid the price.

This mingling of the historical and the mythical means that although Antigone presumably comes from somewhere, and leaves for somewhere else, the image of the beautiful and uncanny boat obscures her origins and destination. Part of the point, I think, is that Antigone does not come by any colonial route; we are not encouraged to imagine her as arriving from ancient Greece, or via Britain, so her advent is attended by none of the anxiety that might be generated if we were to think of her as a sign of the colonial inheritance. Instead, her arrival by boat allows her to bypass this inheritance completely. If Antigone resists being

---

[15] It is not clear from these stage directions that Antigone is on the boat, but in a later scene (24) she descends from it, so that we must retrospectively realise where she came from.

thought of as 'colonial', then the fact that she arrives on the boat of the Yoruba water-goddess invites us instead to think of her as African. At some level it is clear that she does not *arrive* at all; in the boat of an African deity, she is already part of Africa. If we accept this reading, we can see that one important aspect of the play's postcolonial politics is this offer to erase Africa's colonial history, by asserting that the Antigone-tradition is African as much as it is European. Indeed, the play's title announces as much when it describes the drama *Tegonni* as 'an' African Antigone, implicitly invoking plays such as *Odale's Choice* and *The Island*. Antigone in *Tegonni* is one of a plurality, part of an indigenous tradition, and her colonial identity is subsumed within her African.

Works Cited

Boehmer, E. 1995. *Colonial and Postcolonial Literature* (Oxford and New York: Oxford University Press).

Budelmann, F. (2004). 'Greek tragedies in West African adaptations', *Proceedings of the Cambridge Philological Society* 50 (forthcoming).

Crow, B. 2000. 'Tradition as theme and form in three Nigerian dramatists', *A Review of International English Literature* 31, 29-51.

Dunton, C. 1992. *Make Man Talk True: Nigerian drama in English since 1970* (London and Melbourne: Hans Zell).

Etherton, M. 1982. *The Development of African Drama* (London and Melbourne: Hutchinson University Library for Africa).

Gibbs, J. (2004). 'Antigone and her African Sisters: an examination of work based on Antigone produced in Ghana, South Africa, Malawi and Nigeria (1962-1994).' Conference paper, *Classics on Post-Colonial Worlds: an international, interdisciplinary conference*, Open University, Birmingham.

Gilbert, H. and J. Tompkins. 1996. *Post-colonial Drama* (London and NY: Routledge, 1996).

Hardwick, L. 2004. 'Greek drama and anti-colonialism: de-colonising classics', in E. Hall, F. Macintosh and A. Wrigley (eds), *Dionysus since '69: Tragedy at the Dawn of the Millennium* Oxford: Oxford University Press).

Jeyifo, B. 1995. 'Interview with Femi Osofisan', *Yearbook of Comparative and General Literature* 43, 120-32.

Macintosh, F. 2001. 'Oedipus in Africa', *Omnibus* 42, 8-9.

McDonald, M. 2000. 'Black Dionysus: Greek tragedy from Africa', in L. Hardwick, P. E. Easterling, S. Ireland, N. Lowe, F. Macintosh (eds) *Theatre Ancient and Modern*, Milton Keynes: Open University. Electronically available at
http://www2.open.ac.uk/ClassicalStudies/GreekPlays/conf96/ccfrontpage.htm.

Olaniyan, T. 1999. 'Femi Osofisan: the form of uncommon sense', *Research in African Literature* 30, 74-91.

Osofisan, F. 1999. *Recent Outings 1: 'Tegonni, an African Antigone'* and *'Many Colours Make the Thunder-King'* (Ibadan, Nigeria: Opon Ifa Readers).

Osofisan, F. 1999. 'Theatre and the rites of post-negritude remembering', *Research in African Literatures* 30, 1-11.

Quayson, A. 2000. *Postcolonialism* (Cambridge: Cambridge University Press).

Richards, S. L. 1996. *Ancient Songs Set Ablaze: the Theatre of Femi Osofisan* (Washington DC: Howard University Press).

Wetmore, K. J. Jr. 2002. *The Athenian Sun in an African Sky* (Jefferson NC and London: McFarland)

MAKING COLOURS, REMAKING LIFE: SUBVERSION IN THE WRITING OF FEMI OSOFISAN*

SOLA ADEYEMI

I

The publication of Edward Said's *Orientalism* in 1978 and the inauguration of colonial discourse analysis brought into theoretical focus the ways in which Europe has constructed other peoples and cultures as objects of knowledge to further the aims of imperial domination. What Said's analysis of Europe's construction of the Orient brought to the fore was that more than physical conquest, the more profound and lingering effects of colonialism were the *textual* conquest and subjugation by which Europe established a discursive hegemony over the 'other'.

While Said's work focussed on the unmasking of the operations of the European agenda in the Orient, writers and artists from Africa and other parts of the colonised world have always consciously or unconsciously, openly or surreptitiously, challenged this discursive domination by contesting the myths and stereotypes and indeed the image of other peoples authorised by Europe. This challenge and contestation have always been part of the history of resistance to slavery, colonialism and domination. Beginning with the narratives of the freed slaves through to the counter-discursive manoeuvres of the Négritude movement, writers from every part of the colonised world evolved various strategies for countering European representation of the colonial subject. These counter-discursive gestures, which have been collectively classified under the rubric of the Empire writing back to the *Centre*, have become one of the major themes of post-colonial discourse. Bill Ashcroft et al (1989) and most post-colonial critics conceive of the centre as located in Europe, in the metropolitan centres of power from which the 'Empire' was created and controlled. However, in the works of Nigerian playwright and dramatist Femi Osofisan, the idea of a metropolitan locus in which all power is located is de-centred. While acknowledging the historical significance of this centre, Femi Osofisan sees pockets of power in various kinds of 'Empire' authorised spaces and the major impetus of his work has been to question and challenge these. Beginning with *Oduduwa, Don't Go!* (1968) to *A Diary of My Father: A Voyage Round Wole Soyinka's Isara* (2005) and grounding his vision of change in a dialectical reading and re-reading of history and political discourse, Osofisan manipulates the various heritages available to him as a post-colonial as well as

---

* A slightly different version of this essay was first published in *Africa e Mediterraneo: Cultura e Societa, No 40*, 2004.

post-négritude writer to speak to the challenges facing his broad society, and to scrutinise the practice of art in the 'Empire'.

I describe Osofisan as a post-colonial writer based on Helen Gilbert and Joanne Tompkins definition which argues that post-colonialism is, rather than a naive teleological sequence which supersedes colonialism, an engagement with, and contestation of colonialism's discourses, power structures and social hierarchies (1996: 2). While this definition reinforces the idea proposed by Ashcroft et al (1989) that African writers generally continue to privilege the 'centre', a former colonial country in Europe and more specifically Britain and France, by engaging in a kind of counter-discourse, albeit in a subaltern's role, there is however another agenda that African writers pursue and which the definition omits to explain. African writers attempt to confront the various problems of underdevelopment, the threat of alienation and, more important, the erosion of ethnic identity among the people. But even more than being a post-colonial writer, Osofisan is a post-négritude writer whose work has proceeded beyond the rhetoric of Senghorian négritude which responds to the rhetoric of colonial discourse and that has been refined to respond to the post-colonial discourse. Négritude, as propounded and as practised by Senghor, Césaire and Damas, is a racist philosophy, or, as Sartre puts it in *Orphée Noire*, an 'anti-racist racism' but this is opposed to the idea of post-négritudism that seeks to identify with and promotes African cultures that are under the threat of erasure by colonialism, post-colonialism and non-African cultural incursions without conversely mystifying the African past. Osofisan's work, like post-négritude, critically examines Africa's heritage as a dynamic process that needs to be re-appropriated and foregrounded for the benefit of Africans. In plays such as *The Chattering and the Song* (1976) and *Morountodun* (1983), Osofisan challenges the recuperative bias of the négritude ideology which generally classified everything African as noble, and proposes the presence of imperial or pseudo-imperial tyranny as the dictating current behind the popular African myths and traditional practices.

In *The Chattering and the Song*, Osofisan takes a story of power and 'deliberately challenges a specific distortion of historical consciousness' (Dunton 1992: 93). He uses the play-within-a-play technique to expose the fallacy of the received history of Alaafin Abiodun who reigned in the 19th century. Alaafin Abiodun is always portrayed as a benevolent monarch who brought peace and prosperity to his kingdom but Osofisan re-interprets the history to depict the despotic nature of Abiodun's reign. Again, in *Morountodun*, Osofisan adapts the myth of Queen Moremi of Ile-Ife who sacrificed her honour and freedom to save the city of Ile-Ife from the incessant raids of a neighbouring community. Osofisan, while acknowledging the sacrifice of Moremi, interprets her actions as that of royalty who did not want to lose her prestige and is therefore willing to do anything to maintain the status quo, even while depriving the public their rights. As Titubi, the protagonist in the play, states: I am not Moremi! Moremi served the State, *was* the State, was the spirit of the ruling class. But it is not true that the State is always right (1983: 70).

With the eighties, Osofisan embarked on the demythologisation and demystification of the canons of neo-colonialism in dramas like *Once Upon Four Robbers* (1984), *Esu and the Vagabond Minstrels* (1984), *and Farewell to a Cannibal Rage* (1986). The first two examples belong in the category of the 'magic boon' plays where solutions to real life situations are devolved to the intervention of 'magic', or rather the Ifa motif, in the realisation of the theatricality. In *Once Upon Four Robbers*, a play centred around the debate on the public execution of armed robbers in Nigeria, Osofisan advances the argument that it is really the whole society that is criminal. He suggests that there is no rationale behind executing armed robbers while neglecting fraudulent civil servants, corrupt law officers, politicians and profiteers, although he stops short of prescribing an alternative solution. Instead, he throws the argument back at the audience to resolve, a device he uses also in *Esu and the Vagabond Minstrels*. *Esu and the Vagabond Minstrels* is about a group of out of work minstrels who are offered magical assistance that will reverse their fortunes. The only clause is that they must use the power to help only those in need. Osofisan develops characters based on the politicians who were in power during the civilian regime that ruled in Nigeria between 1979 and 1983. As variously documented, the politicians were notorious for the high level of corruption and forfeiture of the mandate they were elected to defend. *Esu and the Vagabond Minstrels* captures the panic that ensued in the country after the military coup d'etat of December 1983. *Farewell to A Cannibal Rage* on the other hand is a play specifically written to encourage reconciliation after the Nigerian civil war of 1967-1970. In it, our dramatist employs folktales and idioms to caution the country about the hegemony of colonial legacy. In these plays, and others written around that period, Osofisan attacks the neo-colonial and colonial attitudes of his people while at the same time advocating a revolutionary discourse that involves the common people.

In the nineties, plays like *Aringindin and the Nightwatchmen* (1992), *Yungba-Yungba and the Dance Contest* (1993) and *Twingle-Twangle, A Twynning Tayle* (1995) reappraise issues of post-colonial/ post-negritude remembering. In *Yungba-Yungba*, Osofisan applies the theme of the sufferings of the poor under ruthless tyrants to Africa's long history of oppression. The popular demands for democracy on the continent are foregrounded in the agitation of a group of young girls for freedom of expression and choice. *Nkrumah-Ni!... Africa-Ni!* (1994), *Tegonni, An African Antigone* (1994), and *A Nightingale for Dr DuBois* (1998) situate the post-colonial and post-negritude discourses in the quest for a pan-Africanist nationalism that seeks to textually challenge and re-construct African neologism, tropes and the relationship of the 'Empire' to the centre, while also re-membering the disjunction created by the binary division of 'us' and 'others'. *Nkrumah-Ni!... Africa-Ni!* examines the dialectics of pan-Africanism as propounded by the late Ghanaian president Kwame Nkrumah. *A*

Nightingale for Dr Dubois continues Osofisan's examination of the continental question and the quest for African unity with an appraisal of Dr W. E. B. Dubois' work during his last years in Ghana.

II

Born Babafemi Adeyemi Osofisan on 16 June 1946 in Erunwon, a little village in the western part of Nigeria, our author won a government scholarship to the University of Ibadan, Nigeria, after a secondary education at the Government College in Ibadan. In 1969, he obtained his first degree in French, after a further year's study at the University of Dakar, Senegal. While in Senegal, he trained with the Daniel Sorano Theatre Company. He also gained additional experience in acting and directing for both theatre and television through his affiliation with the Orisun Theatre, a professional company established by Wole Soyinka as an offshoot of the 1960 Masks. He then went to the Nouvelle Sorbonne in Paris (Université de Paris III) where he started the postgraduate studies he later completed in Ibadan in 1974. His first play, *Oduduwa Don't Go*, was produced when he was an undergraduate at the university. In the theatre, Osofisan is a man of many parts. He has acquired a solid reputation as actor, director, songwriter, critic and a major contemporary playwright. He is as a result frequently a guest or visitor of institutions and governments outside Nigeria. He has also taken his semi-professional drama troupe, *Kakaun Sela Kompany* on tour of the United States of America and Europe. His plays have also won many awards. Osofisan writes under his real name and some pseudonyms, the best known of which is Òkínba Laùnkó. In all, he has written, published and produced more than fifty full-length dramas for radio, television and stage, including *The Chattering and the Song* (1976), *Morountodun* (1983), *Another Raft* (1989), *Esu and the Vagabond Minstrels* (1991), *Twingle-Twangle, A Twynning Tayle* (1995) and *The Women of Owu (An African Re-reading of Euripides' The Trojan Women)* (2003).

An understanding of the political dynamics in Africa is essential to the understanding of the structure of Osofisan's dramaturgy and his mythopoeic quest. The clamour for freedom, which started in the former Soviet Europe and spread to Africa, also affected the literary landscape with a variety of ideas, each promising an alternative to the political situations and 'the dance contests', the seemingly senseless successful relays of political leadership in the various African spaces. Many of these literary and dramatic creations have consistently questioned or challenged political constructs in the various pockets of power in Africa. Some dramatists have also developed, to paraphrase Wole Soyinka, *orisunitis millenicus*,[1] a social circumstance not unlike people's mass protests to

---

[1] Wole Soyinka coined the term *orisunitis millenicus* to describe the spirit of performance at the production of *The Beatification of Area Boy* in Jamaica in 1996, likening it to the enthusiasm against all odds displayed by members of the original Orisun Theatre Company in the 1960s Nigeria.

outwit suppression. According to Soyinka, *orisunitis, millenicus* is a survival tactic employed for the various successes of both the 1960 Masks and The Orisun Theatre that performed political satires in Nigeria in the 1960s. Present dramatists have developed this tactic through an intertextual engagement with mythopoeic materials, using traditional myths to counter the erected or popular versions of the prevalent hegemony.

This recourse to myths and history to question political tyranny serves to distance and shelter the dramatist from the menace of present terrors on the continent. Femi Osofisan has clearly emerged as a revolutionary ideologue and the most consciously intertextual Nigerian playwright in its use of myths. He has often 'adopted a free wheeling iconoclastic attitude to antecedent texts and authors from which / whom he constantly borrows materials', (Garuba 1996) which he then subverts to satisfy his creative impulse. Garuba suggests that this inclination to challenge previous plays, orthodox historiography and conventional wisdom[2] is best done by engaging contemporary historical facts in an intertextual debate. Osofisan couches his dramaturgy in a web of music, dance, songs and rich dialogue to evolve an aesthetics he has often referred to as constituting 'surreptitious insurrection', especially in his constant 'dialogue' with the socio-political hegemonies in his universe. This strategy involves the manipulation of the mechanics and metaphors of playmaking and of performance in such a way that they do not directly expose themselves to immediate repression. Or, to render it in Olaniyan's phrase, 'uncommon sense', 'a concept that retains the dramatist's subversive agenda as well as its stealthy coding but is more descriptive, more accessible, less evaluative, and therefore infinitely more pedagogically resonant' (Olaniyan 1999: 112). This abrogating and appropriating of the works of other writers and cultures sometimes lends a postmodern consciousness that questions and suggests new ways of interpreting ideas, to his dramatic engagements.

Our dramatist's dramaturgy draws heavily on African myths and ritual forms, whose repertory he has raided and subverted to propose an alternative ideological position. He advances this position instead of the accepted historical function of legitimising political and religious orthodoxy. In the words of Olaniyan, Osofisan's plays are 'characterised by deft appropriation and re-interpretation of indigenous performance forms, a fine-tuned materialist vision of history, and a consummate dramaturgic sophistication and openness' (1999:

---

[2] Harry Garuba lists as among Osofisan's 'displaced and disfigured' texts and historiography John Pepper Clark-Bekederemo's *The Raft* (*Another Raft*), Wole *Soyinka's The Strong Breed* (*No More the Wasted Breed*), the myth of Moremi (*Morountodun*), the life and times of Alaafin Abiodun of Oyo Kingdom (*The Chattering and Song*). And we can also add Osofisan's adaptation of Sophocles' *Antigone* (*Tegonni, An African Antigone* 1995), his reconstruction of the Rwandan genocide (*Reel Rwanda* 1996) and his adaptation of Max Frisch's *Andorra* (*Andorra Goes Kinshasa* 1997). For Garuba's seminal discussion of Osofisan's intertextuality and the apt inscription of his dramaturgy into the whole post-modern discourse, see 'The Album of the Midnight Blackout and the Aesthetics of Levity' (published in this volume, pp. 217 - 225).

110). In essence, he has taken drama away from the shrine, metaphorically and symbolically, and brought it to the public square – the market (as in *Once Upon Four Robbers*) or the junction (as in *Esu and the Vagabond Minstrels* – to the gathering of the masses. Osofisan subjects tradition to scrutiny and reinterpretation, using the embedded modes of thought and structure to proffer a counter-official version of myths and history. In virtually all his plays, he advocates radical social changes based on this ideological position. History provides for him a clarifying agent for the present, the critical exposition of which suggests ideas for a positive alternative future by unmasking the anguish created by the unmediated ancient formalistic myths or rituals in the society.

In an early essay entitled *Ritual and the Revolutionary Ethos: The Humanistic Dilemma in Contemporary Nigerian Theater*, published in 2001, the dramatist observes that:

> The dramatic heritage available to us has simply proved to be inadequate. And it is not only that the machinery provided by the old society for dealing with chaos has lost its capacity for total effect, it is also that the very metaphysical *raison d'etre* of that machinery has been eroded with the advent of a new socio-political philosophy. The comprehensive repertory of myth and ritual, particularly of those primal rites of communal retrieval which survived as paradigm, and whose seasonal re-enactments helped to restore harmony in the race, face the prospect of attrition in the contemporary intellectual climate. The flux of social transformation stands unrelieved in the crisis of ritual (2001: 92)

In this piece in which Osofisan meditates on the role of myth and ritual in Nigerian theatre and the guiding principles of his own work, he identifies the idealising and mystifying qualities of myth as one of the problems which the contemporary playwright concerned with the dynamics of history necessarily has to confront. Since myths and rituals were used in traditional societies as tools for 'communal retrieval' and survive into the present as paradigms which transcend their historical origins, writers continually reproduce and represent them in their works, thereby according these tales a hegemonic power borne of insistent repetition. But these myths, Osofisan insists, have lost their efficacy in the face of the social transformation brought about by a new socio-political reality. In his plays, therefore, Osofisan seeks to break this hegemonic hold by using the myths and rituals only as metaphors, as paradigmatic sites from which to conduct an interrogation of contemporary cultural and political issues. The tales, for him, become raw materials to be interrogated and appropriated into the corpus of non-African performance traditions, conventions and cultural styles.

Femi Osofisan is a revolutionary who uses ritual forms, that is, forms that are repeated, that have already been sanctified by time and usage. Therefore, what Osofisan is saying when he states that 'the machinery provided by the old society for dealing with chaos has lost its capacity for total effect' (2001: 92), is that the old rituals have proved inadequate to contend with modern realities.

Individuals or families, known as 'carriers', played the society's scapegoat and ceremonially washed away the sins and diseases, leaving the community purged, until the following year. This is the subject of Wole Soyinka's *The Strong Breed* (1964). The society used rituals to purge itself, creating newness on that basis. However, Osofisan is saying that all these apparatus of myth and ritual can no longer, in the modern time, bring newness or revolution, or change our society.

While other Nigerian playwrights like Wale Ogunyemi, Ola Rotimi and John Pepper Clark-Bekederemo are mostly content with recording or recreating, or reconstructing historical events, rituals and myths, Osofisan instils a revolutionary ethos into these forms. He is not simply recreating them in repeated unchanging forms; he is breaking the cultural and political hegemony that these kinds of rituals impose by re-interpreting them in new ways.

As a contrapuntal to Osofisan's ideology, for instance, in Ovonramwen Nogbaisi, Ola Rotimi, another Nigerian dramatist, tells the story British pacification of the Benin Kingdom in 1897. Rotimi, in the assessment of Chris Dunton, is obsessively concerned 'with the role of the individual leader' (1992: 15), in this case, King Ovonramwen. Rotimi is concerned with chronicling the tragedy of the Benin Kingdom and sustaining the hegemony of cultural and political hold of the king on the people. However, when Osofisan takes a story of power, like in *The Chattering and the Song* (1976), he re-interprets that story; he is not retelling the story in the manner of a chronicle. He deliberately 'challenges a specific distortion of historical consciousness' (Dunton 1992: 93). His ideological stance is diametrically opposed to the ideology of his contemporaries, being intrinsically entrenched in the belief that our present cultural and socio-political realities are distilled from the crystallised creations of the rich and the powerful, and that salvation lies in re-gingering the conscious awareness of the people.

With the older writers, myths go hand in glove with different rituals, and this is reflected in the dramas produced by writers like Ogunyemi (*Obaluaye, Ijaye War*), Rotimi (*Kurunmi*) and Soyinka (*The Strong Breed, Death and the King's Horseman*). Whereas, Osofisan radically reconfigures the familiar history and myth in the light of contemporary realities to stress their dialectical dynamism, to suit his revolutionary view on the political forces of oppression, injustice and corruption, and, to 're-interpret history and myth for our own self-rediscovery' (Awodiya 1993: 47).

If the connecting line between Osofisan's plays and the use of myths and ritual forms appears tenuous, it can only be so at first sight; a phenomenon that can be attributable to various other influences on the dramatist. Osofisan, apart from growing up in a deep Yoruba community, is a product of Western education, where he imbibed the cultural influence which later manifested in his writing. Scholars may therefore view Osofisan from the perspective of a university-trained artiste with a bias towards Western performance models while disregarding the equal, if not stronger, influence of the Yoruba performance culture.

References

Adeyemi, S. 1999. 'A Comparative Study of the Use of Myths and Rituals in Selected Plays by Femi Osofisan and Bode Sowande, and Zulu Myths and Rituals in Selected Plays by Mbongeni Ngema and Gcina Mhlope' (unpublished dissertation submitted to the University of Natal, South Africa).

Ashcroft, B, G. Griffiths & H. Tiffin. 1989. *The Empire Writes Back: Theory and Practice in Post-colonial Literatures* (London and New York: Routledge).

Awodiya, M., ed. 1993. *Excursions in Drama and Literature: Interviews with Femi Osofisan* (Ibadan: Kraft Books).

Dunton, C. 1992. *Make Man Talk True: Nigerian Drama in English Since 1970* (London: Hans Zell Publishers).

Gilbert, H. & J. Tompkins. 1996. *Post-Colonial Drama: Theory, Practice, Politics* (London: Routledge).

Garuba, H. 1996. *The Album of the Midnight Blackout and the Aesthetics of Levity* (rpt. below, pp. 217-225).

Jeyifo, B. 1996. *The Reinvention of Theatrical Tradition: Critical discourses on Interculturalism in the African Theatre,* in Patrice Pavis (ed.), *The Intercultural Performance Reader* (London and New York: Routledge, pp. 149-161).

Jeyifo, B., ed. 2002. *Modern African Drama* (New York & London: W. W. Norton & Company).

Olaniyan, T. 1995. *Scars of Conquest, Masks if Resistance: The Invention of Cultural Identities in African, African-American and Caribbean Drama* (New York: Oxford University Press).

Olaniyan, T. 2004. 'Femi Osofisan: The Form of Uncommon Sense', in J. Conteh-Morgan and T. Olaniyan (eds.), *African Drama and Performance* (Bloomington and Indianapolis: Indiana University Press, pp. 109 -- 125).

Osofisan, F. 1976. *The Chattering and the Song* (Ibadan: Ibadan University Press).

Osofisan, F. 1983. *Morountodun* (in a volume containing *Morountodun, Red is the Freedom Road* and *No More the Wasted Breed*) (Lagos: Longman Press).

Osofisan, F. 1988. *Another Raft* (Lagos: Malthouse Press Limited).

Osofisan, F. 1991. *Esu and the Vagabond Minstrels* Ibadan: New Horn Press)

Osofisan, F. 1991. *Once Upon Four Robbers* (Ibadan: Heinemann Educational Publishers).

Osofisan, F. 1992. 'And After the Wasted Breed?: Responses to History and to Wole Soyinka's Dramaturgy' in U. Schild (ed.), *On Stage – Proceedings of the Fifth International Janheinz Jahn Symposium on Theatre in Africa No. 6* (Gottringen: Arbeiten aus dem Mainzer Institut fur Ethnologie und Afrika-Studien, pp. 59-74).

Osofisan, F. 1997. *Playing Dangerously -- Drama at the Frontiers of Terror in the Postcolonial State* (Inaugural Lecture, University of Ibadan, July 31).

Osofisan, F. 1995. *Twingle-Twangle, A-Twynning Tayle* (Ikeja: Longman Nigeria PLC).

Osofisan, F. 2001. 'Ritual and Revolutionary Ethos: The Humanist Dilemma in Contemporary Nigerian Theatre', in *The Nostalgic Drum: Essays on Literature, Drama and Culture* (Trenton, NJ & Asmara, Eritrea: Africa World Press, Inc.).

Osofisan, F. 2003. *Many Colours Make the Thunder-King* (Opon Ifa Readers, Ibadan)

Richards, S. 1996. *Ancient Songs Set Ablaze: The Theatre of Femi Osofisan* (Washington: Howard University Press).

Rotimi, O. 1974. *Ovonramwen Nogbaisi* (Ibadan: Oxford University Press).

Utudjian, E. 1992. 'West Africa: Ghana and Nigeria', in B. King (ed.) *Post-Colonial English Drama: Commonwealth Drama since 1960* (New York: St Martin's Press, pp. 186-199)

REPRESENTATIONS OF HORROR: THE RWANDAN GENOCIDE AND FEMI OSOFISAN'S *REEL, RWANDA!*

CHRIS DUNTON

I

Written in 1995 and first performed in March the following year in London, Femi Osofisan's play 'Reel, Rwanda!' was one of the earliest attempts to address the 1994 Rwanda genocide through the creative arts (that is, through a medium other than journalism, official reportage or scholarly analysis). In this paper I discuss Osofisan's play in the context of other writing – including journals and novels – on the events of 1994; I explore the stated intentions of writers who have addressed the events and the broader question as to how any adequate account might be rendered of atrocities of this magnitude, and finally I examine the dramaturgical options taken by Osofisan in his attempt to do justice to his subject-matter.

What words can be found with which to address a catastrophe such as the Rwanda genocide is a cardinal question. Tragically, this question is not new, not unique in the context of the Rwanda genocide. One of Andrea Reiter's driving concerns in *Narrating the Holocaust* – a study of memoirs written between 1934 and the present – is to determine how victims and survivors of the Nazi atrocities found words to talk about the unimaginable. It can be argued that, in an absolute sense, no words can be found: that the historical realities are beyond the capacity of language to encompass. As Nigel Eltringham notes 'Elie Wiesel has eloquently argued that the Holocaust is a sacred and incomprehensible event, for which no representation is sufficient' (Eltringham, 58). For those who do believe that words can be found, questions of interpretation and of the judicious choice of language remain profoundly challenging. As Mark Osiel has noted (employing a light ironic touch that might itself be seen to be problematic): 'large scale administrative massacre is not the sort of event in regard to which we feel comfortable about letting a hundred interpretive flowers bloom' (Osiel, 265). Clearly the responsibility of bearing testimony in such a context is one of awesome magnitude. Witness the fact that those who have struggled to achieve representation of the unspeakable have often been deeply traumatized by the effort to be adequate to their subject-matter: Antjie Krog, for example, reporting on the processes of South Africa's Truth and Reconciliation Commission, at one point protests 'No poetry should come forth from this. May my hand fall off if I write this' (quoted in Coullie, 361).

Any writer who undertakes a project of this kind enters into a realm of practice in which, to an unusual degree, professional concerns—questions of technique, of narrative strategy, and so on—become imbued with, even indistinguishable from, ethical concerns. This was the experience of the playwright Peter Weiss when he produced *Die Ermittlung* (*The Investigation*), a dramatization of war crimes trials dealing with atrocities at Auschwitz. When the play was first performed, in 1965, there was an immediate controversy as to whether it did justice to the historical event (see Hilton, 47-54); an editorial in the *Times Literary Supplement* succinctly addressed anxieties the play provoked regarding the relationship between ethics and aesthetics by commenting: '*The Investigation* is not a good play. It would be an obscenity if it was' (quoted by Hilton, 47).

That primary (and Elie Wiesel would argue, finally, unachievable) goal of doing justice both to the victims of genocide and to the attempt to achieve some understanding of the causal factors that underlie such a catastrophe, is acknowledged by virtually every author who has tackled the events in Rwanda.

When, for instance, the Québecois writer Gil Courtemanche produced his novel *A Sunday at the Pool in Kigali* – a work he describes as a fictionalized version of eye-witness reports (Courtemanche, [iii]) – he prefaced his acknowledgements with a statement to his Rwandan friends: 'I have tried to speak for you / I hope I have not failed you' ([i]). As Courtemanche's narrative develops, the emphasis is placed again and again on the necessity of facing up to reality full-square (just before the genocide begins, a priest tells the narrator '"I would like to reassure you and I cannot"'; 66) and on the moral testing involved in an examination of the causes of the genocide and of the world community's notoriously defective response to this.

These preoccupations are echoed by Nigel Eltringham in a profoundly perceptive study titled *Accounting for Horror: Post-Genocide Debates in Rwanda*. One of the first questions Eltringham poses, in his Preface, is: 'How does one "account" for such an event? "Account" both in the sense of "to account for" (to provide adequate explanation) and "account" as in "provide a processual narrative"' (Eltringham, xi). The analysis that follows pays honour to the task of naming, of ensuring the record is kept: quoting V. Das, Eltringham comments 'The survivors' experiences of death and loss must be gathered, preserved and, above all, acknowledged less survivors be "condemned to dwell alone and nameless in the ruins of memory"' (147). Most significantly, Eltringham focuses on the meaning of procedures such as identification and self-identification (in the arena of ethnicity), on the partisan reading of specific historical moments and the construction of competing explanatory narratives: in short his emphasis is not solely on the responsibility of giving account but on those processes that lead us to knowledge or to the belief that we possess this.

It was a sense of these responsibilities that led in 1998 to an invitation to ten African writers to attend a research residency in Rwanda, under a collective project titled 'Rwanda: writing as a duty to memory.'[1]

---

[1] The residency was organized by the African Arts and Media Association, sponsored by the Fondation de France.

A number of published works emerged from this project and, once again, in these the question of adequacy – the question 'how to give account?' – is paramount.

Thus in her book *The Shadow of Imana* Veronique Tadjo, one of the ten, begins by stating 'I am not afraid of knowing. But may my mind never lose sight of what must grow within us: hope and respect for life' (Tadjo, 10: the implied fear being that full knowledge of the enormities that were committed will foreclose the retention of hope). One of Tadjo's interviewees asserts that 'Silence is the worst thing of all... We must destroy indifference' (27) and Tadjo herself draws attention to the title of the 1999 report on the genocide by the organization Human Rights Watch, *Aucun Témoin ne Doit Survivre (No Witness Should Survive)*, a title that refers to the intention underlying the insistence on mass participation in the killings – that no unimplicated witness could be isolated – and to the recognition that derives from this, that to bear witness is primary (84-5). Once again, the emphasis is both on the need to secure record and on the need to examine the processes by which we come to knowing (processes that include the attempt to achieve adequate self-recognition). Thus, as a Côte d'Ivoirienne (a citizen of a country that has been the site of repeated, sometimes violent, campaigns against foreign residents) Tadjo notes 'I am afraid when, in my country, I hear people talk of who belongs there and who doesn't. Creating division. Creating foreigners. Inventing the idea of rejection' (37). The focus is again on self-cognition and on the negotiation of a sense of self in relation to the other, when Tadjo interviews an expatriate African lawyer who insists that what is most needed, post-genocide, is a 'credible justice' (the emphasis being on 'credible', on that which is believed to be valid): 'If people do not recognize themselves in this justice, there will be no national reconciliation' (23).

The task of grappling with ways of knowing is central, too, to the novel *Murambi: le livre des ossements* by the Senegalese author Boubacar Boris Diop, who was, like Tadjo, one of the members of the 1998 research residency. Like the Courtemanche, this is a work of fiction based on eye-witness accounts. It is also a work in which Diop employs multivocality: as Fiona McLaughlin, who has published a detailed account of the novel, points out: *Murambi* 'resembles Diop's previous polyphonic novels in the multiplicity of narrative voices it employs' (McLaughlin, 205). Underpinning – indeed, determining – this technique one imagines there is an ethical imperative: to access all available accounts of events, however skewed and unreliable these may be, as a necessary prelude to the construction of an overview.

At the heart of Diop's narrative is the attempt by Cornelius, a Rwandan exile now returned to Kigali, to find ways of addressing the horror, an attempt made the more acutely painful by the revelation that his father, a highly respected Hutu doctor married to a Tutsi, has been responsible for facilitating the killing of tens of thousands, including his own wife, Cornelius's mother. When the doctor gives account of his actions to his son, there is an overwhelming sense of the wilful cauterization of consciousness: this is a man who has abandoned any notion of the value of self-knowledge.[2] He is a man who has replicated the same willed ignorance recognized in the perpetrators of the Nazi holocaust. As J. M. Coetzee's fictional character Elizabeth Costello puts it (in *The Lives of Animals,* a book that has provoked an extended debate on the ethics of representation): 'The horror is that the killers refused to think themselves into the place of their victims, as did everyone else' (Coetzee, 47); and, on many Germans of a particular generation, 'They lost their humanity, in our eyes, because of a certain willed ignorance on their part. Under the circumstances of Hitler's kind of war, ignorance may have been a useful survival mechanism, but that is an excuse which, with admirable moral vigor, we refuse to accept' (19). That question of the admission of real is, as we shall see, central to Osofisan's play.

II

'Reel, Rwanda!' was commissioned by London's Tricycle Theatre[3] and first performed in March 1996 as part of a programme of new plays commemorating the 50th anniversary of the Nuremberg trials and intended to stimulate awareness and discussion of the responsibilities of the international community in respect of crimes against humanity.[4]

Unlike Courtemanche, Tadjo, Diop and others, Osofisan did not visit Rwanda before planning and writing his play, but researched the events of 1994 and the background to these at the School of Oriental Studies, University of London. He was appalled, as he carried out this research, to discover how inadequately the genocide had been reported by his home press, back in Nigeria.[5] For Osofisan

---

[2] Interviewing members of the Interahamwe ten years after the genocide, Fergal Keane records: 'Most of the men we interviewed described themselves as having been overtaken by emotions they still struggle to articulate or understand' (Keane, 13). Reviewing Keane's retrospective BBC documentary, Andrew Anthony records: 'One man recalled hunting down a 10-year old boy for a week, clubbing him as he begged for his life, then burying him alive. Though haunted by the atrocity, he spoke as if he did not know or understand the person who committed it' (Anthony, 20).

[3] Susannah Clapp notes that 'The Tricycle in Kilburn is the centre of political theatre in Britain. It has investigated political corruption, legal failure and war crimes' (specifically, the Stephen Laurence case, the Hutton inquiry, the Nuremberg trials and the treatment of detainees at Guantanamo Bay). (Clapp, 10)

[4] The Tricycle programme comprised one long play on the Nuremberg trials and three short plays on recent events in, respectively, Rwanda, Yugoslavia and Haiti. All three short plays were given in a single programme and then alternated in conjunction with the Nuremberg play.

[5] This and the following observations in this section from an interview given by Osofisan to the author, Leeds, May 15th 2004. There is a substantial literature on the failure of both governments and the international media to address the genocide with anything like due adequacy. Within the British context, see Melvern and Williams, who note how references to the genocide appear to have been "airbrushed" from the memoirs of key political figures of the day, the British government having been spectacularly inert at the time of the crisis (Melvern and Williams, 12-13), and Richard Dowden, who reported on the genocide from within Rwanda. On the question of representation, Dowden comments 'it was difficult for me to describe what was happening. I had covered nearly 20 wars, but the usual

this kind of neglect, wilful or otherwise, provides the context within which subsequent atrocities can take place. His priority in writing 'Reel, Rwanda!' was, then, to counter ignorance, indifference and amnesia and to address the negotiation of knowledge and self-knowledge. In this context, Osofisan aligns himself with Wilfred Owen's assertion 'All a poet can do today is warn.' He does acknowledge that those that carry out crimes against humanity – or, rather, those who organize and commission such crimes – may well be beyond reach (they will not be warned); nonetheless he believes that writing on events of this kind provides a means both of exploring causal factors and of alerting the potential victims of future atrocities as to how such events occur.

III

Although Osofisan's 'Reel, Rwanda!' is a one-act play, the dramatic action develops through four quite distinct stages.[6]

The single setting for the play is a bungalow in Kigali: both the interior and the exterior can be seen. Though the period is not precisely stated, it clearly falls some time after the cessation of the genocide. The first, fairly lengthy, stage of the action comprises a dialogue between two characters, Rose, a Hutu lawyer, and her friend and former lecturer, Françoise, a retired university professor. Whilst the opening stage picture is harmonious – Françoise is lovingly braiding Rose's hair – within a few lines of dialogue the tone shifts abruptly, as Rose refuses to look at herself in the mirror, referring to the trauma and physical abuse she has suffered during the genocide. Though later developments will drastically alter our perspective on this, Rose's refusal tangibly images that inability to re-secure self-identification recorded extensively in the literature cited above.

At this point the dialogue becomes highly expository as, in a series of extended speeches (Osofisan 1999, 179-93), Françoise and Rose confirm the events that have led to their current reunion. Following media reports on the genocide, Françoise has returned to Rwanda to seek out her old friend and pupil; the plan is that they will return together to France (once again, the possibility of harmony is sounded as they celebrate together the hope that, out of Rwanda, Rose's wounds will heal; 183). For her part, Rose recounts the murder of her husband ('He was a marked man, the moment he dared to criticize Habyarimana's government. All of us who had argued for accommodation with the Tutsis, for a democratic power-sharing, all of us were doomed' 189-90); she then speaks of the subsequent murder of her children and her offering her body for abuse by the Interahamwe militia in an attempt to forestall this. In words that echo the fears

---

clichés of death and destruction mocked Rwanda's horrors. I could find no new words to describe what I was seeing' (Dowden, 285).

[6] As the published play text is not widely available, the following analysis incorporates a detailed summary of the dramatic action.

of Veronique Tadjo, quoted above, Rose tells Françoise: 'It was in your class that I learnt all those grand themes about humanity, culture and civilization. The ideals which the grand poets sang about... They made us dream and we soared like birds. But it's all lies, isn't it?' (187).

The second stage in the action (from p. 193) begins with Rose's exit and the entry of Jean-Baptiste, a Tutsi government official and friend of François, who has brought along with him Alain, a Belgian lawyer appointed to the human rights commission that will eventually report to the Goldstone Tribunal. As François and Jean-Baptiste greet each other, there are a few moments of harmonious relaxation. The dialogue then returns to expository – even didactic – mode with a series of speeches by Jean-Baptiste and Alain that consolidate the recognition of the horror of the genocide and, especially, the role of the Interahamwe; in the background here is an uneasy acknowledgment that Rose, whom François has chosen to rescue, is a Hutu. During the latter part of this dialogue the emphasis turns to the role of Belgian colonial policy and of the French government's support for the Habyarimana regime as causal factors underlying the genocide. Then (201-04) a particular concern of Jean-Baptiste's emerges, namely, the lack of assistance provided the new (RPF) government and the focusing of the world's attention on the Hutus who have fled the country to camps such as Goma.

Jean-Baptiste now argues that François's concern for Rose constitutes an inversion of priorities. Though the two exchange recriminations, peace is restored (on the basis of the solidity of their friendship) and Jean-Baptiste agrees, in the interests of reconciliation, to meet Rose, who is elsewhere in the bungalow. When Rose enters, the third stage in the dramatic action begins, and it does so with a major disjunction between the 'given' as viewed up until now and what is to follow.

On seeing her enter, Jean-Baptiste exclaims 'No! Not Rose!'; he then announces she is going nowhere, certainly not to France. Pulling out a gun, he threatens to shoot her, identifying her as the 'butcher of Butare' (213-14). Rose, though mostly silent during this incident, briefly protests her innocence. The dialogue returns to expository mode, but now within the context of a dramatic reversal, a drama of revelation[7], as Jean-Baptiste asserts Rose's guilt, claiming that, in uniform, in collaboration with the militia, she participated in a massacre of Tutsis. His account culminates in the accusation: 'And when you had finished, Rose, you all climbed into your buses and went for a celebration in the town

---

[7] Earlier in his career Osofisan wrote a series of television plays in which a concern with social issues is embedded in the conventions of the detective thriller (the dramatic action of these plays being left open-ended, the final revelation scene omitted, as the identification of the guilty party was left to the audience to determine). Three of these plays are gathered in Osofisan 1990. For a discussion – and problematization – of the hybrid nature of these plays, see Dunton, 199-200; 203-04; Richards, 55-7; 281-83. For a novel by a Ugandan writer that uses the conventions of detective fiction to explore the Rwandan genocide, see Kyomuhendo.

hall... You did not even pause to change your clothes, clean off the blood... You who were a mother, mourning the loss of your own children, how could you then shoot into the midst of innocent children?' (218).

At this point, with a further, startling disjunction in the progress of the dramatic action, attention is drawn to a Yoruba *egungun* mask, which has begun to dance.

To backtrack, this mask has been visible from the very outset of the play. The opening stage direction notes that it should be suspended from a post standing in the bungalow's garden. The early dialogue between François and Rose establishes that it is a Yoruba ancestral mask; François explains 'It dances, they say, and the dead return' and when questioned by Rose as to why the eyes are open, explains 'It's a statement. About life' (181) – a pointer to the play's concern with knowledge, with connectivity. Further comments in the dialogue provide a strategic reminder – a low-key foregrounding – of the mask's presence. When Jean-Baptiste, for example, comments that the mask frightens him, François defends its presence, stating that 'the Yoruba use it to invoke the spirits of the dead' and adding that the promise the mask represents is that 'humanity never dies' (195).

Now, in the closing moments of the play, the mask becomes performative, an *egungun* dancing masquerade (accompanied by off-stage drums and incantations; Osofisan leaves it to the producer as to how to effect this transition). A number of questions arise here as to the effectiveness of this device, especially in performance to a non-Yoruba audience or to one that does not have roughly cognate masquerade traditions. What one assumes Osofisan to be drawing from here is the recognition that the *egungun* encapsulates a moment of liminality, a point at which in the Yoruba cosmos a window is opened between *aye*, the visible, tangible world of the living, and *orun*, the invisible spirit realm within which the dead reside: a moment of connection that enables a healing, awareness-enriching bond of coherence between the two. (A problem bearing on the question posed above about cross-cultural performance is that, for a western audience, say, the point of masking is that it conceals identity, whilst within *egungun* it enables a recognition of entities not otherwise visible[8]).

As the mask begins to dance, Jean-Baptiste recognizes 'The dead are stirring!' (219). As the ritual patterns of the dance become more distinct, Rose's falsifying attempt to defend herself breaks down and she confesses to her crime. In a lengthy speech she testifies as to how her family had regarded herself and her husband as traitors ('They said we were collaborators with the *inyenzi*, with the detested Tutsis', 220). With the militia everywhere demanding demonstrations of

---

8 There have been a number of recent explorations of this question: see, for example, Jeyifo, who considers productions of Soyinka's play *The Road* (a play in which *egungun* masquerade plays a pivotal role) given in the United Kingdom, India and Trinidad, posing the question 'In what resides the "Africanness" of African literary and dramatioc texts, and how does this "Africanness" fare when African texts travel? . . . how [are] the markers, signs, and codes of Africanness read, decoded, reconfigured, and, above all, appropriated [when this occurs]' (Jeyifo, 449).

allegiance, Rose was first ordered to kill her godfather (presumably identified as Tutsi) and then compelled deeper and deeper into the violence; her account ends with the comment 'all my humanity died that night' (221). The play ends with Rose handing herself over to Jean-Baptiste, who will have her put on trial. The question as to whether that trial will be a just one is left open; over the closing moments of the play one might superimpose the recognition of the lawyer quoted by Veronique Tadjo (and cited above): 'If people do not recognize themselves in this justice, there will be no national reconciliation.'

IV

A large part of Osofisan's purpose in 'Reel, Rwanda!' is evidently to provide, or confirm record: more than half the play's dialogue comprises expository speeches that detail the processes of genocide. An equally important emphasis is on cognition and awareness, and on the reliability of testimonies derived, variously, from adequate or partial consciousness or based on deception (whether that deception is fully conscious or signifies the kind of cauterization of consciousness recorded earlier in this essay). Osofisan's exploration of cognition is played out through the interchanges between the three major characters: Françoise – largely a sympathetic figure but one whose limited perception reflects the deeply flawed response to the genocide by the west; Jean-Baptiste, whose commitment to justice may be compromised by his rage at what has been done; and Rose, whose experience and conduct lie at the storm-centre of this history.

Although the dramatic device of the mask is realized only in the play's closing moments, it does bring to the foreground Osofisan's thematic preoccupation with connection and recognition: it is the catalyst that enables the three major agents, Françoise, Jean-Baptiste and Rose, to speak on common ground. If, as the first part of this essay has suggested, the exploration of the Rwandan genocide through the verbal arts raises acutely difficult questions regarding the value of the aesthetic and the ethics of representation, then the appropriateness of Osofisan's strategy here might be disputed, to the extent that the device of the mask might be considered to be reductionist, that is, too facile a catalyst for Rose's connection with her true self. Yet the recognition that drives the play here is clear enough and is cognate with other explorations of the genocide discussed above: that our future is predicated on the struggle to establish an adequate record of historical process and our ability to reach a consensual acknowledgment of this. Osofisan's stand in relation to these aspirations has always been an optimistic one[9]; at the present time (the close of 2004) events in, for example, Iraq and Darfur suggest they may be as elusive as ever.

---

[9] See, for example, the processes by which truth is arrived at in plays such as *Morountodun* and *Yungba-Yungba and the Dance Contest.*

Works cited

Anthony, A. 2004. Review of BBC documentary by Fergal Keane. *The Observer (Review)*. April 11th. 20.

Clapp, S. 2004. Review of play on Guantanamo Bay. *The Observer (Review)* May 30th. 10.

Coetzee, J. M. 2000. *The Lives of Animals*. London: Profile Books.

Coullie, J. L. 2004. *The Closest of Strangers: South African Women's Writing* (Johannesburg: Witwatersrand University Press).

Courtemanche, G. 2003. *A Sunday at the Pool in Kigali* (Edinburgh: Canongate).

Diop, B. B. 2001. *Murambi: le livre des ossements* (Abidjan: Nouvelles Editions Ivoiriennes).

Dowden, R. 2004. Response to Melvern and Williams. *African Affairs* . Vol 103, no. 411. 283-90.

Dunton, C. 1998. *Nigerian Theatre in English: A Critical Bibliography* (London: Hans Zell).

Eltringham, N. 2004. *Accounting for Horror: Post-Genocide Debates in Rwanda* (London: Pluto Press).

Hilton, I. 1970. *Peter Weiss: A Search for Affinities* (London: Oswald Wolff).

Jeyifo, B. 2002. 'Whose Theatre, Whose Africa? Wole Soyinka's *The Road* on the Road.' *Modern Drama*. XLV: 449-465.

Keane, F. 2004. 'How did we allow this to happen?' *Radio Times*. April 3rd – 9th. 13.

Kyomuhendo, G. 1999. *Secrets no More* (Kampala: Femrite Publications).

Melvern, L and P. Williams. 2004. 'Britain waived the rules: The Major government and the 1994 Rwanda genocide.' *African Affairs*. Vol. 103, no.410. 1-22.

McLaughlin, F. 2002. 'Writing the Rwandan Genocide: Boubacar Boris Diop's *Murambi: le livre des ossements*' in T. Falola and B. Harlow, eds. *Palavers of African Literature* (Trenton, NJ and Asmara: Africa World Press).

Osiel, M. 1997. *Mass Atrocity, Collective Memory and the Law* (New Brunswick, NJ: Transition Press).

Osofisan, F. 1990. *Birthdays are not for Dying and other plays* (Lagos: Malthouse).

Osofisan, F. 1999. 'Reel, Rwanda!', in Osofisan, *Recent Outings II* (Ibadan: Opon Ifa Readers, pp. 177-223).

Chris Dunton

Chris Dunton

Reiter, A. 2004. *Narrating the Holocaust* (London: Continuum).

Richards, S. L. 1996. *Ancient Songs Set Ablaze: The Theatre of Femi Osofisan* (Washington: Howard University Press).

Tadjo, V. 2002. *The Shadow of Imana: Travels in the heart of Rwanda* (Oxford: Heinemann).

142

'CENTRING THE MARGINAL'? NOTES TOWARD A QUERY OF WOMEN AND GENDER IN THE DRAMA OF FEMI OSOFISAN

TEJUMOLA OLANIYAN

Do not be content with little fires
set the dawn ablaze!
-- Femi Osofisan

The Embrace

Femi Osofisan, critics now agree, is the leading and most significant African playwright after the generation of Wole Soyinka, Athol Fugard and Tawfik Al-Hakim. In technique, Osofisan is robustly experimental, constantly searching for new and appropriate forms, from popular to elite and arcane traditions, to express his concerns. In the popular Yoruba Travelling Theatre tradition, he inherits a form that has many features of Bertolt Brecht's Epic theatre – songs, dance, mime, and other estranging devices – but, not surprisingly as a popular form, not much of the critical attitude. Osofisan as a Marxist, and Brechtian, stands this form on its feet. The result, as critics have agreed, is an 'innovative form' and 'revolutionary content' that is second to none on the African continent. This playwright, a blurb on one of his early plays agreeably summarises and prophetically forecasts, 'has an incisive vision which he puts at the service of oppressed humanity. His over-riding theme is that the machinery of oppression in human society is created by man, and man is also capable of demolishing it. His is about the first body of plays in Nigeria with a clear ideological perspective. He is already on the way to doing for us what Bertolt Brecht did for Europe'.[1]

Osofisan is also uniquely significant for something else in African drama: right from the beginning of his career in the 1970s, he has been consistent in his non-condescending representational emphasis on women as equal and worthy partners with men in the struggle for a just society. And that was well before the emergence in the 1980s of a grudging tolerance of feminist perspectives by a handful of African male writers and critics. Through that representational emphasis, Osofisan charted an alternative course for the portrayal of women in Nigerian, indeed, African drama. This course, to borrow the early but still

---

[1] Distinguished poet, Niyi Osundare, reviewing *Once Upon Four Robbers* and *Morountodun* in *West Africa*. See the back cover of the former play.

refurbishable feminist activist conceptual rallying cry, is 'from the margin to the centre.'

I will explain the concept I just borrowed but as a preliminary note, it needs to be emphasised that the truly worthy goal is not so much to move 'from the margin to the centre' but to critique the very idea of margins and centres, to struggle for a world where there are no such borders and hierarchies. By 'margin' I do not necessarily mean total absence or invisibility, peripheral visibility, or simply, poor statistical presence but at the same time, I am not excluding these. More importantly, I mean the representation of women as objects: objects of social derision, foil for the affirmation of stifling customs and archaic traditions, objects of the gaze and pleasure of men. By implication, 'centre' for me no longer means the visibility or rich statistical presence of women on the stage, but the imaging of women as subjects: individuals capable of cognition, endowed with consciousness and will, capable of making decisions and effecting actions. By and large, this latter is the category of women dominant in Osofisan's drama, from Iyabo in *A Restless Run of Locusts*, Yajin and Funlola in *The Chattering and the Song*, Alhaja in *Once Upon Four Robbers*, Titubi in *Morountodun*, Olabisi and Folawe in *Farewell to A Cannibal Rage*, Moni in *The Oriki of a Grasshopper*, to Yobi in *Aringindin and the Nightwatchmen*, and more.

Feminist scholars have pointed attention to the gendered nature of space and attitudes in most *contemporary* societies, in which, for instance, woman is figured as the homemaker (even if she is a career woman), confined to the 'private' sphere, while an active, 'public' and social life is considered the prerogative of men. Other binary oppositions are mapped on to gender, in which emotion is female and reason is male. The drama of Osofisan traverses and undermines our contemporary gendered absolutes and, by inference, reveals them as neither natural nor inevitable but as partisan, ideological constructs that can and need to be altered. For Osofisan, this is primarily an ideological claim, but he may be even more profoundly right at a deeper cultural level, for the sad irony is that in many African societies, the sources of many of these specific and now generalised contemporary gendered divisions are external to the societies and are to be found very often in their colonial heritage. The story of the en-gendering of Yoruba culture – Osofisan's cultural background – which autochthonously privileges age and not sex/gender as mode of assigning hierarchy, is a case in point.[2] Yajin and Funlola mature as lovers as well as committed social activists. As Morountodun, Titubi has become not only a loving wife but also an indispensable revolutionary colleague of the farmers. Folawe in fact, ditches her apolitical artiste-boyfriend for a more socially-aware and committed companion. Moni is not just the socialist Imaro's girlfriend but also a 'fellow socialist.' And Alhaja's contributions to the various robbery

---

[2] See Oyeronke Oyewumi's useful work, *The Invention of Women*.

operations equal that of any male member of the gang. In short, the women generally refuse to be closeted into a restrictive, gendered space.

A point needs be emphasised: even though the socially-conscious, self-sacrificing, committed activist women are centralised in Osofisan's drama, they are never de-eroticized: a charge to which even the legendary Bertolt Brecht, one of Osofisan's main influences, is susceptible. On the contrary, they love and have personal love lives, even while in the forefront of the agitation for justice and social equality. The personal, to repeat the battle-cry, is political. The foregrounding of the personal is an acknowledgement that it be a point of scrutiny in female-male relationships and the social allocation of roles within those relationships.

There are indeed some stereotypical women figures in Osofisan's plays, but these are mostly figures of satire – Tolu, Abeni Mailo, Kaokudi Animasaun in *Who's Afraid of Solarin*, and Mrs Asibong in *Midnight Hotel*, to cite a few examples – and the satiric swipe in these plays neither spares the men nor respects the boundaries of gendered attributes in popular discourse. The dumb Tolu is no more negative than the stammering, incoherent Alade-Martins. Mailo and Animasaun are no more vain and corrupt than their male colleagues. And Mrs Asibong and Pastor Suuru are pronounced as equally guilty of prostitution.

We must underline the fact that Osofisan is without compare in Nigerian drama in the foregrounding of women and their representation as able battle-mates with men in the fight for social justice and equality. This is indeed a big political gesture, given the Nigerian context in which that gesture is made. However, this process of 'centring the marginal' which I have only briefly and incompletely sketched above is, not without some equivocations. Let us for the moment focus on a few of these I call 'Osofisanian ambiguities.'

The Query

Femi Osofisan, I have said, pays attention to the private lives of women. The relationship between men and women is constantly thrown into focus but this focus is, however, NOT in terms of the existing sexual arrangements, but usually in terms of a larger, that is, group or class struggle. This is the crucial point that has been missed by nearly all Osofisan's critics, overly worshipful as they are of his 'radical' attitude to gender relations.[3] *Morountodun* is more concerned with the liberation of the peasants. Perhaps we are to assume that the relationship between the sexes among the freedom fighters is perfect, since this issue is barely broached, or that whatever imperfections there are will go away with the victory of the peasants against their oppressors.

---

[3] See, for instance, Onwueme, 'Osofisan's New Hero'.

Like Morountodun, Yajin committed class suicide by joining the peasant/proletarian struggle against oppression. Yet her relationship with Sontri, her intended and a leader of the Farmers' Movement, is governed by a kind of 'oppression' – harassment and fear, due to Sontri's unnecessary, unpacifiable, insanely volcanic anger. The play never problematizes this relationship, rather what hangs spectrally is the larger class struggle in which the contributions of both are measured. In fact, this play that is the beloved of traditional Marxist critics is at the same time really disturbing for feminists. The exquisitely constructed love scene that opens the play shows Yajin matching Sontri wit for wit, but they are cast in the accepted and traditional role patterns in courtship, suffused with ideologically complicit (with the patriarchal order) proverbs, riddles and metaphorical constructs. Sontri is the 'hawk,' the 'stag,' while Yajin is the 'hen,' the 'doe.' Furthermore,

SONTRI: A straight oak is the pride of the forest.

YAJIN: Young leaves are the pride of the oak.

SONTRI: A brave hunter is the pride of the tribe.

YAJIN: A good woman is the pride of the - no, no! You go too fast, hunter! (4)

Here, you won't miss the accumulation of the images of ferocity (traditionally taken to be masculine) 'hawk,' 'stag,' 'straight oak,' 'brave hunter' to describe Sontri, and the opposite images of gentility (and therefore femininity) 'hen,' 'doe,' 'young leaves,' 'good woman' for Yajin. These images should be incongruous in any revolutionary play: they are divisive and, worse, elitist. In a useful moment of self-consciousness at least, Yajin refuses to complete her last line in the quote above, a completion that would have made her metaphorically surrender as the pride of Sontri. The revolution will ultimately make distinctions, but will it be according to these guilty overly conventional categories of measurement?

In both *Oriki* and *Farewell to A Cannibal Rage*, Moni and Folawe both ditch their boyfriends because the men's commitment to the struggle against class oppression has come to serious doubts. Never is the issue of their relationship as women with their men in question or focus. The same is true of *Altine's Wrath* in which the focus of the play is corruption in government and high places symbolised by Lawal, Altine's husband, rather than the Altine-Lawal relationship. Yet, this play comes really close to opening the cupboard of our patriarchal skeletons, but alas, it backs away too soon. See, for instance: Dr Aina is a medical doctor just arrived from abroad. She is a spinster, a radical and an old-time friend of Lawal. She is in this scene the farmers' advocate come to complain to Lawal, the government official, for the government's uncompensated acquisition of the farmers' lands. We start from where she wonders why Altine can't speak:

AINA: Who caused it, I mean. You men can be terrible, I know you now. You all think marriage is the modern version of the Slave Trade.

LAWAL: Ah, a feminist! You won't get far with that kind of talk in this society, you know.

AINA: Are you telling me! Why do you think I took to medicine? I'm not a combatant I heal, and that compensates.

LAWAL: For what?

AINA: For everything. Healing the sick compensates. I no longer miss the affection which I thought men alone could provide.

LAWAL: I see. Is that perhaps because you're sick yourself? (Laughs.)

AINA: Oh laugh on. Maybe you'll call it a sickness. But I feel. I feel pain. And more than that, I fight it.

LAWAL: Hm, *Eji Ooro*!

AINA: I fight pain. And sometimes I win over pain. That compensates.

LAWAL: But the pain here? (Points to his heart.) How about the pain of loneliness?

AINA: I have risen above it.

LAWAL: That's what you think. You've just come back, and we'll see. Whether any woman, or man even, can rise above the pain of loneliness.

AINA: There are other ways, Lawal, of fulfilling oneself. I've discovered that. And that brings me back to my mission this evening (62-63).

A lot is revealed about Lawal's crass sexist attitudes, and Aina ably holds her ground. But the author appears unable to sustain the argument, so the focus is shifted from a problematic rooted in the existing sexual arrangement to the 'mission,' the issue of the dispossessed farmers (the two farmers shown in the play are men). Perhaps we should revise our earlier suggestion that Osofisan does focus on the private, personal lives of his women.

Repeatedly in Osofisan's dramatic universe, the relationship between men and women is shown only in their connection with the larger social struggle, rarely in terms of the tension-soaked issue of unequal sexual arrangement and genderization of roles and attitudes. By a sleight of hand, Osofisan succeeds beautifully in foregrounding male-female relationships but at the same time escaping a questioning of the basic assumptions of such relationships: love or friendship or kinship and their gendered distribution of roles within such relationships. The public, that is, class struggle, is carried into the private, that is, love affairs, and really examined there, making it seem as if it were the private that is brought up for scrutiny. But it is not.

In *Once Upon Four Robbers*, 'Market Women' appears in the cast list as a category of characters separate from 'Traders, Customers.' Why this distinction?

Soon enough into the play, we find that the market women symbolically represents the institution of commerce and its retainers, and in larger terms, the social entity as a whole governed by the doctrine of private enterprise and untethered private accumulation. The song which the market women sing and which they call their song, is revealing enough, and most suggestively, it is not titled 'song of the market women' but 'Song of the Market.' Let us see just two verses:

> The work of profit
>
> brought us into this world,
>
> this life that is a market.
>
> Some sell with ease and flourish
>
> and some are clients
>
> who pay their greed in gold!
>
> Edumare Oba toto!
>
> ....
>
> The lust of profit
>
> keeps us in this world
>
> this life that is a market:
>
> refuse to join and perish,
>
> rebel and quench!
>
> For those who spit at gold,
>
> Otosi asiniwaye!
>
> (33-34)

Now the major question is this: why the mapping of the institution of commerce onto women? Those who share the ethnic background of Osofisan would know that buying and selling and the market as an institution are really not gendered among the Yoruba, though contemporary Yoruba popular discourse of 'Iyaloja' (head of market women), women and market, might deceive one into thinking so. The play uncritically appropriates this stereotype. Also, considering the venality of the institution of commerce in the Nigeria of the play's first production (1978), what effect is the mapping of that institution onto women supposed to have on the image of women? Were women that visible in the really determining commercial transactions of the country at that time?

One final 'Osofisanian ambiguity' for now. In a superbly moving and theatrically effective final scene in *Morountodun*, Titubi becomes the wife of Marshal. With her two knees firmly on the ground before her warlord husband, Marshal names her 'Morountodun' (I have found a sweet thing). At the end of *The Chattering and the Song*, the earlier unattached Funlola becomes the lover of Leje. In

Farewell, Folawe leaves Fatai, but only to attach to a revolutionary young man who has lately changed her beliefs. Aina in *Altine's Wrath* is an exception to these quick-to-marry strong women, but even then, she is ridiculed for that. The question then is: why these consistent images of what we can only call 'obligatory matrimony'? Can we regard this as neutral and harmless in a society that disparages the spinster and the single mother, that considers the 'end of a woman' to be a man's home, that says the highest educational degree a woman can attain is 'Mrs'? Is male-female revolutionary solidarity dependent on being lovers? Moni in *The Oriki of A Grasshopper* successfully rebels against this trend but see below, from the stage direction, the effect on the ditched boyfriend, Imaro:

> He turns, only to find that Moni is gone. A pause, in which we see his pain. Lights begin to fade. He walks round slowly, like one searching in the sand. His voice is broken when he speaks again.

To say the truth, to be loved is a great and soothing thing, and to be abandoned by one's lover could be quite painful. So Imaro is certainly right to feel lost. Of course, revolutionaries could be lovers, but my point is that this need not be necessarily so, and that the vision of an obligatory matrimony is a male fantasy which all cultural workers must quickly outgrow and leave to the monopoly of the 'fathers,' the patriarchs, the chauvinists.

The Recess

Here is the more exemplary, praiseworthy feature of Osofisan's art: far more than many Marxists of his generation, Osofisan was highly sensitive to the issue of including women and their concerns in artistic portrayals of the present inequities and of the possible coming revolution. It is clear that in the just world he envisions, women and men would be equal and contribute efforts and share rewards equally. To the extent that this theme of social equity and equality of *all* in society irrespective of gender is also one of the central concerns of African feminism,[4] Osofisan is, without question, helping in African women's specific struggles. However, the specific lens through which Osofisan addresses the struggle, class, assumes that class inequity is the most important problem to address and therefore, by implication, all other problems would be solved or easier to solve after that. We know now that that is an unacceptable illusion. Class equality is *not* the sole content of 'social' equality. Osofisan's class lens goes blurry when it comes to capturing another content of the social relations between men and women: the specificities of gender difference and inequity between them. It is as if the struggle for class equality will have little or no implications at all on the relations between men and women at the level of

---

4 See, for instance, Ogundipe-Leslie, *Re-Creating Ourselves*, especially the classic essay, "Stiwanism: Feminism in an African Context" 207-241 ('Stiwa' is an acronym for 'social transformation including women in Africa' (229) - ed).

gender. The relations between women and men are certainly not exhausted by the matter of their equal placement in the realms of struggles for economic production and reproduction. From the point of view of African feminism, this is where the limitation of Osofisan's art lies, his emphasis solely on a class-based approach to history and analysis of oppression. To be sure, the class question is extremely important, and it is doubtful if any genuine solution to those other struggles could be found outside its context. But this does not mean that class struggle must come before gender struggle: they ought to be fought side by side. After all, what is a socialist society – if at all that is the goal of Osofisan's marxism – that is a patriarchal, sexist, chauvinist? As Osofisan himself has said again and again,

Do not be content with little fires

set the dawn ablaze![5]

Bibliography

Launko, O. 1987. *Minted Coins: Poems* (Ibadan: Heinemann Educational Books, Nigeria).

Ogundipe-Leslie, M. 1994. *Re-Creating Ourselves: African Women and Critical Transformations* (Trenton, NJ: Africa World Press).

Onwueme, T. A. 1988 Summer. 'Osofisan's New Hero: Women as Agents of Social Reconstruction,' *Sage: A Scholarly Journal on Black Women* 5.1: 25-28.

Osofisan, F. Spring 1999. 'Theater and the Rites of "Post-Negritude" Remembering.' *Research in African Literatures* 30.1: 3-11.

Osofisan, F. 1998. '"The Revolution as Muse": Drama as Surreptitious in a Post-Colonial, Military State,' 11-35 in *Theatre Matters: Performance and Culture on the World Stage*. Ed. R. Boon & J. Plastow (Cambridge: Cambridge University Press).

Osofisan, F. 2001. *Literature and the Pressures of Freedom: Essays, Speeches and Songs* (Ibadan: Opon Ifa Readers).

Osofisan, F. 2001. *The Nostalgic Drum: Essays on Literature, Drama and Culture* (Trenton, NJ: Africa World Press).

Osofisan, F. 2001. *Insidious Treasons: Drama in a Postcolonial State. Essays* (Ibadan Opon Ifa Publishers).

Osofisan, F. 1975. *A Restless Run of Locusts* (Ibadan: Onibonoje Publishers).

---

[5] See Osofisan under the pseudonym, Okinba Launko, *Minted Coins*.

Osofisan, F. 1977. *The Chattering and the Song* (Ibadan: Ibadan University Press).

Osofisan, F. 1978. *Who's Afraid of Solarin* (Ibadan: Scholars Press).

Osofisan, F. 1980. *Once Upon Four Robbers* (Ibadan: BIO Educational Services).

Osofisan, F. 1982. *Morountodun. Morountodon and Other Plays* (Ikeja: Longman Nigeria).

Osofisan, F. 1986. *Midnight Hotel* (Ibadan: Evans Brothers).

Osofisan, F. 1986. *Altine's Wrath. Two One-Act Plays* (Ibadan: New Horn Press).

Osofisan, F. 1986. *The Oriki of a Grasshopper. Two One-Act Plays* (Ibadan: New Horn Press).

Osofisan, F. 1991. *Aringindin and the Nightwatchmen* (Ibadan: Heinemann).

Osofisan, F. 1986. *Farewell to A Cannibal Rage* (Ibadan: Evans Brothers Limited).

Oyewumi, O. 1997. *The Invention of Women: Making an African Sense of Western Gender Discourses* (Minneapolis: University of Minnesota Press).

FABULOUS THEATRE: A RE-ASSESSMENT OF OSOFISAN'S REVOLUTIONARY DIALECTICS

OLU OBAFEMI & ABDULLAHI S ABUBAKAR

Introduction

The debate over the extent of ideological and aesthetic dependence of radical African playwrights on established European cannons and models refuses to abate. In rather uncritical circles, there is a wholesale attribution of radical Nigerian dramaturgical aesthetics to Brechtian epic. It is indisputable that there are correspondences and coincidences in the Brechtian canons and the African folk performance in the areas of audience participation, style of acting and the use of music and songs. Yet, the critical question of chronology – of which theatrical style precedes the other – remains indeterminate. This fundamental question prompts a fresher look at Osofisan's dramaturgical experiment in his resolve to pioneer a 'new way' (Awodiya 1993: 67), which we refer to in this discourse as 'fabulous theatre'.

The concept is borne out of the realization that a hybrid product is necessarily different from any of its genealogies. But some critics of Osofisan's dramaturgical patterns align him with the Brechtian epic theatre (Awodiya 1995; Amuta 1989; Gbileeka 1997) while others apply the 'folklorist' parameters (Ukala 2001). These taxonomies have however fallen short of a rounded study of Osofisan's dramaturgy. It is obvious that some aspects of Osofisan's style agree with materialist precepts, but these also coincide with African folk performative aesthetics. Therefore, Osofisan's approach could be said to be a fusion of African thought-structures and foreign forms. This observation is partly made by Olaniyan where he states that Osofisan's theatre is 'characterized by deft appropriation and reinterpretation of indigenous performance forms, a fine-tuned materialist revision of history and a consummate dramaturgic sophistication openness that takes us a few steps beyond Bertolt Brecht' (1999: 74). The choice of the 'fabulous' notion in describing Osofisan's experiment is informed by his combinations of absurd situations, total theatre and myth/legend.

Basic Concepts

'The created world', states Sha'aban Robert, 'repeats itself within the nations of human being in order to show their common origin and their great unity'. (Mapanje and White 1983: 1). In spite of this close association in human origins and descent, certain peculiar features abound in the superstructure of every human community. While the end may be to create a world where peace and justice reign, the means will vary because of obvious contextual differences in the superstructures. The Brechtian dramaturgy is stimulated by Erwin Piscator's new perception of the theatre as an objective political laboratory, which he describes as epic. As a participant in Piscator's experiment with new theatrical devices, Brecht was part of the early attempts to evolve 'a (new) drama, which could be used for public "discussion" of political and social issues' (Styan 1981: 128-130). However, while Piscator's emphases are on multi-dimensional stage design and projection of background images, to counteract acted scenes, Brecht's inclination toward poetry makes language his major focus. All the same, Brecht owes his politico-theatrical tutelage to Piscator.

Osofisan creates a link between the socio-political functions of the African performers – court poets, griots and bards – on the one hand, and modern dramaturgies, on the other, to effect dialectical reforms in modern Africa. This, to him, is expedient because in Africa the

debate between pure aestheticism and socio-political commitment is largely mute. Such is the force of history in our environment that those of us who come into the shrine of Art, either as acolytes or worshippers, enter into an already predetermined space. The dominant and seductive tradition is of an art fully entrenched within the survival rituals of the community, consciously and ideologically catalytic. Whereas, in the West, politics is theatre, in Africa theatre is politics. (Osofisan 2001: 87).

Consequently, while Brecht, in line with Piscator's precept, subverts theatrical antecedents (theatre as imitation, or impersonation and empathy- driven) and replaces them with epic theatre, Osofisan links the political functions of traditional folk performance with modern theatrical forms to fashion out a new dramaturgy aimed at socio-political reforms in modern Africa. This new approach by Osofisan is what we have consciously and deliberately elected to christen fabulous theatre. By fabulous, we do not simply refer to the art of constructing astonishing fables. We also establish the coinage of theatrical artistry from a creative interrogation of the connecting nexus of the empyrean with the terrestrial – the recurring metaphor and presence of mythical and legendary figures in the mundane life of the human society, from which new visions are etched as basis for socio-economic and political codes in contemporary society.

There are closely related elements in the dramaturgies of these playwrights that suggest a great influence or even a suspicion of an outright adoption of the dramaturgical approach of the former by the latter. However, through a subliminal investigation, the distinctions between the two dramaturgies become obvious, in spite of the general tendency to link Osofisan with the Brechtian epic theatre.

To start with, Brecht's epic theatre of revolutionary change subverts Aristotle's empathic concept of literature (Needle and Thompson 1981: 187). However, Osofisan's theatrical precept advocates changes that are pedestal on a desire to provide an alternative to war and bloodshed, tendencies found among the ruling class and engendered by first generation Nigerian playwrights. He particularly opposes Soyinka's adoption of Ogun's philosophy of war and opts for Orunmila's wisdom and justice (Obafemi 1981 and Awodiya 1993: 67-70). Essentially, while Brecht advocates change through subversion of the past, Osofisan champions a change through a synthesis of the past revolutionary ideals and modern dialectics, since as he aptly avers, 'no nation can grow after all, which abandons its roots' (Osofisan 2001: 159). Osofisan thus defines his theatre as praxis and post-Negritude. He expatiates on this.

> Unlike Negritude, post-Negritude does not ... believe in, or promote, a willful mystification of the African past, the blanket exorticisation of which people like Senghor were often guilty of ... But post-Negritude does not reject the past either, it only demands a critical attitude to the exhumation of our heritage that will not just present it as a static, nostalgic monument, but rather, as a dynamic process, hybrid and sometimes, even self-contradicting (Osofisan 2001: 172).

It is this attempt at hybridism that necessitates this new effort.

To further explicate on the dissimilarities in the aesthetic prognosis of both playwrights, here is a table:

	EPIC THEATRE	FABULOUS THEATRE
1.	Brecht finds inspiration in Piscator's political theatre and Marx's revolutionary dialectics, the latter supports a proletariat struggle against capitalism as the only veritable means to a classless socialist state.	Osofisan's source of inspiration is Orunmila's principle of justice and wisdom, which is founded on Africa's concept of retributive justice as panacea to social insecurity. Osofisan explores historical antecedents and mytho-metaphysical beliefs of his people to propound a theory of struggle against oppression and dehumanization
2	Epic theatre polarizes the society into a class of oppressors and the oppressed on the basis of economic interests	Fabulous theatre bases its groupings on attitude towards social relations, justice, freedom and collective responsibility, which are considered pre-requisites to equity, peace and tranquillity.
3	It is purely with the proletariat whose plan is to totally annihilate existing oppressive	It is not concerned with class interests; its focus is to reform the entire society through collaborative efforts, in order

	structure, and replace it with a classless society.	to eradicate all forms of oppressions and injustices culminating from disorientation and wrong value judgement.
4	Eschews 'theatre of imitation' for theatre of 'interruption' of actions to achieve alienation- effect.	Adopts Africa's traditional story telling patterns to distinguish the world of fiction from the world of reality through the association of the empyrean and the terrestrial.
5	Meanings are derived through un-discussed possibilities made available in the displayed actions.	Meanings are drawn by analogy through a replication of human activities in the animal or spirit world (fabulous world).
6	Appeals to audience's sense of reasoning rather than its sense of feeling, to discover the un-discussed possibilities.	Tests the audience's intellectual ability through riddles, proverbs, witty expressions and questions, in order to relate the world of fiction to the world of reality.
7	Elicits audience participation through songs and casting, to enhance audience/actor relationship.	Adapts widespread tales and history, popular songs and cultural values that provoke audience participation as in traditional performance.
8	Actors are trained to shock the theatre audience (not cajole it) through detached performances. They show actions without replicating the characters they play.	Adopts the style of Africa's disguised world of the animals and personification of the empyrean to give the necessary impetus for analogy between theatrical actions and the reality.
9	Uses narrators and casting on stage to de-mystify the theatre and objectify theatrical actions	Borrows the folktale's style of multiple roles: the narrator leads/expatiates the roles, thereby de-emphasizing the characters and accentuating the encoded actions.
10	Denounces the concept of tragedy and considers a loss of life in a struggle as a necessary	Adopts the traditional concept of death (in a struggle) as a process in societal rebirth.

	sacrifice.	
11	Attitude towards religion is negative because it is perceived as a hindrance to change.	Aligns with Africa's pragmatic approach to the interaction between the empyrean and the terrestrial in which man is the initiator and regulator and can challenge all forces, including the supernatural.
12	Subverts existing history because it is marred with capitalist tendencies. He creates another version which thought-content is aimed to shock the masses to unprecedented awareness.	Re-analyses existing history to emphasize past revolutionary tendencies: collectivism, communal survival, humanism and heroism, and de-emphasizes the individuation of success.
13	Classifies myth as unscientific and superstitious because it negates all progressive wills.	Approaches myth dialectically with exclusive aim of de-mythologizing (non-progressive myths) and mythologizing (providing alternative versions) in order to re-awaken tendencies that culminate into heroism in the past to suit present dispensation.

Fabulous Theatre And Political Commitment In Many Colours Make The Thunder King.

The Yoruba belief in the intermittent associations between the celestial and the terrestrial bodies is the springboard to Osofisan's M*any Colours Make the Thunder-King.* The gods, it is believed, seldom come to human communities to restore and cleanse the earth (of human plundering and excesses). In one of such rare missions, Alagemo, Yoruba primordial god, transforms into the human form to assist Shango, the then king of Igbeti, to restore sanity to the war torn community. Osofisan uses an abridged myth, curled from the myths of the Shango-king and the Shango-god, an anthropomorphic essence, to express his concern for the political blunder and the desecration of humanity, which permeate the Nigeria polity. Osofisan assumes the traditional role of Igunnu, the masquerade-story-teller, who features annually in the Yoruba festival of communion (with the ancestors), to emphasize the continuum in leaders' crave for excessive power and their predatory desire to subdue others. The similarities in the characteristics of Shango, the king, and civilian/military leadership in Nigeria, since independence, empower Osofisan to explore the legendary/mythical figures of Shango, Oya, Osun and Alagemo (Esu's messenger) to draw attention to the unhealthy political development that

157

threatens the country because, 'the ancestors, you forget, were very much like us! We remember their virtues. But we have inherited all their foibles'. (Osofisan 2003: 69)[1]. Shango's misadventure is the lesson the playwright wants to teach modern African leaders in their palpable misrule.

Shango's vaulting and inordinate ambition nudges him onto many adventures without recourse to their societal effects. He seeks to surpass his predecessors in achievement by accepting to marry spirits – Oya, Osun and Oba. These symbolic figures represent the three stabilizing forces a leader must be identified with: prosperity, humanity and humility. Instead, Shango pompously recounts his present successes:

> Shango: I have conquered more territories than any of our ancestors, but it is not enough! Pushed further the frontiers of Yorubaland, yet that isn't enough! I have slaves in my compound, enough to populate an entire city, yet that isn't enough. Oranmiyan is still the father! I, Shango, I am king! Today I will take up the challenge! I will marry a river...
>
> Igunnu: ..Kabiyesi,... You cannot pay the price...; it is too dangerous. No ordinary man can marry a river, your majesty.... Let me warn you of the consequences, Kabiyesi! If you succeed and marry a river, you will....
>
> Shango: Tell me afterwards. After it is done. (18-19)

As a conqueror of human societies through bloodshed and terrorism, Shango's insatiable quest for power urges him to explore the world of the spirits as a mark of his supremacy over his predecessors. He marries the river, a symbol of prosperity, with the aid of Alagemo, the agent of the empyrean. With the natural endowment dug from the waters, Igbeti becomes a centre of attraction to world trade, as exportation of the resources and mass importation of foreign finished goods flourish. But just like Oya, who is unproductive, the economy of the city is equally not based on productivity. This development agitates the mind of Shango and he begins to worry about Oya's barrenness, because his genealogy is threatened with extinction, just like the feeble economy built on imported finished products. In spite of the prosperity that is synonymous with Oya's reign as the queen of Igbeti, a serious vacuum is left unfilled. Alagemo sums it up:

> For many seasons the kingdom knew peace and stability and grew rich.... Its markets drew traders from all points of the compass. All the historians agreed and chanted it in their songs that indeed Shango had surpassed his father. Wealth had come to the land like never before. But why was the king unhappy? (28).

The emptiness and lack of fulfilment in Oya turn her into a treacherous and selfish woman, who could sacrifice the interest of the kingdom for personal and prurient interest; for example, she would not hear of Shango's marriage to the

---

[1] Subsequent references to this text will only indicate page numbers

mountain, even as Alagemo explains the implication of the latter's absence on the kingdom (38-39). She begins to feel threatened by anybody who has access to Shango. Alagemo incurs her wrath because he suggests Shango's marriage to Osun, the forest spirit, if the childless situation in the palace is to change. Osun's offence is her fertility and the abundant food and healing power, symbolized by the fruits, roots and flowers that accompany her. Gbonka and Timi are also considered a threat, having known too much of her secret plans and therefore they too must be eliminated. To achieve this, she tags them traitors before Shango. Oya and Shango, symbolizing wealth and power respectively, strive to bend one another for each to achieve his/her personal desires; both have arrogance and selfishness as their second nature, and they eventually destroy themselves. The high handedness with which Shango rules and the restlessness of Oya in dealing with anything that stands in her way, portray the duo as merciless, thereby insinuating that a combination of power and wealth spells doom for the ruled. The presence of Alagemo and Osun tames the duo's excesses and specially constrains Oya. This, she finds uncomfortable and thus she begins her designs to eliminate or ostracize them from the community.

> Alagemo: Ah! Shango, Olukoso mi! My king terrible you are in your anger! I am walled up in this dreadful hole! But what did I hear! Drum? A song of lament? Ah! It's Osun's procession... A tragic day indeed for the people of Igbeti! (62).

With the exit of Alagemo and Osun and the setting of Shango against Gbonka and Timi, Oya assumes the role of a sole adviser to Shango. She perfects her plan to dominate affairs in the kingdom. Using her whims and caprices, she lures Shango into hasty decisions that have adverse effects on the community and Shango's security as a leader. The sacking of Gbonka and Timi is later to show that, after all, Shango is vulnerable.

Oya's dominance and pre-eminence in Igbeti after her successful plans of oustering Alagemo, Osun the generals can be likened to our leaders' dependence on a resource at the expense of other equally beneficial resources, which would have better sustained the country.

It is equally note-worthy that Gbonka and Timi are conscious of the Yoruba moral code, which forbids a soldier from raising his arms against the people he is employed to protect, and they, therefore, exercise caution when Shango orders them to use force in quelling the people's revolt against Shango's leadership (70-71). Thus, Oya deceives Shango into misinterpreting the generals' caution as a conspiracy against him. The death of Timi and the expulsion of Shango from Igbeti, cannot bring an end to the people's woes, if Gbonka succeeds Shango; except the former is affected, positively, by the general cleansing at the end of the play and he engages the people in a more productive venture rather than war, the domination of the weak by the strong shall not abate.

Osun symbolises food security, self-reliance, love and peace that are pre-requisites to happiness. Her presence in Igbeti transforms its aridity to fertility and its economy assumes a productive turn. The city ceases to be a dumping ground for all sorts of surplus, imported goods. Through agriculture, the teaming population of able-bodied people that depended on war for survival are now endowed with productive sources of livelihood. With everybody engaged in productive ventures, Igbeti becomes self-reliant and secured. Everyone is gainfully employed as the economy is no more manipulated by the metropolitan elite and the leadership. She extends friendship to all and sundry and the palace ceases to be a dreadful place, trodden only by the influential and the bourgeois. The yawning gap between the seat of power and the populace prior to, and during, Oya's reign (as the favourite thins out) ceases. The common people have access to their leaders, could tender their requests and voice out their frustrations and aspirations. Osun is an epitome of compassion, an attribute which Shango and Oya lack. The absence of this and Shango's failure to marry the mountain, which symbolises humility, are the two major defects that make him fail as a leader. A combination of Osun and mountain would have provided the needed succour and control, but Oya would not hear of it, even when Alagemo reiterates the importance of such a step to communal peace and stability.

> Olori, you're prevaricating. You know as much as anyone else that the mountain is your senior sister! Her breasts feed and suckle all of us. Your waters begin from the mountain springs. If they dry up, your rivers will die, Oya.Your forests, *ayaba* Osun, feed on the ores of the mountain.... (39)

Osofisan's interest in Shango's legend/myth is not the belief in the content of the story but the philosophical essence of the whole experience. He uses the story as an analogy to political leadership in Nigeria (since independence), with the observation that the 'Shangoistic' tendencies are still prominent in the corridors of power and this has jeopardised the growth and development of the country, in spite of her resources. All succeeding leaders have failed to channel the course to national prosperity. Rather, they are constrained by personal ego and complacence. The intention is to draw attention to the continuous injustice, lack of foresight and witch-hunting that have transformed preceding hopeless leadership-experiences into veritable source of nostalgia, due to worse, subsequent leadership manifestations, since independence.

The people's revolt against the tyranny and cavalier attitude of Shango to their plights is pertinent to awakening revolutionary tendencies in the audience. At the peak of Igbeti's misfortunes, the terrorism of the generals could not stem people's reactions to the tyrannical regime. Also, to promote a joint revolutionary action against oppression, the rank and file soldiers, whose initial complaint was their dwindling fortune as a result of stoppage in the attacks on innocent people, now join the populace in the struggle to free all from the strangulating hold of Shango and his generals. The presence of Osun has opened their eyes to an alternative to warfare (service to humanity and selflessness).

Timi: The people Kabiyesi! The people of Igbeti have run amock! They're attacking anything in sight!

Shango: What happened?

Gbonka: We don't know, Kabiyesi! But the whole town's in revolt!... The men are angry, Kabiyesi, because their families are hungry, and they cannot feed them! (70-71)

The above justifies the earlier claim that the traditional society believes only in productive leadership; any failure on the part of a leader is vehemently challenged. Not even a leader like Shango with his furious and fiery nature is spared.

This revolutionary impetus informs Osofisan's concept of myth and legend, a device intended to recreate the past with the main aim of appealing to the inherently revolutionary tendencies that made leaders accountable. The ruler and his associates have to be sacrificed to atone for the sacrilege committed against the earth, while the children of Osun remain succour for the community in the future. The death of Osun serves as a caution for excessive sympathy for unrepentant leaders as represented by Oya and Shango. When given the chance to make his last request, Shango thinks, not of the return of Osun to Igbeti, in order to restore hope; his sympathy rests with Oya over the 'plight' of a son that is destined to plunder the world. Alagemo could not have had any choice but to meet this demand so as to complete his mission on earth. However, Osun's refusal to obey Alagemo's order- that she should flee- amounts to a ruinous and uncritical show of sympathy.

The submission by Alagemo at the end of the tale summarizes the message of the playwright to a world torn apart by wars, poverty, oppression, disrespect for human life, dignity and pollution.

My people, it is time to go. I hope you have all been strengthened again, for the challenges of the coming year! Remember, whatever you do, and whatever choices you make in your lives, the earth is older than all of us. And after we are gone, she will still be here. Let us strive therefore always to nourish her, and not despoil her (92).

This follows the completion of the cleansing exercise by Alagemo, with Osun and Oya's blood transforming into rivers that join forces with the god of the sea (Olokun), to rejuvenate and propitiate the spirits of the earth, who, in turn, would restore her sanctity. This lesson humanity has to learn the hard way. It is a situation that could have been saved, if Oya had overcome her jealousy and Shango had acted rationally and thoughtfully. Ordinarily, Shango's marriage to Oba mountain would have subdued the mountain within him, which robs him of passion and humility, qualities necessary to checkmate the excesses of power and material wealth.

Narrating/Acting in Fabulous Theatre

Osofisan's stage directions avoid any form of disguise as to the real personalities of the actors. They occupy the position of observers who merely re-tell and re-enact a story outside their personal experience. Thus, their identity is disclosed to the audience from the outset, as a folktale narrator will do. The combination of acting and narration in Osofisan's plays is a folkloric device that is effective for time maximization. The narrative aspect of the performance offers background information, fills in the gaps between events and enhances audience's direct interaction with the stage. Osofisan's narrator, as in folktales, displays oratory power and corresponding body movements that motivate the fabulous theatre audience; the narrator is also empowered to direct other stage actions. In some of Osofisan's plays, the functionality of the plays is engendered by the use of narrator, who appears before the audience as its guide to the story land. But rather than tell the story verbatim, the narrator calls for a dramatization of the events. While the narrator's appearance removes all forms of illusions about any direct relationship between the story and the audience's reality, the dramatization of events mellows down the fantasy attributed to fairy tales. Furthermore, the interjection of the story with the narrator's appearances and disappearances, at intervals, assist, in no small measure, in constantly reminding the audience of the other world. The narrator brings the audience back to its reality before it is plunged into the 'wonder land' again. These entrances and exists are deliberate devices, which have become popular among playwrights who belong to the radical school in Africa. With Osofisan, however, it goes beyond a mere fulfilment of existing radical ideological practice. It is borne out of the need to popularize modern African drama, which has hitherto been restricted to the academia, by contextualizing it ; this desire is intensified by the urgent need to facilitate the social relevance and function of modern drama in modern Africa, as the oral narratives was, in pre-industrial African societies. The pursuance of this vision is strengthened by the playwright's close observation of a wide range of the target audience and the discovery that it is strongly attached to pre-industrial belief in the empyrean and it has recourse to religion on contemporary socio-economic and political issues.

In *Many Colours*, for instance, Igunnu doubles as the narrator and Alagemo in the play, the stage direction is specific on this. This assists in the demystification of both the empyrean figures and their actions, thereby emphasizing the relevance of the events on stage to the human community and allowing for inferences to be drawn by the audience from the story. The shift in role is captured thus:

> (*taking out his sword, he (Shango) attacks the tree, joined by his generals. Soon, we hear a loud groan, and a fruit comes crashing down. Shouting in triumph, Shango goes to the fruit. As soon as he touches it, it splits open, and Alagemo, the human incarnation of the chameleon dances out. It is, preferably, the same who played Igunnu)*

Alagemo: Master, I'm here to fulfill all your wishes!

Shango: You again, Igunnu? How did you-

Alagemo: No, not Igunnu any more, that was only one of my masks! Call me Alagemo, Kabiyesi. (21).

The description of the change in role-playing as a process of masking, unmasking and re-masking in the full view of the audience replicates the traditional concept of man/ ancestor communion, which is never perceived from a real physical presence but in a representational or symbolic interaction through masking. The bearer of the mask is human, with flesh and blood, but his words and actions while in the mask are representational of the opinions in the spiritual world. We witness the transfiguring process of the mask into the masque and back to the masque, through role-playing/performed narration.

The Audience In Fabulous Theatre

It is indisputable that formalized modern style of playwriting necessitates the authorial monopoly of plot and stage directions, which serve as serious impediments to audience participation in performance. Osofisan defies some of these constraints to create an active audience within the purview of what modern theatre anticipates and enables. The first step is to 'de-formalize' the stage, the actions and the actors, in order to relax the usual tension that punctuates the actor/audience relationship in a modern theatre. This innovation witnesses a resurrection of interactive moments between actors and their audience; a step that creates similar effects, as in the oral narrative performance tradition (Sekoni 1998: 139-159). The coterie nature of modern theatre (pre- Osofisan) makes it a mere means of escape for the elite and therefore unpopular outside the class. To change the theatre to a medium of social instruction (as is customary to Africa) its audience has to be made active, hence the step to modernize pre-industrial performance by extending some of its practices to modern playwriting.

The effort at recreating the pre-industrial 'dialectics' of narrative performance in modern theatre is a transposition process that has two dimensions. The first seeks to transpose a style common to all open performance to a formalized theatre, which is restricted to the auditorium. The second is the transposition of the European concept of theatre (theatre for leisure) to fit into the African concept of a socially relevant theatre. This experiment seeks to transform the docility of the audience of modern theatre from zero interaction to an appreciable level of involvement by minimizing the rigid stage forms. The aspect that affects the audience is our concern here.

Osofisan tackles the problem of audience participation in his dramaturgy by categorizing his audience into what we describe as 'integral' and 'integrated' audiences. The integral audience forms a corporate part of the play, while the integrated audience is the theatre audience, which is also sporadically drawn into the performance. These are aimed at changing the audience's aloofness, which is an inhibiting feature of the modern theatre.

In the prologue to *Many Colours*, the Songleader, Drummer, Women, Elder and Voices form an integral part of the play, (as audience to Igunnu, the master story-teller). They partake in the opening of the narrative by approving of Igunnu as a narrator and consent to the choice of Shango's adventures as a story.

> Song leader: Igunnu, it is because of your scintillating tales that each year, after harvest, we embellish street and shrine, clear the debris from home and market, and wear our finest clothing.

> Drummer: It is because of your stories, so rich in wisdom and laughter, that children abandon school, women their stalls, and men their tasks on the farm, to throng the square.

> Song leader: Why should a man even think of marrying a river?

> Igunnu: Suppose he does, my people? What step must he take next? ... The answer is simple: If a man dares and marries a river, then he must also bring in a forest as her co-wife. (12).

Songs, Music And Dance in Many Colours Make The Thunder-King

Songs are core to performance in most African traditional settings. Hardly can a performance subsist (be it ritual or mundane) without its being embellished with songs music and dance. Obafemi (1986: 14) reiterates that no traditional performance can be conceived outside poetry (songs) and folktales, on the one hand, and music and dance on the other hand. It could be added that of all verbal arts (folktales, proverbs, riddles, incantations etc.), song is the commonest. It features frequently in and outside performance because it is easily accessible. Events are recorded and are easily recalled through a song. Its brevity and musicality make references to it and inferences from it easy. Thus songs, in a performance, are not about entertainment only. They encode, and decode the messages therein. As a theatrical medium in modern time, Ogundeji (2003: 23) observes that songs can form sub-structures to acting. In Osofisan's fabulous theatre, there is a resourceful use of songs, music and dance as tropes to meaning, in manners that make them pre-emptive, proactive and interactive.

The two categories that are relevant to *Many Colours* are largely the use of songs, music and dance to pre-empt actions or events in the story and those that proactively advance the plot. The third category usually consists of songs with refrains (and music and dance), which require the active participation of the audience, but this style is not featured in the play under consideration as we find in other plays of Osofisan, such as *Once Upon Four Robbers* (1980). *Many Colours* opens with song, music and dance to welcome a mask as part of annual communion with the ancestral spirit, Igunnu. The drumming, singing and dancing before an expectant mammoth crowd, which consist of the old and the young, pre-empts a big event crucial to the existence of the community. Also, the appearance of a mask, the applause and the celebration, which greet the appearance, suggest positive reactions and fulfilment of a desire (that motivated a confluence of colourfully dressed youths and the aged to throng the market centre on a day other than the market day). The celebration equally suggests a long awaited reunion, from which much is expected. The song goes thus:

Welcome, welcome!

Welcome, we greet you!

Do as you (only can) do!

Strut as you (only can) strut!

Jump as you (only can) jump! (10).

From the content of the song, the visit is a recurring one and it has usually brought desired things, which the crowd converges for. If the expected thing is from an ancestral spirit, it is obvious then that it should be something of common interest to both the living and the visiting ancestors. Also, since the ancestors are considered the representatives of the community in the spirit land, it must be good news that accompanies the dancing mask; news that will benefit and advance the communal course. This opening equally pre-empts the mythical base of the story enacted in the play.

In other instances, songs, music and dance are used proactively as part of the plot development. One of such is the song of departure by Osun, after her expulsion from the palace on the false allegation of immorality with Alagemo (60.) The song covers the period of her departure with her retinue. Another one is the 'Clothe Changing Play' performed during Shango's courtship with Oya and the 'Colour Embellishment Songs' in which Alagemo endows the birds with colours in exchange for 'their voices'. The honey-filled container with the voices is used to prepare concoction for the return of Osun's lost voice (34).

Conclusion

This essay re-examines the extent to which one can justifiably tie Osofisan to the apron- string of Brechtian/Marxian praxis as done by many critics. It acknowledges virtual and actual coincidences and influences in the dramaturgies of both playwrights, due to their motivation towards a functional, dialectical theatre, a factor that might have compelled Osofisan to look inward for a way of addressing the teeming potential audience that do not find the works of his predecessors relevant to its situation. The result of the experiment with Africa's populist theatrical tradition for European stage designs is described as a hybrid of two theatrical experiences to create the fabulous theatre. It establishes this by accentuating the differences in Brecht's and Osofisan's dramaturgical concepts. Osofisan's dialectics are found to align more with Africa's functional theatre than with Brecht's political theatre.

References:

Awodiya, M. P. 1993. 'Talk in 1986', in Muyiwa Awodiya, (ed.). *Excursions in Drama and Literature* (Ibadan: Kraft Book).

Awodiya, M. P. 1995. *The Drama of Femi Osofisan: A Critical Perspective* (Ibadan: Kraft Book).

Mapanje, J. and L. White. 1983. *Oral Poetry from Africa: An Anthology* (London: Longman).

Needle, J. and P. Thompson. 1981. *Brecht* (Oxford: Basil Blackwell).

Obafemi, O. 1986. *Contemporary Nigerian Theatre* (Bayreuth: Bayreuth African Studies Series).

Obafemi, O. 1981. 'Revolutionary Aesthetics in Recent Nigerian Theatre' in *African Literature Today*. No12.

Ogundeji, D. 2003. 'Introduction' in A. Dasylva. *Dapo Adelugba on Theatre Practice in Nigeria* (Ibadan: Culture Study Group).

Olaniyan, T. 1999. 'Femi Osofisan: The Form of Uncommon Sense' in *Research in African Literature*. (30:4) Winter 1999, 74 – 91.

Osofisan, F. 2001. *Insidious Treasons: Drama in a Postcolonial State* (Ibadan: Opon Ifa Readers).

Osofisan, F. 2003 'Many Colours Make the Thunder King', in *Major Plays 1* (Ibadan: Opon Ifa Readers).

Sekoni, R. 1988. 'Oral Literature and the Development of Nigerian Literature', in Y. Ogunbiyi (ed.). *Perspectives on Nigerian Literature Vol. 1: 1700 to the present* (Lagos: Guardian Books (Nigeria)).

Styan, J. L. 1981. *Modern Drama in Theory and Practice* Vol. 31 (Cambridge: Cambridge University Press).

Ukala, S. 2001 'Politics of Aesthetics' in M. Banham, J. Gibbs, and F. Osofisan, (eds.). *African Theatre Playwrights and Politics* (Oxford: James Currey)

ORAL TRADITIONS AND CONTEMPORARY HISTORY IN FEMI OSOFISAN'S *ONCE UPON FOUR ROBBERS*

AYO KEHINDE

The reworking of forms of oral traditions in contemporary African drama is a deliberate and necessary attempt at indigenising the genre. Modern African playwrights graft elements from their cultural backgrounds unto their plays so as to give such works a local flavour. This is desirable since it imbues their dramatic texts with a certain identity code and signification. The commitment of Osofisan's plays is, without any doubt, to the cause of the masses and society in general. The Marxist overtone could be detected in his writings, like in the works of other African radical writers with ideological motivations such as Ngugi wa Thiong'o and Sembene Ousmane. His handling of African oral traditions is peculiar because of the re-orientation of such elements of artistic forms of communication (oral story-telling mode, myths, legends, folktales, songs, riddles, jokes and oral poetry) in a new creative milieu. This is a proof that the playwright is breaking a new ground in the radical use of oral traditions to meet the challenges of contemporary socio-historical situations and to espouse his socialist vision of society.

Thus, to most of contemporary African playwrights, oral tradition is an excellent instrument in the treatment of their thematic considerations. To a great extent, the drama of Osofisan appears conscious of itself as a linguistic act; it has a pertinent correlation with the indigenous tradition that preceded written/scribal drama in Africa. This view is corroborated by Barber (1995):

> It (orality) is treated as both a source – the origin and precursor of 'modern' literature – and a resource – a rich heritage or fund of themes, motifs, images, and techniques upon which the 'modern' author can draw (6)

Therefore, we can conclude that there exists a symbiotic relationship between culture, tradition and modern drama in Africa. This relationship is highlighted by Irele (1990) who believes that the 'distinctive mark' of written African literature in European languages is the striving to attain the condition of oral expression, even within the boundaries established by western literary conventions. This is to claim that the admixture of oral traditions and western models of drama by modern African playwrights is a giant step towards solving the problems emanating from the use of foreign languages by African writers.

Quayson (1995) also dwells on the issue of the crossing-point of literary practice and oral traditions. He draws illustrations from the works of Amos Tutuola and Ben Okri and identifies two factors that are responsible for the 'interface between orality and literature' (175). The factors are both ideological and aesthetic. In a similar vein, Ahmed (1995) identifies the influence of orature on the novels of Ngugi wa Thiong'o. He states: 'This paper sets out to examine Ngugi's adaptation of the devices of the oral tradition in his novels' (46). Also, the influence of oral literature in written literature is discussed by Isola (1981). Although his thesis is based on Yoruba drama, it has a universal appeal. He sees modern Yoruba plays as having something in common with other genres of Yoruba written literature. He believes that Yoruba plays borrow a lot from oral literature, especially from oral poetry.

It can be argued that the reconstruction of culture and tradition by African writers has a utilitarian value. It propagates and re-invigorates African cultural values. Jeyifo (1981) asserts that the reconstruction of oral tradition and culture in modern African drama is a weapon for popularizing the so-called literary drama. Furthermore, many literary critics have examined the issue of re-enactment of culture and tradition in contemporary African drama. For instance, Ogunba (1982) vividly highlights the traditional content of Soyinka's plays. Also, Ilori (1988) attempts an analysis of the use of oral tradition in Osofisan's plays while Wilentz (1988) also discusses the use of orature and tradition in Efua Sutherland's *Foriwa*.

However, the concern of this essay is to isolate and foreground the various traditional forms, which are employed in Osofisan's *Once Upon Four Robbers* to depict socio-historical realities of Nigeria, in particular, and the African continent in general. In the play, Osofisan dwells on his country's neo-colonial inequities, most especially the impoverishment of the masses and its consequences, such as armed robbery. As a writer who operates from a materialist socialist perspective, Osofisan in the play uses drama as an ideological weapon. He is unmistakably partisan as he makes use of his play to conscientize the suffering masses. This makes his play to be potentially revolutionary. The contribution also seeks to examine how culture and tradition have been integrated, in the play, through the medium of English language, to produce a powerful work of art, which gives character and strength to African writings. The justification for noticing the culture and tradition employed in the play becomes more valid when it is realized that this is an era of cultural nationalism and rejuvenation. In the main, Osofisan leans much on the traditional Yoruba performance modes and mythology. This is an effective weapon that makes the play accessible beyond the precinct of the English-speaking elite.

Here, I define tradition as that complex corpus of verbal or spoken art, based on the ideas, beliefs, symbols, assumptions, attitudes and sentiments of a people, created as a means of recalling the past. Vansina (1961) enumerates two basic groups of oral tradition that can be utilised by modern African playwrights. These are: literary group (poetry, songs, formulae-proverbs, incantations and parables), and historical categories (narratives based on myths and other historical plays or anecdotes). This is further amplified by Adedeji (1971) who sees tradition as:

An ensemble where the conscious and unconscious; the real and the unreal; poetry, song and dance, intermingle with elements of traditional theatre both sacred and secular (107).

In a similar vein, Okpewho (1983) identifies some ways through which African writers rework the materials from the folklore into their works. These include the following:

a) Tradition Preserved – a straightforward transfer of oral art to a literate tradition. Thomas Mofolo's *Chaka* is a good example;

b) Tradition Observed – the transfer of concepts and motifs from the literate tradition into the oral tradition, incorporating same within the latter, for instance, Wole Soyinka's *The Forest of a Thousand Demons* (a translation of Fagunwa's *Ogboju Ode Ninu Igbo Irunmole*);

c) Tradition Refined – the tales, in their old forms, are dropped; only their figures are adopted for the essences or values that they embody. Wole Soyinka's works evince this practice.

Osofisan has once admitted that modern African playwrights do restructure oral traditions in their works. He asserts:

The playwright takes the figures extent legends or myth, and brings them on stage, mostly to revive a tradition, identify with a glorious past, and reclaim a heritage (1974: 110).

However, unlike many other African playwrights, Osofisan maintains a distance from the elements of oral tradition to achieve a dialectical treatment of them, with a view to conveying his political viewpoint. He stresses:

Obviously, I may use myth or ritual, but only from a subversive perspective. I borrow ancient forms specifically to unmask them, to use theatrical magic to undermine the magic of superstition. All these gods and their inviolability… one is tired of them (1991: 12).

Thus, in *Once Upon Four Robbers,* Osofisan dwells on the problem of escalating armed robbery and the public execution of 'convicted' offenders instituted by the then military regime of General Yakubu Gowon. However, the myths of African magic are subjected to a test in the play with a view to exposing their limitations and the foibles of their practitioners.

To a great extent, Osofisan uses an experimental and dialectical treatment of oral tradition by demystifying and adapting them for progressive, artistic and ideological effects. In fact, the enduring brilliance of his dramaturgy lies in the concurrence of oral tradition with western techniques. This view is corroborated by Gbilekaa (1988) who declares that Osofisan reconstructs the elements of oral tradition to achieve his socialist vision. Thus, the thematic preoccupations of his plays centre on the plight of the masses, the oppressed, dehumanization, man's inhumanity to man and the institution of jungle justice.

In *Once Upon Four Robbers*, Osofisan borrows from contemporary history to pass a comment on the social ills plaguing the Nigerian society. The play shows the playwright's radical approach to historical and social realities. It is a confrontation of contemporary reality – a metaphorical treatment of the phenomenon of armed robbery.

In the play, Alhaja, Angola, Major and Hassan are portrayed as by-products of an extremely materialistic and unjust society. The programme notes of the play reinforces this:

> It is obvious that as long as a single, daring nocturnal trip with a gun or matchet can yield the equivalent of one man's annual income, we shall continue to manufacture our own potential assassins. For armed robbery, on the scale we are witnessing, are the product of an unjust society.

Therefore, Osofisan traces the origin of excessive armed robbery in Nigeria to the problem of neglect of the able-bodied masses by Nigerian neo-colonial rulers. Since the youths of the nation are not well catered for, they take to armed robbery. The play shows an unfamiliar treatment of familiar history and cultural elements. In it, a dialogue ensues between the armed robbers tied to the stake and their executioners. This gives a theatrical twist to the arm of contemporary history. There is a process of self–justification by all the segments of the society – firing squad, the market women, and the robbers – in a heated argument, which is a condemnation of the system that produces such mental and social consciousness.

Also, magical effect through incantations, taught by Aafa to the four robbers, brings emancipation – not war or sanction or coup! The 'unexpected phenomenon', namely the chanting of Angola's formula of *Ofo*, bewilders Sergeant, and the death sentence is not enacted. Dance replaces shooting. Therefore, a stalemate is produced, enabling a democratic involvement of the audience in resolving the plot. The audience are required to give a referendum, having heard the reasoning of the robbers. This treatment of history evokes reasoning rather than empathy, because Osofisan does not merely document reality, he subverts it. The contemporary phenomenon of armed robbery in Nigeria is thus treated objectively in an unconventional way to shock the audience into awareness.

Furthermore, the play relies heavily on the story-telling tradition of the Yoruba people. Actually, the title of the play, *Once Upon Four Robbers*, reveals that a traditional story is about to commence. It is apparent that traditional story-telling technique features prominently in Osofisan's dramatic ideas. The setting and stage effects are highly suggestive of the traditional village story-telling scenes and situations. The story-telling motif is used to generate a full-blooded audience involvement in the theatrical process. Osofisan employs the traditional story-telling techniques with a narrator who is also a performer, telling a contemporary tale in an acted form.

In the prologue, a storyteller is revealed in the moonlight, in a performing mood. He comes with *Sekere* (castanets) to announce, with a shout, the formula beginning of a sung-fable in the contemporary mode. This technique is traditional, although the content is modern. Everything in the technique suggests the narrative act of story-telling: the moonlit night, the call - response introduction or opening, the intimate rapport between the audience and the performer, interventions, digressions, meta-narrations, dramatic illustrations, and critical interplay with the audience. Suffice it to highlight the traditional introductory formula employed by Osofisan in the play:

> . . . ALO O! As usual everybody replies: AAALO! He (the story teller) repeats this, gets the same response, and playing his instrument, starts his song. The audience picks up the simple refrain – ALUGBINRIN GBINRIN! after each line. As the song gathers momentum, the musicians and actors, hitherto lost within audience, begin to assemble on the stage (1).

The story-telling technique is not inadvertently utilised; rather it is deliberate. It is a means of bending the conventions of the imported genre (scripted drama) towards the more communal conventions of orality. The dramatic text is rooted within a known tradition. Again, the story-telling technique is used for didactic effect (Okur 1998; Nwachukwu-Agbada 2000; Ogundele 2003); it points out a simple moral. Osofisan expands this didactic function by using the folk-tale to project an ideological viewpoint. The play is about the disruptive violence produced by an aggressive society. By this Brechtian technique, whereby the actors come out of the audience and seem part of them, the playwright puts the message across that the criminals are there to dramatise an aspect of common experience. Also, the characters are initially part of the audience but come out, after the play begins, to act out the role of the four robbers. By this, an effect has been achieved, By making the actors come out from among the audience and pick up their costumes from the stage to get themselves into the roles they are to play, Osofisan makes the conscious effort of implanting into the actors' minds the fact that they are not to immerse their personalities in the roles they play. It also intimates the audience with the theme and subject matter of the play.

Moreover, the use of the entrance – song is significantly 'a theatrical device of social consequence' (Adedeji 1971: 110). This opening song, which may also be referred to as the opening glee, serves the purpose of identification, thus communicating the aim and intent of the performance that is to follow it. The storyteller's song in the play begins thus:

Itan mi dori o dori

O dori dori

Dori olosa merin o

Danondanon akoni ni won

Ajijofe apanilekun

Awodi jeun epe

Arinko sole dahoro

Ran ni sorun apapandodo! Etc (1/2).

Translation

An ancient tale I will tell you

Tale ancient and modern

A tale of four armed robbers

Dangerous highwaymen

Freebooters, source of tears

Like kites, eaters of accursed sacrifice

Visitors who leave the house desolate

Dispatchers of lives to heaven, etc (98/99).

The storyteller's song, like all other songs in the play, foreshadows the major thematic interest of the playwright. It also passes a critical comment on the acquisitive and materialistic tendencies of the capitalist society where the play is set. Thus, music/song plays a crucial part in Osofisan's dramaturgy. Actually, the play is realised to a great extent in music. The plethora of songs in the play artistically privileges accumulation of details, statements and imagery. Songs and dances in the play energise the potency of Aafa's incantatory magical formula used by the robbers for unarmed 'robbery', as well as producing the stalemate at the end of the play. Songs are also used for satirical effect; all the songs of Aafa, which provide the plot of the play, are satirical. They condemn armed robbery and human greed that bring misery to the robbed families. The other songs analyse the evil of armed robbery and the reasons that lead men to get involved in the business – the race to get rich quick in an exploitative society. Music is therefore used for aesthetic and political purposes.

In the play, Aafa is used as a votary of Orunmila. This hint is given by Gbilekaa (1988):

> Orunmila enters the dramatic universe of Osofisan in three different perspectives: through votaries, through the Ifa motif (*Iwori Otura*) and in person (245).

Alhaja, Angola, Major and Hassan are expected to give a dramatic meaning to Aafa's story. They dramatise the story so as to give it theatrical significance and dimension. The story-telling idea is further reinforced by Aafa's statement in the Epilogue:

AAFA:

(Walking round the auditorium) A stalemate?

How can I end my story on a stalemate?

If we sit on the fence, life is bound to pass

us by, on both sides . . . (96).

The play ends 'unconventionally'. The audience must decide the outcome of the conflict. This underlies the importance of individual decision-making rather than distanced spectatorship; it also provokes critical thinking and debate. The audience is thus brought into the performance through a series of questions from Aafa to them as to who should win the contest – the robbers or soldiers? Hence, the play has an indeterminate ending – it may end for or against the armed robbers. The audience is, in this manner, allowed to participate in the creative process, and also in the search for solutions to pressing societal problems. The inconclusiveness of the play is based on the indigenous tradition of story telling .A narrative event is supposed to be continuously in circulation with variations as many as there are skilled performers. A narrative event itself may wind up at a point in time, but the story hardly ends. This is because another narrator will continue the same story with slight or major variations elsewhere.

In the play, Osofisan also employs the oral poetic form of incantation chants and magic. Aafa teaches the four robbers an incantation and magic formula for smooth robbery operations without hindrances or molestation. This is done by teaching each of them a part of the formula, not the whole because of the ravenous nature of man. Aafa chants the following verse, while the robbers repeat antiphonally the same lines:

Omo Enire

Omo Enire

Omo enikan saka bi agbon

Ifa karele o

Ewi nle Ado

Erinmi lode Owo

Ifa karele o! (31).

Translation

Son of Enire

Son of Enire

Of those who strike sudden and sharp

Ifa, we invite you home!

Ewi of Ado

Onsa of Deta

Erinmi of Owo

Ifa we beckon you here!, etc (103).

The incantation chant is supposed to avail the four robbers with great power to overcome their victims in public places like markets and banks. Throughout the play, song dance, drumming and music advance the message therein. It is therefore inevitable to recall Achebe's assertion about proverbs being the palm-oil with which conversation is *eaten* among the Igbo people. Also, the Akans of Ghana say that a wise child is spoken to in proverbs, not by banal /prose statements. The point here is to establish the primacy of the proverb as an ingredient in the literary make-up of Osofisan. In *Once Upon Four Robbers*, Osofisan makes use of proverbs for aesthetic effect. For examples:

> Major: Aafa, nobody quarrels so much with his head that he wears his hat on his knees (21).

> Aafa: Ah, if only one way led to the stream, how many women would fill their pots? (30).

> Major: When the man walking in front stumbles into a pit, what should those behind do? (51).

Also, the use of African oral poetry in the play is worth isolating. Osofisan employs oral poetry for aesthetic and ideological purposes. For instance, Alhaja chants a dirge to commemorate the death of her husband, Alani, who has just been publicly executed:

> Alhaja

> (Singing) Eni lo sorun kii bo

> Alani o digbere, o darinnoko o

> Eni lo sorun, aremabo o

> Alani o digbere, o doju ala o!

> Ohun won n je ni o bawonje,

> Ma jokun, ma jekolo o,

> Alani o digbere, o darinnoko o...(4).

> *Translation*

> The traveller to heaven never returns

> Alani, goodbye, till we meet over there!

> The journey to heaven

Is a one-way route,

Alani, goodbye, till we meet in dream

Whatever is food in heaven

You will share

You will not eat worms

Or centipedes

Alani, so fondly remembered (100).

Therefore, in the play, Osofisan borrows from contemporary history and adapts the oral story-telling mode to his drama to advocate his socialist vision of society. The advantage of the reconstruction of oral tradition in Osofisan's plays is viewed by Ibitokun (1995) thus:

Little by little, in the plays of Osofisan, through subverted, fissured myths, Nigeria (Africa) affirms her stand from the pantheistic, monarchical, deterministic universe to a revolutionary, nationalistic, Nietzchean cosmos where man's potentials or possibilities are great (97).

In this essay, I have attempted a discussion of the reconstruction of oral tradition in Osofisan's *Once Upon Four Robbers*. In the play, one can sense the commencement of a story even with the framing of the title along the traditional model of folktales in the traditional African setting. I have also observed that in the play, Osofisan is more indebted to the indigenous African traditions than to the imported tradition of play writing from the West. He borrows extensively from the oral traditions of his culture in order to develop an indigenous idiom of drama which is neither apishly Euro-Western nor foolishly traditional. The playwright has taken up certain traditional African ideas and explored them beyond the traditional boundary. Therefore, Osofisan, through the play, has contributed immensely to the preservation, observation, refinement and revision of fast-dying art forms of Africa in the face of crippling technology. What he has done for the oral traditions of Africa is bringing it forward, something more than merely updating folkloric materials. The predominance of oral traditions in Osofisan's play does not only illustrate the power of the spoken word, but serves as an educational tool and emerges as a narrative strategy in his writing.

References

Adedeji, J. 1971. 'Oral Tradition and Contemporary Theatre in Nigeria' in *Research in African Literatures*.2.2 (Fall), pp. 103-116.

Ahmed, K. 1995. 'Orature, Politics and the Writer: A Case Study of Ngugi wa Thiong'o's Novels' in S. Brown (ed.), *The Pressures of the Text: Orality, Texts and Telling of Tales* (London: B. P. C. Wheatons Ltd., pp. 47-59).

Barber, K. 1995. 'Literacy, Improvisation and the Public in Yoruba Popular Theatre' in S. Brown (ed.), *The Pressures of the Text:Orality, Texts and Telling of Tales* (London: B. P. C. Wheatons Ltd., pp. 6-27).

Gbilekaa, S.E.T. 1988. 'Radical Theatre in Nigeria (1970-87)' (unpublished dissertation, University of Ibadan).

Ibitokun, B. M. 1995. *African Drama and the Yoruba World-View* (Ibadan: Ibadan University Press).

Ilori, K. A. 1988. 'Oral Tradition and the Playwright: The Case of Femi Osofisan' in *Nigerian Theatre Journal*.2.1, pp. 68-82.

Irele, A. 1990. 'The African Imagination' in *Research in African Literatures*.2.1, pp. 59-80.

Isola, A. 1981. 'Modern Yoruba Drama' in Y. Ogunbiyi (ed.), *Drama and Theatre in Nigeria: A Critical Source Book* (Lagos: Nigeria Magazine, pp. 399-410).

Jeyifo, B. 1981. 'Literary Drama and the Search for a Popular Theatre in Nigeria' in Y. Ogunbiyi (ed.), *Drama and Theatre in Nigeria: A Critical Source Book* (Lagos: Nigeria Magazine, pp. 411-421).

Nwachukwu-Agbada, J.O.J. 2000. 'Nigerian Literature and Oral Tradition' in E. Emenyonu (ed.), *Goatskin Bags and Wisdom–New Critical Perspectives on African Literature* (New Jersey: Africa World Press, pp. 67-89).

Ogunba, O. 1982. 'Traditional Content of the Plays of Wole Soyinka' in *African Literature Today*.Nos 1,2,3 and 4, pp. 2-18.

Ogundele, W. 2003. 'Early Yoruba Cultural Nationalism Contra Nigerian Nationalist Historiography: A Reassessment' in W. Ogundele & G. Adeoti (eds.), *Iba: Essays on African Literature in Honour of Oyin Ogunba* (Ile-Ife: Obafemi Awolowo University Press, pp. 257-272).

Okpewho, I. 1983. *Myth in Africa* (Cambridge: Cambridge University Press).

Okur, N. 1993. 'Ritual, Tradition and Reconstruction in Contemporary Nigerian Drama: Femi Osofisan and Tess Akaeke Onwueme, a Dramatic Analysis in Afrocentricity', a Paper Presented at the Sixth Annual African Studies Consortium Workshop, University Of Pennsylvania, (October 2).

Osofisan, B.A. 1974. 'The Origin of Drama in West Africa: A Study of the Development of Drama from the traditional Forms to the Modern Theatre in English and French' (unpublished dissertation, University of Ibadan).

Osofisan, F. 1991. *Once Upon Four Robbers* (Ibadan: Heinemann Publishers).

Quayson, A. 1995. 'And the Relationship of Literary Practice to Oral Traditions' in S. Brown (ed.), *The Pressures of the Text:Orality, Texts and the Telling of Tales* (London: B. P. C. Wheatons Ltd., pp. 96-117).

Vansina, J. 1985. *Oral Tradition as History* (London: Heinemann Publishers).

Wilentz, G. 1988. 'Writing for the Children: Orature, Tradition Community in Efua Sutherland's *Foriwa*' in *Research in African Literatures*.19.2 (Summer), pp. 182-196.

MYTHOLOGICAL AND PATRIARCHAL CONSTRAINTS: THE TALE OF OSOFISAN'S REVOLUTIONARY WOMEN

VICTOR UKAEGBU

Introduction: Femi Osofisan's Theatre

Osofisan's theatrical style derives mainly from the selection and integration of features from traditional African and Western performance aesthetics, transformed into a form that is characterized by among other features, its instigation of stage-audience dialogue instead of providing answers to social conditions or explanations for them. Osofisan employs minimal staging, themes contextualized in socio-historical contexts, myths, storytelling and narration and presents his theatre as a parable on contemporary situations. Other features of the theatre are the use of alienation techniques in the forms of flashbacks, 'play-within-the-play', the incorporation of dance and music, symbolic language, gestus and visible scene changes. Amuta 1989, Obasikene 2000 and Asiedu 2001 among others have commented on Osofisan's Marxist leaning and have for good reasons, compared his theatre to Brechtian theatre. Osofisan's plays offer a revolutionary view and interpretation of events and like Brecht's, his dramaturgy provokes and demands audiences' intellectual engagement with the events on stage.

1

Morountodun

The play is about the Agbekoya uprising of 1969, an actual historic incident 'in which ordinary farmers, in the west of the country rose up and confronted the state' (Osofisan, *Morountodun*, 1982: 6). It celebrates the heroic struggles of poor courageous farmers who, armed with crude implements and conviction in their cause fought the state to a standstill before peace was restored through dialogue. *Morountodun*, interrogates the extent to which collective actions provide an antidote to oppressive patriarchy but Osofisan is not merely concerned with the presentation of history; his re-interpretation of this particular incident through the legend of Moremi draws attention to the lessons that history, myths and legends offer contemporary Yoruba and Nigerian societies. His dramatic decision to contextualize the Moremi legend and Agbekoya uprising as related incidents in Yoruba history is a way of privileging revolutionary option over impotent silence.

According to legend, Igbo warriors invaded Ile-Ife kingdom repeatedly, leaving a path of wanton destruction. All efforts to understand the mystery behind their terrifying physical appearance fail. As the kingdom is paralysed by fear of impending attacks, Moremi, the king's favourite wife, volunteers capture by the invaders in order to discover their secret(s). Captured as intended, she discovers the invaders were masked Igbo warriors. Moremi escapes her captors and returns to a hero's welcome. The knowledge she brings saves Ile-Ife but in sacrificing her safety and royal privileges for her community, Moremi displays rare courage and bravery deserving of the mythical status reserved for national heroes/heroines and deities.

In the play, Titubi and her wealthy mother Alhaja lead protests to stop a group of performers from staging their interpretation of the Agbekoya uprising for implicating their privileged, moneyed class in the state's attack on the poor farmers. In the process, she comes face to face with the very corrupt Superintendent Salami responsible for stopping the uprising and arresting its leaders. Baited and challenged by the superintendent, Titubi, who relishes herself as legendary Moremi ignores her mother's warnings of dangers to her life but instead, agrees to infiltrate the farmers and to deliver their leader to Salami. Aware of plans by the farmers to attack the Police station to free their arrested comrades and all other detainees, Salami puts Titubi, now pretending to be a vagrant with the arrested farmers. Titubi is captured but is shocked by the farmers' deprivation and suffering. After winning their trust, she lures and leads their leader, Marshal to Superintendent Salami but at the last minute, aligns herself with the farmers' revolution. She returns to the forest with Marshal who marries her just before his death and peaceful settlement of the uprising.

Moremi and Titubi: Mythological and Cultural Barriers to Women's Revolution.

Titubi captures the endearing public stature of her legendary inspiration, Moremi, whose epic service to the state Osofisan re-contextualizes to show History as possessing the stimulus for revolution in contemporary Yoruba and Nigerian societies. Like Moremi, Titubi breaks role and gender boundaries as her bravery is not only exemplary, her siding with the oppressed farmers disrupts those traditional class and gender constructs that marginalize women and the poor in cultural process. *Morountodun* is not only revolutionary for eulogizing women's contributions to society, it is dramaturgically significant as in it, Osofisan avoids character simplism and tokenistic presentation of women, creating instead, strong, complex women who command similar ideological and intellectual statures as men. They fight beside men as equals and resist marginalization from decision-making on gender grounds as men attempt to do in the trial and execution of Buraimoh and Isaac, their male relatives and traitors to the farmers' cause.

Osofisan conceives Titubi, Mama Kayode, Wura, Mosun and Molade as no ordinary women in peripheral, decorative roles but as part of the inner circle of revolutionary ideologues. He places women further up the revolutionary ladder and in place of simplistic, one-dimensional characters, he opts for complex individuals whose ideological motives are no different from those of their men counterparts. This approach enables Osofisan to link the play's ideological conflict to both gender and class whilst introducing Alhaja, Titubi's class-conscious mother as the representative of the corrupt, political upper class, a role reserved for men in *Another Raft, Once Upon Four Robbers* and in *The Oriki of a Grasshopper*. Alhaja, like her namesake in *Four Robbers* disrupts the notion of the noble dignified woman and exhibits all the excesses of the corrupt moneyed class.

According to Amuta, Titubi commits 'class suicide' (1989: 172) by rejecting her upper class background for a radical vision of society. Her ideological bridge-building between traditionally opposed classes challenges assumptions about class relations. Titubi's marriage to Marshal is ideological and revolutionary, however, by maintaining a patriarchal form of gender relationship with its separation of roles, Marshal objectifies Titubi in the name, *Morountodun* (I have found a sweet thing) and raises searching questions about how traditional institutions such as marriage are used to disadvantage women. In effect, the cultural ramifications of the marriage changes Titubi's place in the revolution.

MARSHAL: ...That's better! Now I am a man again... Morountodun, *I have clothed you in a name of honour*... My fists to a superb woman! (my italics) (p. 78)

The farmers' revolution achieves its main goals of restoring productive capacity to the farmers and ensuring their livelihood, but it fails to negotiate gender relations either within the working class or society in general for although her marriage and *re-naming* are cultural acts, it changes Titubi's strategically significant position as ideological comrade and co-revolutionary to the collective, subordinate norm of *women* where her voice in silenced. This raises other questions: Why was Marshal's relationship with Titubi uneasy and why was marriage between them an option? Did marriage effectively move Titubi to a secondary platform where she no longer competed with Marshal as the voice and face of the revolution? Despite the significance of their actions, the women's occupation of the ideological high ground with men is short-lived and although Obasikene has rightly suggested that Osofisan's 'radical transmutation of an established myth is meant to provoke debate and arouse the docile consciousness of an audience to a revolutionary action' (Obasikene 2000: 43), Titubi's marriage brings her revolutionary idealism to a pre-mature end.

Like legendary Moremi who returns to the role of silent wife, the women do not challenge gender constructions; mother/wife and domestic serf, implied by marriage. Their collusion and uncritical acceptance of Titubi's marriage as a reward and logical by-product of the revolution is disturbing, if not disappointing. If anything, such actions play into the emerging power dynamic that their presence as co-revolutionaries threatened to re-order but which Marshal was too eager to restore. The women return to domestic spaces, surrendering political power to Marshal who seizes the opportunity to sideline them from decision-making. By undermining and relinquishing their own political positions, the women, especially the usually eloquent Titubi fail to challenge the same stereotypical gender constructions that patriarchy has traditionally used to oppress them:

> MARSHAL: Are we to argue this out in front of the women?

> WOMEN: We want to hear this too, Marshal (p. 76).

Marshal's marginalisation of the women is a form of cultural repression based on 'distinct ideological interpretations and political strategies' (Doolan 1991: 3). He diminishes Titubi's heroism, rises to the dizzy heights of revolutionary idealism and ignores her plea for inclusion in the forthcoming battle; 'Marshall... what about me?' (p. 78). The women discover it is too late to reassert their position for on becoming 'a man again' (*Morountodun*, 78) Marshal marginalizes them altogether from collective decision-making. Although the play re-contextualizes the Moremi legend and history, it repeats a pattern of gender displacements and a conservative worldview different from the one Amuta's considers as reconstructing 'myth and history in the service of contemporary reality with specific reference to the issue of social and political change' (1989: 172). For the women, the resulting contemporary reality is shaped by patriarchal forces while the envisioned political change perpetuates gender dis-equilibrium and men's strategic dominance of the revolution as Marshal's unilateral decision to continue the war epitomizes.

The Oriki of a Grasshopper

This is one of Osofisan's shorter plays in which the revolutionary agenda is located in a contemporary context. In the play, undergraduates respond to the arrest of their colleagues by arresting and detaining one of the policemen patrolling students' demonstrations against the government. Tensions mount as university authorities fear violent clashes between students and the police intent on freeing their colleague. To avert violence, Claudius, wealthy capitalist, ex-student and political operative organises the arrest of all socialist agitators amongst the students and lecturers except their leader, Imaro. Claudius' spares Imaro, his best friend, ex-classmate, leading socialist and lecturer from detention in a subtle political move designed to undermine Imaro's leadership and Marxist claims. Although aware of the arrests, Imaro anticipates the arrival of his faithful disciple and the brother of his mistress Moni, to rehearse Estragon in Samuel Beckett's *Waiting for Godot* only for Claudius to confirm his friend's arrest.

On her arrival, Moni is shocked to discover her lover and his best friend collude in the detention of her brother and other socialists. In the resulting heated debate Moni challenges Imaro's commitment to socialism and is understandably disappointed that despite their class and political difference, Imaro and Claudius place personal friendship over ideology. The combination of personal disappointment and ideological betrayal by Imaro and Moni's realisation that

Imaro's instinct for self-preservation is not different from Claudius', the self-confessed, unashamed capitalist, ends her emotional and ideological romance with socialism and her lover.

Moni: Personal Failings, Gender Inequality and Patriarchal Domination.

Moni is the play's only woman character, a victim of personal betrayal, patriarchal domination and institutional limitations. Her contribution to the socialist cause is both emotional and ideological; with her long association with Imaro as former student, mistress and comrade, Moni's place in the socialist cause is strategically significant but as she proves through her actions, the emotional costs and gender imbalance associated with her subsidiary role of mistress affects her ideological commitment. Moni's revolutionary standing is in some respects, compromised by her emotional entanglement with Imaro mainly because Osofisan bases the relationship between the two on conservative hierarchical gender and class relations; leader-follower, teacher-student, man-woman, and lover-mistress. Moni is not only an uncritical follower trapped in the throes of emotions, Imaro's hierarchical relationship with her is quite different from the revolutionary comradeship she believes sharing with him. Unlike Imaro whose attempt to distinguish personality and ideology is puny, Moni has real difficulties separating ideological commitment and affections for Imaro. Both characters claim the same ideological platform, but adopt different strategic views *vis-à-vis* the relationship between personality and ideologue:

IMARO: Claudius restored my faith not in socialism but in myself.

MONI: And where's the difference? You know, Imaro, if I closed my eyes…, I would not see you as you are now, a wreck, but only as I first knew you and grew to love you –….like an echoing dream, your voice urging us not to despair, to rise up and carry the burden of our destiny. Teaching us that…

BOTH: "….Rise! Rise up now and shake off your slumber. History waits for our footsteps, for the command of our voices, for we have a special role to play…" (1986: 37-8)

The ideological and emotional arguments favour Imaro as Moni discovers with her lover's betrayal. Her bid to regain the ideological high ground by challenging Imaro's commitment is couched in ideological terms, yet Moni reveals two uncomfortable truths about herself; accommodating Imaro's double-standard when deemed appropriate and her ignorance of his readiness to betray filial and ideological loyalties for personal comforts. Imaro is an unproven dreamer but Moni's predication of her entire ideological position on his fickle vision or personality is a weak premise for an enduring revolution. This exposes her own more fundamental personal failings, especially her inability to separate love for ideologue from commitment to socialism and her misreading of Imaro's intentions and methods:

IMARO: Moni, dreams are a wall which every man builds to lean his life on. But I did not promise to be strong all the time, at every hour of the day...., because we are only human, sometimes the wall cracks....

MONI: I needed someone who could fly. And you gave me a promise of wings. But alas!, you're only a grasshopper, powerless before the wind. When the forest begins to burn, you're just as trapped as all the crawling things.... (p. 39)

Osofisan is unkind to Moni by presenting her as Imaro's bedfellow, an object of material comfort, a muse that inspires Imaro without figuring in his notion of freedom. Imaro mistreats her but Claudius is less harsh, preferring the less painful route of indifference to the ideological humiliation to which he subjects Imaro. Moni's relationship with the two male characters reveals obvious evidences of gender and patriarchal domination. Claudius reduces her stature as a credible threat to capitalism while using her to dismantle Imaro's socialist pretence. Her *anagnorisis* ennobles without strengthening but the collusion between Imaro and Claudius destroys whatever faith she had in socialism. If anything, Osofisan treats her as a peripheral player *unworthy* of the revolutionary stature reserved for her arrested comrades. Spared by Claudius for no other reason than for Imaro's comfort, Moni is *objectified* as an emotional prop; her objectification is by men who duly defend their actions while her charges against them are more likely to be viewed as the wounded shrieks of a lovelorn woman. Osofisan contextualizes Moni's place in the revolution as dependent on Imaro's utilitarian needs of her than by a shared political vision as he declares:

IMARO: .... I need you, but not as you are this moment. Only as you are when you dream, when you turn the world into fairyland. (p. 43)

Osofisan provides us with little justification to view Moni more positively. She is emotionally compromised and *morally* flawed like Imaro. Her emotional investment clouds her judgement as her collusion in Imaro's unconscionable betrayal of his marriage damages and denies her the platform to attack his socialist credentials. Their emotional relationship was always a warning of Imaro's propensities for self-indulgence and self-preservation. This is a serious failing on both parts, but while Osofisan uses her reaction to Imaro's betrayal to undermine her political commitment and judgment, in comparison, Claudius occupies a stronger, less complicated position from which he launches his subtle but devastating attack at the very heart of the socialist group. Moni is betrayed and undermined on all fronts, but by ending her association with socialism on personal grounds, like Imaro, she sacrifices collective goals for personal interest. Moni's political commitment is difficult to fathom especially as she loses the will to continue the struggle. In Moni Osofisan creates a woman character that is unable to rise above the human frailties she berates in others and although these shortcomings are found wherever unproven polemics and self-preservation collide, in her case, it is debilitating and hardly enhances her revolutionary credentials.

Another Raft

In *Another Raft*, the nation is once again adrift. Angered, Yemosa, the sea goddess floods communities along the coast. Houses are destroyed, lives are lost, cultivated farmlands are washed down the lagoon to the sea. As custom demands, the community's representatives are to take a raft bearing a virgin girl to be offered to Yemosa where the lagoon enters the sea. The sacrifice is a restorative ritual designed to arrest drift and restore cosmological harmony. The ritual is threatened with subversion and failure; unknown to anyone, the ritual scapegoat is replaced by her brother intent on exerting vengeance on the priests and custodians of ritual who selected his sister for the role and the politicians that hired him to kill their rivals on the journey. Violence surface on the raft; some representatives die from their own thoughtless actions while two are killed for flimsy reasons. With fewer hands to work the ropes, the chances of survival are slim especially as Yemosa offers no divine solution. Mysteriously, the raft moorings break loose, paddles are lost to fast currents but cataclysmic disaster is averted when the three survivors, Reore (hardworking farmer), Oge (his assistant) and Orousi (chief priest of Ifa) solve a riddle posed by the goddess about a king faced with the thorny problem of choosing a successor from his three equally-endowed sons.

In the riddle, the king sends his three sons on a quest, decreeing that whoever returns with the best evidence of his love and devotion to the king would ascend the throne. Setting out, the sons agree to meet to compare notes before their return to the town. Each son returns with one each of See-Far/See All, Fly-Fast and Heal–At-Once. While going over their gifts, See All discovers their father at death's door, Fly-Fast takes them home instantly where Heal-At-Once restores his health. Applied to Nigeria, each son or *section* has something unique but the solution to disunity and social fragmentation is to combine the three gifts. Each gift is inadequate on its own, peaceful co-existence depends on the three sons combining their individual attributes and realising that they are much richer in a *collective context*. In the end, Reore, Oge, and Orousi realise that collective action is more important than individual sacrifices, successfully guiding the raft to safety:

YEMOSA THREE: ....And if you were king, who would be your heir?...

REORE: I have the answer! We're saved!

OROUSI *(to sprites)*: Who are you?

YEMOSA TWO: The answer first! ....

REORE: None of them! None of the sons!

OROUSI: Yes, how dumb! I'm with you now! None of the three sons of course! Or rather, all of them together!....

REORE: All of us! That's the answer to the riddle!

YEMOSA THREE: At last! At last you've got it! (Osofisan, *Another Raft*, 1988: 82)

The survivors realise that ritual sacrifices may massage human fears, but ultimately, they excuse individual and collective failings.

YEMOSA ONE: But if you abandon yourselves

recklessly to our caprice

as most of you insist on doing

we have no power anymore

except to drift with the currents

of your cowardly surrendering

and choke up the fresh springs, and

the waterways of your lives. (*Another Raft*, 83)

The Limitations of Ritual as Revolutionary Impulse

Another Raft has no female characters other than Yemosa, the goddess and the ritual scapegoat replaced before the journey by Agunrin, her brother and subversive soldier. Yemosa wields ritual influence but like the hapless, faceless ritual scapegoat offered to her to restore socio-sacral harmony, she has little political power outside the ritual context. The sacrifice of a woman to the goddess has ritual significance and gender connotations because in substituting the scapegoat with a man whose antipathy to traditional religious and political authorities subverts the spirit and conduct of the restorative ritual, Osofisan transfers the revolutionary imperative from women to men. The scapegoat, the goddess are their associated rituals do not therefore, constitute a revolutionary impulse of any description for while the scapegoat may be unwilling, coerced or induced, Yemosa merely acquiesces with prescribed rituals. Trapped and bound to a ritual structure and order, Yemosa and scapegoat may be deemed revolutionary only if they step outside prescribed ritual corridors, yet when they do, they are destructive rather than constructive. Yemosa and scapegoat have less to do with political authority than with ascribed ritual functionality, as it were their positions are determined by the very conservative structures that dominate them. Like the ritual scapegoat whose sacrifice is restorative rather than revolutionary, Yemosa is driven by the need to perpetuate traditional cultural order and is implicated in a ritual in which women are the victims.

The play highlights collective survival but women are not only absent from the raft, they are trapped in a mythological alley and subsumed in a latent ritual state until activated. Despite men's obvious shortcomings, Osofisan invalidates the revolutionary capacity of the scapegoat, the one woman whose sacrifice in ritual terms at least, is potentially more powerful than the combined might of men; politicians, priests, soldier, farmers, etc. Although the play reveals men's destructive and redemptive propensities, it is less complimentary of ritual, demonstrating instead, its irrelevance and by implication, the inefficacy of scapegoat and Yemosa to society's survival. Osofisan's handling of Yemosa and ritual scapegoat in this hugely topical play hardly frees women from patriarchal domination. Other than placing responsibility for redemptive action with men, women's ritual involvement produces, not a new order but the old restored with little contributions from women.

Once Upon Four Robbers

Set in the 1970s after the Nigerian civil war of 1967 to 1970, the play recounts the ideologically-motivated escapades of four robbers, one woman and three men. The robbers; Alhaja (wife of group's executed leader), Major (greedy opportunist), Hassan (ideologue) and Angola (convert to the group's cause) earn their living by violent robberies. Constantly chased by the law in an unending dance with death and near death encounters, the robbers are thrown a life-line by Aafa, would-be victim, traditional medicine man, priest and storyteller who offers them a thoughtfully contrived magic formula whose efficacy depends on their acting *collectively* to rob only thrice but without violence. In their penultimate outing, Major betrays his colleagues and makes away with the loot. He is caught and condemned to death by public execution. In a brave act of sacrifice and commitment to group cause reminiscent of socialist/Marxism, the other three robbers forgo retribution and deploy their last outing to saving Major. Arrested and condemned to die with Major, their execution is interrupted by Aafa's invitation to the audience to debate whether the robbers should be freed or executed in the final action of the play.

Alhaja and the Market Women: Contemporary Revolutionary Contexts

The play has two types of women characters: Alhaja, who assumes *de facto* leadership of the robbers and the market women who collude with the soldiers. Osofisan presents the two sets of characters in stark contrast to each other, using them to sustain the class debate that runs throughout the play.

Alhaja makes no pretensions contextualizing herself in the revolutionary role of the legendary Moremi in her willingness to sacrifice personal safety for group interests and a new social order. Although motivated by anger at social injustice and the loss of her husband and friends, Alhaja exhibits the selflessness, compassion and revolutionary zeal of Osofisan's other Moremi. Titubi. She throws her lot with the robbers to keep her late husband's dreams alive when it would have been safer to abandon them. Resolute in her defiance of authorities and personal dangers, she draws on the lessons of legend and history willingly immersing herself in a dangerous ritual trance in which she is both legendary Moremi and her modern equivalent (see trance scene in *Once Upon Four Robbers*, 1991: 80 - 81). She deliberately transforms the Moremi story with biting irony, giving it cultural and contemporary relevance. Claiming to be the very Moremi who purportedly saved the colleagues of soldiers she attempts to seduce, Alhaja uses the more recent history of the Nigerian civil war to draw the soldiers' attention to their complicity in the social inequities plaguing the nation. Her evocative use of trance and legend to convince the robbers to stick together and the soldiers to free Major are revolutionary.

Osofisan presents the market women's mindless, exploitative capitalism in ideological contrast to Alhaja's selfless sacrifice. The market women – Mama Toun, Mama Alice, Bintu, Yedunni, etc. – are a diverse group of individuals united by a common concern for exploitation and profiteering. The methods employed by both sets of women define their ideological differences: Alhaja is motivated by collective interests while the market women celebrate their transformation into exploitative agents of capitalism and the ruling classes. In fact, while the latter justify their self-seeking materialism on purely economic grounds, Alhaja views the robbers as a legitimate response to social inequalities. Alhaja challenges the status quo, her identification with the poor exposes the market women, not as powerless pawns but as people who as their choric manifesto reveals, have chosen selfish individualism over collectivism:

Song of the Market:

…..The lure of profit has conquered our souls

and changed us into cannibals;

oh praise the selfless British

who with the joyous sound

of minted coins and gold

brought us civilization!

We make inflation and hoard away

as much as we may relish….

….

Let's also say

as we collect our profit

that life is heaven on earth! (pp. 45 – 46)

The market women's material needs are no different from those of the rest of society but they and the soldiers who defend and exploit them in equal measure privilege individualism over the collectivism espoused by Alhaja. Osofisan is not uncritical of Alhaja; he questions her violent methods as well as exposing her and the market women's abuse and misuse of the collective platform for sectional interests. Both groups defend their actions but the market women's exploitation of customers and their implication in the corruption of the soldiers collapse before Alhaja's idealism and demand for a common front for challenging social inequalities. Alhaja's greatest revolutionary achievements are therefore, neither her daring attacks on corporate victims and market women nor her commitment to the fractious group of robbers, but her ideological belief in the re-distribution of wealth even if this is achieved by violent means. She retains her revolutionary edge and critical objectivity in the face of Major's treachery and even when it is obvious that time is running out for the robbers. As a true leader, she leads from the front but it is the sheer conviction of her argument and her demonstration of personal sacrifice in forgiving and risking her life for Major that encourages Hassan and Angola to forgive the traitor and follow her example. Alhaja understands the value and advantages of group solidarity and it is to her credit that her persistence and commitment earn the robbers the opportunity of a public hearing about the nature of justice and punishment.

2

Women's Revolutionary Platform: Mixed Fortunes

The women in *Morountodun* are revolutionary in form and purpose; they participate in a class conflict in which they share centre stage with men. They are markedly different from the politically naïve market women of *Four Robbers* that come across as willing agents of the ruling class and whose opposition to revolutionary change makes Alhaja the sole woman representative in the commoners' struggle. In distinguishing Alhaja from the market women in *Four Robbers* Osofisan marks a cultural shift from the collective presentation of women as a homogeneous group to acknowledging their individual contributions to society as well as suggesting that their roles should neither be determined by gender nor be constituted as inferior to men's. At one stage, *Morountodun's* women disrupt traditional gender constructs but because Titubi's revolutionary actions are primarily motivated by collective consciousness and a conservative cultural order, it is in Alhaja in *Four Robbers* that women come of revolutionary age, convincing us of their individualism and displaying the self-assurance and commitment that characterize strong ideological beliefs.

In *Oriki of a Grasshopper*, Osofisan diverts attention from legendary to contemporary women and indirectly, to gender relations. The power structure still favours men and although in Moni, he creates an independent woman whose actions counter gender constructions, her ideological position is unfortunately, bound by the very conservative forces she challenges in Claudius' capitalism and Imaro's self-seeking opportunism. In tracing the development of his revolutionary women, Moremi plays a topical part in highlighting Osofisan's respect for women's contributions to society but in Moni, they leave the cloisters of legends and myths, emerging like their men counterparts, with warts and limitations. This similarity does not necessarily make Osofisan's men and women equal; despite their frailties men like *Morountodun's* Marshal occupy the public space where they continue their heroic struggles while Titubi and other heroic women exchange their position for secondary domestic roles where they are unlikely to effect changes prejudicial to men. Osofisan repeats this practice in *Oriki* where the emotional relationship between Moni and Imaro is used to shunt the former from centre-stage as Titubi experiences in *Morountodun*.

In comparison to other women discussed in this essay, Alhaja is Osofisan's most developed woman revolutionary endowed with both critical faculty and ideological stature. She continues the struggle when significant circumstances such as her husband's death, Major's treachery and arrest would suggest otherwise. Her association with the executed gang leader may be emotional but it is also strongly ideological. In these respects, She is a much more sophisticated ideologue than her namesake and ideological opposite in *Morountodun*. She is more understanding of the effect of human shortcomings on revolutions than the university-educated Moni in *Oriki* who terminates her association with socialism on account of her lover's shortcomings. Alhaja's emotions do not impair her revolutionary vision for while Moni abandons the cause because of betrayal and treachery by men, she responds to Major's treachery with vision and pragmatism. Alhaja rises above traditional constraints and dispenses with the emotional and ideological weaknesses that limit Osofisan's other heroines. She is an updated version of Moremi and unlike Titubi and Yemosa in *Another Raft*, who are defined mainly by their cultural and ritual roles, Alhaja is a further development in the emergence of Osofisan's women from patriarchal construction and domination.

3

Conclusions: Shackled in Suspended Revolution – Osofisan's Women

Decades of social developments have neither engineered a sufficiently radical presentation of African women nor has gender relations figured prominently in contemporary Africa's cultural discourse. For a Marxist playwright, other than the Moremi legend and its contemporary interpretations, the cultural setting of Osofisan's plays is characterized by the under-representation of truly revolutionary women. Women's liberation from traditional constructions must embrace the ideological responsibility of dismantling patriarchal representations as well as contesting their cultural marginalization. The four plays have not necessarily achieved this; Osofisan's retention of mythological and traditional paradigms has meant that while his women undertake revolutionary actions, they rarely threaten patriarchy. Dramaturgically, he leans toward archetypal gender constructions; 'the penitent whore', 'the speechless heroine', 'the wilful woman', and 'the golden girl' (Ferris 1990) for he captures elements of these in

Titubi who comes closest to the 'speechless heroine' and 'golden girl'. Other than Alhaja (*Four Robbers)* whose make-up challenges Ferris' character types, Osofisan's other women come in the kind of historically conservative images that Sue-Ellen Case (1988) blames for the biased representation of women on the modern European stage in which 'the form of the narrative itself is complicit with the psychocultural repression of women' (cited in Gibson 1993: 8).

Morountodun is primarily about collective revolution and class struggles than it is about women's liberation but in it, Osofisan reinvests Moremi with her legendary status and revolutionary vision. However, by defining her progressive, anti-conservative impulse on grounds of nationalistic idealism instead of gender, Titubi subordinates her revolutionary zeal to the collective struggle without negotiating gender relations after the uprising. In true revolutionary spirit Titubi steps away from Moremi's shadows but not necessarily from the gendered roles of mother and wife:

> TITUBI: I had to kill the ghost of Moremi in my belly. I am not Moremi. Moremi served the state, was the state, was the spirit of the ruling class.
> (Osofisan, *Morountodun*, 1982: 70)

Osofisan does not link gender with class struggle but Titubi's marriage and subsequent relegation from the revolutionary council, Moni's eventual rejection of socialism and the market women's complicity in sustaining social dis-equilibrium almost succeed in 'making the ruling order seem a 'natural' condition ('there is no alternative')' yet each of these conditions demand 'justification by political argument' (Holderness 1992: 14). This is a legitimate expectation given Osofisan's Marxist ideology for as Holderness points out, the primary 'responsibility of a progressive drama' is to challenge dominance, 'by showing that the existing order is not 'natural' but politically constructed and fundamentally unjust' (1992: 14). Alhaja, Moni, Titubi and some of the women are undoubtedly progressive, but their challenges of the social order are merely tentative without re-contextualizing those dominant structures that under-represent and oppress women. In a way, Alhaja is being ironic and cynical when she summaries women's lot in *Four Robbers* as one of 'nothing changing.... Only my story starting anew. Like before, like always, like ever more' (p. 80).

Other than Alhaja and Moni, the women generally act 'passively before the specter of male authority' (Doolan 1991: 2) but more significantly, their depiction as 'marginal and curiously irrelevant, except as a tacit support system or as a decoration that enhances and directs the pleasure of the male spectator's gaze' (p. 2) raises important questions as to the extent to which Osofisan's women may be viewed as truly revolutionary. Broadly-speaking Osofisan's women confirm Doolan's view that women are usually presented as empathising 'with men's romantic exploits' (p. 2) as we see in *Morountodun* and *Oriki* and that by their own actions as in the cases of the market women and the ritual scapegoat in *Four Robbers* and *Another Raft* respectively, the women are implicated in the 'objectification or erasure of' their 'own gender class' (p. 2).

Osofisan denies his women the capacity to challenge patriarchy. Unlike Ferris' strong-willed, 'evil' women who 'are punished for daring to question, to seek autonomy, to make their own choices' (1990: 130), the incorporation of 'speechless heroine' and 'golden girl' renders most of Osofisan's women incapable of defining themselves in enduring revolutionary light. Alhaja in *Four Robbers* and to a little degree, Moni in *Oriki* are unique for falling outside this muted revolutionary framework.

References

Amuta, C. 1989. *The Theory of African Literature: Implications for Practical Criticism* (London: Zed Books).

Asiedu, A. 2001. 'Once Upon Four Robbers: A Review'. *African Theatre: Playwrights and Politics*. Ed. M. Banham, J. Gibbs, and F. Osofisan (Oxford: James Currey, pp. 57 – 61).

Doolan, J. 1991. *The Feminist Spectator as Critic* (Ann Arbor: University of Michigan Press).

Ferris, L. 1990. *Acting Women: Images of Women in Theatre* (edited by Jo Campling) (London: The Macmillan Press).

Gibson, G. C. 1993. *Performing Women: Female Characters, Male Playwrights, and the Modern Stage* (Ithaca & London: Cornell University Press).

Holderness, G, (ed). 1992. *The Politics of Theatre and Drama* (London: Macmillan).

Obasikene, J. I. 2000. 'Ideological Transmutation of Myth and History in Contemporary Nigerian Theatre: The Example of Femi Osofisan and Bode Sowande' in *Enyo: Journal of African Theatre and Drama*, Vol. 1 No. 1 (Enugu: ABIC Books; pp. 41 48).

Osofisan, F. 1982. *Morountodun and Other Plays* (Lagos: Longman).

Osofisan, F. 1986. *The Oriki of a Grasshopper* in *Two One-Act Plays* (Ibadan: New Horn Press).

Osofisan, F. 1988. *Another Raft* (Lagos: Malthouse Press).

Osofisan, F. 1991. *Once Upon Four Robbers* (Ibadan: Heinemann Educational Books Nigeria Plc.)

A DEBATE ON TACTICS FOR THE BEST WAY TO OVERTHROW VILE REGIMES: OSOFISAN WRITES BACK TO NGUGI AND MUGO.

JANE PLASTOW

It is well known that Femi Osofisan has written a number of plays in response to and critique of other Nigerian playwrights. His *No More the Wasted Breed* (1981) is a reply to Soyinka's *The Strong Breed*, while *Another Raft* (1989) equally overtly speaks to J.P. Clark's *The Raft*. Osofisan freely admits that he is 'an incorrigible plagiarist'[1] who has, like so many great playwrights before him, also plundered the classics and European theatre in search of good stories to reinterpret. It has not however, to my knowledge, been seen that Osofisan's first stimulus for writing a play in response to another African playwright came not from Nigeria at all, but from Kenya. This essay will argue that Osofisan's *Morountodun* is, at least in part, a homage, critique and at times a satire on Ngugi wa Thiong'o and Micere Mugo's *The Trial of Dedan Kimathi*.

The Trial of Dedan Kimathi was written in 1976 and was taken in 1977 to Lagos to be performed as one of the Kenyan offerings at the second FESTAC, the 'Black and African Festival of Arts and Culture'[2]. It is inconceivable that the young Osofisan did not see or at the very least hear about and then read this play from Kenya's leading writer. He then goes on in 1979 to write a play that has a whole series of similar scenes, characters and events, but he sets his play in Nigeria, and uses it to come up with a very different critical analysis of the way forward to achieving equitable social transformation. It is intriguing that Osofisan has not chosen to discuss his debt to Ngugi and Mugo. The nearest reference I have found to an acknowledgement of the inspiration is in an interview with Biodun Jeyifo where he says:

> Sometimes…I feel the urge for adaptation comes from ideological disagreement, when I am provoked to contest some point of view a playwright – usually one I admire – puts forward. That is why I signify as I do on African texts and authors (Jeyifo 1995).

The reference to African as opposed to Nigerian texts may well have been made with the Kenyans in mind, especially since it seems to me that *Morountodun* does precisely discuss an ideological disagreement with *Dedan Kimathi* about how to mobilise people to demand democratic change, while at the same time

---

1 Biodun Jeyifo, 'Interview with Femi Osofisan', p 131, in *Comparative and General Literature*, No 43, 1995, pp. 120-132

2 The other Kenyan play taken to FESTAC was Francis Imbuga's *Betrayal in the City*.

Osofisan patently admires the socialist drive and many of the staging techniques employed in the Kenyan play.

Ngugi and Micere Mugo write from a largely African socialist perspective[3]. Their Dedan Kimathi is a people's hero par excellence. He is of the people, though in this representation he also moves towards an apotheosis as a Christ-like figure resisting both temptation and death. His function is to lead the peasantry and the proletariat so that they will be transformed into egalitarian beings working together in solidarity to resist capitalist forces, of which colonialism is seen as just one aspect. He is also, of course, an historical figure, and *The Trial of Dedan Kimathi* is a play that seeks to re-write a history previously dominated by the sensationalist imperialist view of the Mau Mau struggle as portrayed by a whole raft of Western writers[4]. As Ngugi and Mugo argue at end of their Preface: 'the challenge was to truly depict the masses (symbolised by Kimathi) in the only historically correct perspective: positively, heroically and as the true makers of history'[5].

The iconic figure of Dedan Kimathi and the post-colonial state's betrayal of the ideals of the Mau Mau struggle are leitmotifs running throughout Ngugi's work. Osofisan does not have such a heroic figure or historical moment recurring in his work, though his abhorrence of and resistance to a whole series of corrupt post-colonial Nigerian regimes is equally and consistently the foundation of his theatre. However, the Agbekoya peasant's uprising of 1969 does figure in two of Osofisan's major plays, both *Morountodun* and his 1976 piece *The Chattering and the Song*. Is it that after one theatrical treatment of this peasant's revolt, in which, possibly paradoxically, no peasants appear, Osofisan saw *Dedan Kimathi* and was moved to re-examine Agbekoya as a parallel to the Kenyan Mau Mau experience – albeit on a smaller scale – and as a vehicle for discussing whether such mass revolts could ever lead to effective social transformation?

Crucially all three writers have strong socialist sympathies. They are united in supporting the people's struggles they portray and in condemning the duplicity, brutality and rampant capitalism of their national ruling classes and their scions; the lawyers, religious leaders, businessmen, police and military. Where Osofisan

---

[3] For information on African socialism see A. M. Babu, *African Socialism or Socialist Africa?*, ZED Press, 1981.

[4] The Mau Mau struggle for liberation from British colonialism has been written about from an essentially white imperialist viewpoint, often portraying the Kenyan Mau Mau fighters as barbaric, by a number of writers. Ngugi and Mugo quote a number of examples of this kind of writing in their Preface to *The Trial of Dedan Kimathi*. See, for example, I. Henderson and P. Goodhead, *The Hunt of Dedan Kimathi* (Hamish Hamilton, 1958), E. J. Huxley, *A Thing to Love* (Chatto & Windus, 1954), R. Ruark, *Something of Value* (Doubleday, 1955).

[5] Ngugi wa Thiong'o and Micere Githae Mugo, *The Trial of Dedan Kimathi*, Heinemann, 1976. All quotes given in this essay are taken from this edition of the play. No page numbers are given for the Preface.

departs from the Kenyans and from conventional African socialist theory is that he argues that peasant revolts have never won lasting victories and that the only group capable of effecting change is the educated elite. This analysis however immediately runs up against the unpalatable evidence that it is these very educated classes that have time and time again sold out their fellow countrymen and women to benefit from their education for personal enrichment. Indeed in a parody of the rousing Kikuyu solidarity songs that open *Dedan Kimathi* Osofisan has a first song where the market traders join together to declare their right to fight for wealth.

Stand! Stand!

Fight to be rich

For happiness:

Oh fight for your right

To rise in life!

With good luck and stubbornness

With sweat, sweat, and cleverness

De-ter-mi-na-tion!

Ma-ni-pu-la-tion!

Oh fight for your share

And do not care![6]

In his essay '"The Revolution as Muse": drama as surreptitious insurrection in a post-colonial military state'[7,] Osofisan explains this dilemma.

The educated class is at the core of development in any modern economy, and...the failure of our society in Nigeria, and in other African countries, is to be traced to the lamentable decadence of that class...As a playwright, therefore, it is this question that obsesses me. Almost all of my plays, since I became a self-conscious dramatist, have been passionately devoted to it, and dominated by it. (p. 15)

Osofisan sees his mission as using theatre to reach these educated classes before they become set in their ways, in order to change their orientation.

---

6 Femi Osofisan, *Morountodun and other Plays*, Longman Nigeria, 1982, p. 131. All quotes given in this essay are taken from this edition of the play.

7 Femi Osofisan, '"The Revolution as Muse": drama as surreptitious insurrection in a post-colonial military state', pp. 11-35 in *Theatre Matters: Performance and Culture on the World Stage*, eds Richard Boon and Jane Plastow, Cambridge University Press, 1998.

I divide this class into two – between those whose ideas are already formed, whose positions are therefore already secure on the social ladder, and those whose minds are still in formation, but who will be potential recruits into the class. And it is to the latter, mainly, that I direct my work...Students are young and dynamic, alert to injustice and wrong, capable of compassion, quick to learn or unlearn...Assembled from disparate backgrounds and cultures, they comprise the various ethnic, gender and social types and along with the army, are the ones who most truthfully constitute a 'nation' in more than just a geographical sense. Furthermore and perhaps most important of all, students are also ideologically pliant and hence neutral...For me therefore this is the ideal moment to reach them as growing citizens...The committed dramatist who is able to reach that undergraduate student before s/he fully matures therefore, while his or her allegiance is still fluid, is obviously taking a more than decisive step in the work of communal rehabilitation. (p. 16-17)

I quote Osofisan at length here because while Ngugi's position as a champion of grassroots protest and local language publication and staging is well known and has been written about at length by the playwright himself[8], Osofisan has published considerably less about the philosophy informing his theatre[9]. His position in being so specific about the audience he seeks to reach – one he sees in the same article as drawing on Frantz Fanon's idea of a 'distorted consciousness' (p. 15) in the educated class – is, I think, unique amongst African playwrights.

'The Revolution as Muse' essay dates from 1998, but we can clearly see from a close examination of how *Dedan Kimathi* and *Morountodun* mirror each other, that Osofisan's philosophy was already formed in the 1970s. I have mentioned the relationship between the songs that lead into the main action of the plays, but I think the same distorting mirror applies to how the playwrights set up their action. In *Dedan Kimathi* after the charge against the eponymous hero has been read out the 'First Movement' opens with a great pageant of the historic oppression of black people. In contrast Osofisan shows us no heroic illusion but the banal reality of actors preparing to go on stage. The Brechtian influence so common to his theatre forbids lulling the audience into a primarily emotional response. Osofisan's director declares that he and his actors are horrified by the atrocities taking place in Agbekoya and that: 'We decided to go and rouse people up by doing a play on the subject' (p. 130). What this play, which would

---

[8] See, for example, *Decolonising the Mind: The Politics and Language in African Literature*, James Currey, 1986 and *Moving the Centre: The Struggle for Cultural Freedoms*, James Currey, 1993.

[9] Apart from the essay in *Theatre Matters* and the interview in *Comparative and General Literature* already referred to, the only text where Osofisan talks at length about his views on his own theatre is *Excursions in Drama and Literature: Interviews with Femi Osofisan*, Muyiwa P. Awodiya ed, Kraft Books, 1993; a collection of interviews held with the playwright between 1978 and 1992.

presumably be agitational along the Ngugi/Mugo lines, is we never see for 'reality' in the shape of Titubi and her supporters breaks in to object to any contestation of the right of the individual to accumulate wealth without thought for the poor.

Both plays give an 'heroic' woman centre stage for much of the action, and here there is unanimity of purpose. Osofisan explains that 'female heroines are so prominent in my plays, since the empowerment of women is crucial to [the] prospective programme of liberation and modernisation' (p. 16). Micere Mugo is an avowed fighter for African women's rights[10] who says that in *Dedan Kimathi* the intention was:

> To show that what Kimathi was fighting for was the same thing that a lot of our women were fighting for. Our concern was that whereas, the part the men played in the struggle has been recorded by historians and biographers, the women on the whole have been simply forgotten... research revealed a lot of women who had actually served in the Mau Mau war as generals or lieutenants. (Adeola James 1990)

Ngugi has repeatedly put poor women at the heroic centre of his writing, though in *Dedan Kimathi* in particular I wonder if the nameless 'Woman' is not so perfect that she is unintentionally disempowering to necessarily flawed actual women. 'She is', we are told:

> between thirty and forty years of age, with a mature but youthful face, strongly built. Goodlooking...Though apparently a simple peasant, the woman is obviously world-wise, and perceptive of behaviour and society.

Throughout her actions are under control: her body and mind are fully alert. Fearless determination and a spirit of daring is her character. She is versatile and full of energy in her responses to different roles and situations. A mother, a fighter, all in one. (p. 8)

What a contrast with our first vision of Titubi, 'the one born in softness', who is 'a pretty, sensual and obviously self-conscious woman' (p. 131). Yet Titubi who is, in keeping with Osofisan's target audience, young and educated, will be transformed in to just as great a heroine as Ngugi's 'Woman', contending with the mythic heroine Moremi as she is transformed in to 'I have found a sweet thing', Morountodun. The central difference is that whereas in *Dedan Kimathi* we are *told* that 'Woman' has become the ideal revolutionary as the result of her previous sufferings and then finding 'the call of our people' (p. 19) but we only *see* the finished result, in *Morountodun* we *see* how a pampered rich girl gains her revolutionary consciousness by sharing the reality of the sufferings of the Agbekoya peasants.

---

[10] See Micere Mugo interviewed in Adeola James, *In Their Own Voices: African women writers talk*, James Currey, 1990, pp. 92-101.

As the plays develop a fundamental difference becomes apparent in the means the playwrights use to educate and agitate their audiences. For Ngugi and Mugo the tools are polemic and emotion through the vehicle of representative rather than individualised characters; as Woman, Boy and Girl tell us of the sufferings they have endured, Kimathi offers great set pieces of rhetorical defiance and 'the people' sing and dance their refusal to accept oppression. Osofisan prefers Brechtian alienation and an appeal to the questioning intellect. The audience is never allowed to relax into simple emotional identification as understandings of 'reality' are constantly undercut, and individualised characters reveal themselves as flawed beings with a whole range of complicated motivations for their actions. Leading the pack is the witty, cynical yet fundamentally decent Superintendent Salami, (one of Osofisan's greatest creations and a flawed hero reminiscent of Bertolt Brecht's similar anarchic and brilliant law dispenser, Azdak in *Caucasian Chalk Circle*), who teases and tricks Titubi and her mother, Alhaja Kabirat, into, for the most part, following his plan for infiltrating the peasant movement.

At the same time both plays acknowledge the importance of using popular culture to maintain the interest of their audiences. As Ngugi showed in his subsequent move into community arts with *Ngaahika Ndeenda* (*I Will Marry When I Want*) (1977) and *Maitu Njugira* (*Mother, Cry for Me*) (1981) he became a master of using not only the people's language, but also their music and dance forms to entertain, include and uplift his mass audiences. *The Trial of Dedan Kimathi* is interesting in part because it marks the beginning of Ngugi's move into the use of local form and languages, with some Kiswahili prose and extensive song passages. I cannot help wondering whether Osofisan was at least encouraged in some of his techniques for interpolating Yoruba songs into his work by Ngugi and Mugo. Though *The Chattering and the Song* does include three Yoruba songs the early 'realist' plays[11] have none of this aspect of Yoruba popular culture in them, and *Morountodun* marks a distinct move towards the kind of 'total theatre' that Osofisan later espouses as the most appropriate vehicle for reaching Nigerian audiences[12]. For *Morountodun* he commissioned Tunji Oyelana to compose nine Yoruba songs, though nearly all the prose is in standard English, a factor which reflects Osofisan's wish to speak to primarily university rather than mass audiences. Indeed in Scene Three where Marshal and Bogunde pose as market sellers – surely a direct lift from the plotting-in-the-

---

[11] I have taken this definition of early works such as *A Restless Run of Locusts* and *Red is the Freedom Road* from Sandra L. Richards, *Ancient Songs Set Ablaze: The Theatre of Femi Osofisan*, Howard University Press, 1996.

[12] See 'The Revolution as Muse', p. 20, where Osofisan says, 'The drama which our people savour is still one in the mould of "total theatre", that is, a multi-media production, in which dialogue is no more important than other paralinguistic signs. There must be music and song, dance, colour and spectacle. The only problem here, however, is that unless the playwright exercises control, the message can be subsumed by the theatrical game itself.'

market scenes in the second movement of *Dedan Kimathi* – I find the attempt to play with appropriate use of pidgin clumsy and lumbering. Osofisan certainly lacks Wole Soyinka's dexterity in playing with Nigerian language registers and for the most part all his characters, whether peasants or professors, speak a version of standard English.

Osofisan has, however, a number of other techniques he has developed to facilitate popular access to his theatre. Like so many Nigerian playwrights he is happily at home with the witty metaphoric, proverbial and riddling exchanges that are such a feature of Yoruba conversation, and in which Salami especially loves to indulge. He also uses humour, particularly mockery of the pompous and self-important, to great effect – a potent weapon that Ngugi wields only seldom and then rather ponderously.

However, Osofisan's strength in utilising popular culture comes in to its own in his appropriation of the rich resources of Yoruba myth. His ability to take legend and rework it for his own, progressive purposes is surely one of Osofisan's great contributions to Nigerian and indeed African theatre, and is beautifully handled in the interweaving of the Moremi/Titubi/Morountodun stories. A number of commentators[13] have discussed how Osofisan subverts the myth of Moremi as champion of the state in his portrayal of the transmutation of Titubi with her fashionable Moremi dagger necklace, via an identification with her iconic heroine, into Morountodun who symbolically becomes a dagger in the corrupt heart of the contemporary state and a source of succour and love to the people. Even here I think we can see parallels with the Kenyan play. The domination of missionaries and a settler state effectively cut many Kenyans off from their own mythic history, but Dedan Kimathi himself, like Moremi, appears to have transcended mortality in the popular imagination and acquired divine characteristics. In the Preface to their play Ngugi and Mugo talk of a research trip where they went to Kimathi's home area and met a woman who told them 'Kimathi will never die', and of course in *Dedan Kimathi* we never see his death. Kimathi is equated with Christ in the temptation scenes, but just as Osofisan sees the myths and gods of the Yoruba through anthropomorphic eyes, as ways of explaining and revitalising his world, so in *Dedan Kimathi* the popular belief in Kimathi as supernatural is revealed as a manifestation of the revolutionary, liberationist spirit of the people.

Boy: [*becoming really excited*]: They say…they say he used to talk with god.

Woman: Yes. The fighting god in us - the oppressed ones.

---

13 See Chris Dunton, *Make Man Talk True: Nigerian Drama in English Since 1970* (Hans Zell, 1992); B.M. Ibitokun, *African Drama and the Yoruba World-View* (Ibadan University Press, 1995) or Sandra L. Richards, *Ancient Songs Set Ablaze* (Howard University Press, 1996).

Boy: They say…they say that he could crawl on his belly for ten miles or more.

Woman: He had to be strong - for us - because of us Kenyan people.

Boy: They say…they say that he could change himself into a bird, an aeroplane, wind, anything?

Woman: Faith in a cause can work miracles.

Boy: They say…they say that the tree under which he used to pray fell to the ground?

Woman: There are people, my child, with blessed blood. And when something happens to them, the wind and the rain and the sun will tell. Even hyenas. Their death can shake mountains and give life to the volcanoes long thought to be dormant.

Boy: Maybe they only captured his shadow, his outer form…don't you think?… And let his spirit abroad, in arms.

Woman: Your words contain wisdom, son. Kimathi was never alone…will never be alone. No bullet can kill him as long as women continue to bear children. (pp. 20-21)

The African world view allows for an inter-relationship, a co-dependence between gods and men. Just as failed gods can be disenfranchised, exceptional people can attain divinity and, as in both *Morountodun* and *Dedan Kimathi*, these beliefs can be held simultaneously at a metaphorical and a literal level. Moremi can be brought back to earth, Kimathi does not die, Titubi can become Morountodun, people and societies can really change. This is surely the underlying message of hope that mingles happily with the socialist analysis of all the playwrights and allows the audience in differing measures, intellectual, emotional and spiritual understanding of either play.

To return to the parallels in construction between the two plays, both choose - in conscious contrast to the moments of mythic heroism - to give us scenes that celebrate the humanity of the revolutionaries and their leaders. It is notable in both plays that when we are taken into the camps of the fighters a new tone of warmth and affection comes into the action. In *Dedan Kimathi* this is particularly notable because of the superhuman status accorded the revolutionary hero throughout the rest of the play. The Third Movement scene in the forest lets us see Kimathi as a son and brother, fallible in his merciful judgement when he holds back from executing his treacherous brother. Osofisan's Scene Nine has many parallels. We see the peasant leader, Marshal, (and Kimathi is consistently referred to as Marshal by his men) first tending a wounded Titubi, and then called upon to judge the treachery of the religious leader Alhaji Buraimoh and Lawyer Isaac, both sons of Agbekoya who have prospered through their education, been trusted to help intercede with the authorities, and have then been bought by the state and betrayed their own people. Just like Kimathi, Marshal shows mercy, though in this case the traitors are subsequently killed by government forces.

It is surely pertinent that the traitors are a lawyer and a religious businessman. For Osofisan, Ngugi and Mugo the religious establishment is terminally corrupt. In *Morountodun* that establishment is Islamic, as represented by Alhaja Kabirat who sees a trip to Mecca as simply a means of re-establishing control over her daughter and Alhaji Buraimoh who invokes Allah only to mock those he has betrayed and their socialist aspirations:

> Buraimoh: What is our crime? I demand to know.

> Baba: Your betrayal of our cause.

> Buraimoh: Hear that! Allah-akbar! Where do you think you are? China? Cuba? Mozambique? Or some lunatic asylum? Who's been teaching you these funny words. (p. 168)

In *Dedan Kimathi*, as throughout Ngugi's oeuvre, it is the Christian priests, black or white, who are the sellouts, as illustrated by the priest in the 'Third Trial' whose life-denying God Kimathi rejects in favour of the god of his ancestors and the spirit of the Kenyan people. Businessmen and their attendant lawyers are obvious targets for those lambasting post- and neo-colonial corrupt states, and neither Ngugi and Mugo nor Osofisan hold back form painting pictures of men ruthless in the pursuit of power and wealth.

The final part of this essay is a comparison of endings. In each case a major assault on a stronghold of state power is planned. In *Dedan Kimathi* the plan is to smuggle a gun in to the court in order to provoke mayhem and allow Kimathi to escape in the ensuing confusion. In *Morountodun* Marshal announces his intention to attack the Central Police Station. Both are desperate plans. However the reaction from those to whom they are revealed is markedly different. When the Woman asks Boy and Girl to join her in daring 'Great risks' they do not hesitate but, as becomes these representatives of Kenya's future, each leaps forward declaring, 'I am ready!' (p. 60). The tone Osofisan evokes is far darker. Marshal has just declared his love for Titubi and renamed her Morountodun to popular acclaim. The people are preparing to implement a truce agreed with the police prior to negotiations they hope will lead to peace, when Marshal announces that he has no trust in words and intends to attack and destroy the Central Police Station where so many of his people have been held and tortured. The old civil leader, Baba, and Titubi are horrified, with Baba declaring 'You're insane all of you! That place is almost a fortress! You'll never get in!' (p. 191). Just like Woman, Marshal has his young, unquestioning followers; Bogunde and Kokondi who mouth revolutionary rhetoric: 'Let all prisons fall!' (p. 191), but whereas in *Dedan Kimathi* we are evidently intended to approve of the action being planned, in *Morountodun* daring has become dangerous madness.

In each case the playwrights must expect that their audience will know the bare historical facts of what happened to Kimathi and the Agbekoya peasantry; that both were defeated by the forces of the state. What is fascinating is the response each seeks to evoke to the assault plans. Ngugi and Mugo create a world of almost miraculous heroism, encouraging their audience to rise up and follow the examples shown them in the play to their evident destiny of freeing Kenya from the shackles of capitalist oppression. By contrast Osofisan forbids such emotional identification. Marshal is seen usurping in non-democratic fashion the acknowledged authority of the father figure, Baba, and denying the voice of his beloved, Titubi. Although Bogunde and Kokondi mimic their leader's words in true sloganeering fashion, they cannot look at or answer Baba when he challenges them. Osofisan does allow Marshal and his warriors to exit with a war song reminiscent of the songs of revolt at the end of *Dedan Kimathi*, but any hint of triumphalism is undercut by Baba, whose final line within the world of the inner play is a sighed, 'They will not come back' (p. 192).

In his last scene, which functions as an epilogue, Osofisan further deflates any possible mood of heroic exaltation by returning to the Director who casually informs the audience: 'the old man was right. Marshal and his men did not come back. It was you'll admit, a suicidal mission?' He then launches in to one of the few moments of polemic Osofisan allows himself, when, as in so many of his plays, he puts the onus for future action firmly on the audience. 'This is a theatre, don't forget, a house of dream and phantom struggles. The *real* struggle, the real truth is out there, among you, on the street, in your homes, in your daily living and dying' (p. 192).

In these two concluding scenes it appears to me that Osofisan is speaking in direct debate with Ngugi and Mugo. For them the finale is the trial of Dedan Kimathi; built up to ever greater levels of tension as Woman is bundled out of the courtroom singing her defiance, as Kimathi makes a great polemic speech, is sentenced to death, and the Boy and Girl reveal their gun shouting 'Not dead!' Here the Kenyans, like Osofisan, break the illusion of stage reality, in their case with a gunshot and a blackout. But when the lights come up the forces of oppression have been banished and 'a mighty crown of peasants and workers' fill the stage with a 'Peoples' Song and Dance' of triumph and resistance (p. 84).

Osofisan's peasants try a last gasp similar song of hope, but he cuts them off with a freeze, before raising the lights on the audience and spotlights on the opposing figures of Moremi and Titubi. It seems to me apparent that Osofisan found Ngugi and Mugo's ending an impossible fantasy, and that he has set himself the challenge of mirroring their structure in order to challenge its solution which he finds naïve, manipulative and perhaps even irresponsible. Every possible moment of crowd identification and emotional agitation is teasingly denied his audience who are instead left, in the limelight, to consider their own roles in relation to the issues that have been raised about individual responsibility and the demands of the state.

I am left wondering why Osofisan did not acknowledge what close reading of the two texts reveals as not only obvious thematic and structural influence from the Kenyans but also such an interesting debate about how to achieve the writers' joint aim of mobilising their audiences to act against the forces political oppression and economic inequality. Maybe the young Femi Osofisan did not have the confidence to declare his borrowings without fearing that they would be seen as plagiarism. Maybe he worried about the reaction of Ngugi wa Thiong'o, who was, after all, already one of Africa's most famous writers, to the borrowings and critique of *Morountodun*. Perhaps he felt in the end that the strength of his play lay in its relevance to contemporary life in Nigeria sand that acknowledging the Kenyan link would only weaken its impact. Or possibly, in the end, Osofisan felt he had used *The Trial of Dedan Kimathi* in a deeply personal way, to sharpen his own wit, brain and force of argument, and it was his own creation he wanted recognised, his own points he wanted to get across to audiences without the intermediary text muddying critical waters or audience reception.

My exploration of the parallels between these texts has not led to any dilution of my considerable respect for either play. Rather the process of comparison has forced a re-evaluation of the playwrights' theatrical techniques and intentions that only adds another layer of interest to the process of critical discussion. I have been fascinated by Femi Osofisan's views on just who needs to be conscientised and roused to bring about empowering change in the nations of Africa – or anywhere else for that matter – ever since we debated that matter at a meeting in Germany in the 1990s at a time when I was deeply involved in peoples' theatre in Eritrea, the only country in Africa where I think one could possibly argue, at least recently, that a peasant revolt was ultimately successful in bringing about profound political change. Possibly one conclusion that one could draw from that discussion and the debate embodied in *Morountodun's* debate with *The Trial of Dedan Kimathi* is that African arts would probably be invigorated, performatively and ideologically, by far more cross-country and cross-regional debate that would allow artists to hold up useful and provocative mirrors to the situations they find obtaining in their own nations.

RIDING OSOFISAN'S *ANOTHER RAFT* THROUGH THE SEA OF NIGERIAN HISTORY: THEATRE FOR AGENCY

YVETTE HUTCHISON

Gbebe: My duty is ended, which was to lead you through the hidden channel in the wave of history to the turning edge of knowledge (*Osofisan,* Another Raft 1988: 69).

One of Osofisan's most intriguing and significant contributions to African drama has been his provocative linking of history to knowledge and myth, which he sees as pivotal in challenging and conscientising post-independent Nigeria. This article explores Femi Osofisan's particular contribution to the use of history and myth in Nigerian theatre by looking at *Another Raft* as a specific example.

Arabic accounts of northern Nigerian, dating back to the 9th century, are of the earliest records of West African and Nigerian history and cover events as far back as 1800 A.D. As Oyewese points out, while they are limited insofar as they focus on the history from a very particular Islamic perspective, they do belie the claim that the Nigerians are a 'people without a history' and 'they have demonstrated that the meeting of the various Nigerian peoples was neither a colonial creation nor a recent event' (1988: 12-13).

In a post-colonial period one of the first tasks historians set themselves is to refute the colonial claim that 'the African past was not historical' (Temu/Swai 1981: 21). Thus 'the purpose for which postcolonial historiography was constituted: (was) first and foremost as an ideological rejoinder to colonial historiography' (Temu/ Swai 1981: 28). African historiography was seen as part of the building of nation and creating a sense of 'continuity with the world and ourselves' (Cesaire 1969: 160), as a means of both curing the alienation caused by colonialism and retracing an African identity. The historian Dike says: 'African Studies will be a means to the achievement for the African, of greater self-respect, the means to the creation of a surer African personality in the face of the modern world' (Quoted in Kapteijns 1977: 25).

Thus new myths were created; and ancient civilisations, like that of Egypt, and Empires of the past, like the Malian Empire, were highlighted as the roots of African civilisation. History became a means of contributing to the unification of a nation, and even extended to unifying Africa as a continent. It served to suggest autonomy and originality, although this was less idealistic in west

Africa than east Africa.[1] What is interesting in this process is to compare to what extent the writers and playwrights paralleled the positions of the historians in 're-writing' African history and identity.

The overt use of history as a frame in Nigerian drama began with the Mbari Club in Ibadan. Artists and intellectuals including Wole Soyinka, J.P. Clark, Chris Okigbo, D.O. Fagunwa, Uche Okeke, Demas Nwoko, the South African Ezekiel Mphalele and German Ulli Beier founded this club.

Inspired by this club in Ibadan, Duro Ladipo created a similar club in his basement in Oshogbo, called Mbari-Mbayo ('when we see it, we shall be happy'). The Centre opened with the musical drama *Oba Moro*. Demas Nwoko writes of Ulli Beier's contributions at this time:

> Ulli Beier is not an artist, but he ... created by suggestion, a theatre troupe basically after the style of the existing Ogunmola and Ogunde vernacular troupes. He suggested a historical theme from the legends... Through further suggestions during production; original indigenous music and appropriate dances (along with poetry) were used... (quoted in Ogunbiyi 1981: 338).

Thus from Ladipo's acceptance of Ulli Beier's suggestion to explore the use of legends and history, came a series of historical plays. Soyinka's *Death and a King's Horseman* follows Ladipo's *Oba Waja*, which is an earlier version of the same event. Thus the meeting of African oral legend and western European notions of history meet in Nigerian theatre.

It would seem that there is a greater tendency to blend what may be perceived as history and myth, with a greater emphasis on the ritual, mystic dimension in Nigerian theatre than is the case with the East African writers. This may be because of the modes of colonisation and the extent to which Christianity did or did not make inroads into the two cultures.

Osofisan, though, has made a particular contribution in his use of history in the Nigerian context, involving his use of form to challenge and conscientise post-independent Nigerian audiences in *Another Raft*.

Another Raft (written 1986, first performed 1987) was a direct response to J.P. Clark's *The Raft* (1964), which has as a central metaphor the raft representing Nigerian history. Clark has moved beyond the noble tragic figure of Soyinka, to focus on the workers. Nevertheless, these people are disempowered. They float helplessly down to sea on the raft, unable or unwilling to save themselves or

---

[1] See the Nigerian historian Tamuno's inaugural lecture of 1973 where he does not scruple to suggest that not all were heroes in the struggle for independence, he identifies collaborators and states the failures of the Nigerian amalgamation of 1914, and the hypocrisy of the national leaders (1985: 113).

even attempt to direct the raft. In Clark's play the men are victims: unable or unwilling to act, or define what their doom means, or take responsibility for themselves and their futures. Osofisan challenges this confusion and passivity and extends Clark's cast of workers to include all classes of Nigerian society: including an old Priest, two boatmen (Waje and Oge); Lanusen, the Prince of the palace and current Chairperson of the Local Government Council who oversees the expedition; aided by Chief Ekuroola, a successful Lagos tycoon who holds the prestigious title, Abore: principal Priest of Rituals. Reore is the reigning Farmer King; and the Carrier Agunrin is a disguised soldier. Thus in one place and in crisis Osofisan has representatives of all strata of contemporary Nigerian society: the political, military, religious, farming and working communities. All are held responsible for their own, and by implication, for Africa's history and future.

This expansion of cast reflects Osofisan's more radical approach to and use of history. Being greatly influenced by Marxist thinking and in particular by Marxist Materialist dialectics, he, like Jeyifo, has challenged Soyinka's use of myth and focus on individual heroes as being static and reactionarily backward. In an interview with Olu Obafemi, Osofisan says:

> I think it is inevitable that he (Soyinka) arrives at these tragic conclusions because if you are always thinking of individuals creating, history will always look like a series of tragedies. The revolution itself is a mass of people always doing things together (Obafemi 1982: 119).

This statement suggests that Osofisan is closer to Ngugi wa Thiong'o than Soyinka on the uses of myth and history. While acknowledging the individual in processes of change, he sees them as being less important than the combined forces of the group. Osofisan argues for a change in how the ordinary person is perceived in society, and calls for resistance to using tragic figures to act for or represent their societies. Both Jeyifo and Osofisan object to the 'Kabiyesi syndrome'[2]. Jeyifo argues that the work of Hussein, and Cesaire probes the archetypes of tragic action and the socio-cultural milieu 'within the framework of real historical circumstances and confrontations' (1985: 107). And this is not just the confrontation of individuals and society, but individuals and societal forces, which embody aspirations, or goals of particular social groups, classes or nations. Jeyifo argues that this reveals 'the dialectical operations between politics, material existence and the superstructural categories - the morality, the myths and the metaphysics of the society' (1985: 107).

---

2 Jeyifo has outlined his objection by comparing Soyinka's elite hero in *Death and the King's Horseman*, Elesin Oba, to Hussein's Kinjeketile whom 'is not a man apart, he lives and speaks and acts for the people' (Jeyifo 1985: 105). This is important, Jeyifo argues because it challenges the assumption of a lone tragic hero who is a great historical personage or cultural hero whose connection to their audience is 'never dialectical; it is symbolic' (1985: 107).

Within this frame Osofisan, tends towards Jeyifo and Ngugi's approaches to the uses of history and myth in his work. In an interview he says: 'I may use myth or ritual, but only from a subversive perspective. I borrow ancient forms specifically to unmask them' (Enekwe 1980: 78).

This critical use of myth, ritual and theatrical form is perhaps why Osofisan is said to have produced some of 'the most imaginative and powerful works in the Nigerian English language theatre' (Dunton 1992: 67). Like Brecht, Osofisan understands the use of the dialectic and aesthetics. He is strongly committed to both exploring the options of the theatrical form, while concentrating on awakening the consciousness of his audience to the possibilities for change, and he has intrinsically related these two objectives in a number of ways: Firstly, the plays are all set in recognisable socio-political realities of contemporary Africa. Secondly, he uses a variety of aesthetic strategies that signal the texts as contemporary traditional dramas, including of elements of story-telling, masquerade, the folk-tale, Yoruba song and popular rhythms and proverbs, and the repetition of scenes other stories, and even plays within his play; and then he disrupts these forms. Finally, by the way he constructs and deconstructs himself as *auteur* Osofisan challenges constructed reality and narratives and forces his audience to engage with how they make meaning, and decisions, and thus suggests how they may realise their own power and agency.

One of the ways Osofisan engages with recognisable socio-political realities of contemporary Africa is by situating his plays clearly in the context of the post/neo-colonial. The plays are framed by events in history that Osofisan sees as profoundly influential on Nigeria's current situation, like the civil war and socio-political instability that followed independence in 1960. He also looks at the lack of government engagement with the economic injustices of colonialism and the redistribution of wealth and resources to poor. A particular event to which Osofisan often refers in his plays is the Agbekoya Farmers' Revolt (1968-1970) where small illiterate farmers of the western region mounted an armed resistance against government imposed taxes and other restrictions which made impossible their development or survival. Although they withstood counterattacks for several months, they were finally defeated by infiltration of their leadership. Critics such as Richards argue that the young Ibadan intellectuals like Bode Sowande and Femi Osofisan 'seemingly viewed the Agbekoya Farmer's Revolt as a prime example of the national liberation struggle yet to be waged in Nigeria' (Richards 1996:94). They thus view art as a means to highlight issues and encourage, even teach, the mass audience to critique the ruling hegemony and also to realise their own power and agency.

These events are referred to in *Another Raft* in the references to their 'troubled times' (Osofisan 1988: 24).[3] As the story unfolds corruption is evident on all

---

[3] Subsequent references to this play will be to this edition and signals AR, with page numbers following.

levels and even the workers criticised for not helping themselves, but remaining passively trapped in the hegemonic constructs that underpin the power structures that oppress them. The leaders, like Lanusen and Ekuroola, are depicted as comfortable in the cities, while seeing their peoples' plight on television (*AR*, 14). Lanusen 'grew rich on council contracts and city funds' (*AR*, 12, 24). Ekuroola too has grown rich in the city, absent from the land, sending his agents 'to collect our harvest, leaving us chaff...' (*AR*, 26) and not performing any rituals. The people believe that the disasters follow as a consequence. Orousi lists the disasters: 'The people have experienced accidents on the highway. Fires in the market. A cholera outbreak, followed by yellow fever! And now, before we have fully recovered from those disasters, the flood!' (*AR*, 13). Oge's wife and child was lost in a fire of the Council building (*AR*, 23) and it is suggested that this is as a consequence of the money that had been approved to build a drainage system, having disappeared and been spent elsewhere (*AR*, 24).

Gbebe, the son of priest, is accused of having abandoned the service of the goddess for material things (*AR*, 30). The priest was also complicit in suppressing the farmers' uprising and causing the massacre of more than 2000 people. (*AR*, 47-8) Even the soldier Agunrin is said to have 'milked the land' as a soldier (*AR*, 63). Gbebe argues that they are all human predators, feeding off one another and the people (*AR*, 64). The people floating on this raft are thus metaphoric representatives of a recognisable contemporary Nigeria in which the ropes of direction have been cut, the steering pole and paddles have been lost in a storm, a fog rises and they are lost, and no-one is taking responsibility for their direction or survival (*AR*, 10).

Having set the historic context, Osofisan frames this image of Nigeria's people and 'troubled times' within recognisable forms of contemporary traditional dramas. The conscious reference to Clark's play in the title and first act, in the programme notes which the audience are invited to read, is important as the play 'came to symbolize the troubled situation of our newly-independent country' (*AR*, 4). This frame shifts the focus of the play from the basic plot outline, the narrative trajectory, to a more critical engagement with how and why the events take place, and with the issues and alternatives offered the characters.

However, this focus shift does not suggest foregoing the performative aspects of the theatre. Osofisan overtly signals his use of both traditional and fantastic performance forms in the Masque and folk tale in the opening act with the Yemosa who each introduce their roles in the play and signal the constructed nature of the event. They are the pilot of the evening's show, the narrator, and the writer and singer of the songs. They insist: 'Nothing you see will be real, or pretend to be. Nothing you hear will be true. All is fiction, the story is false, the characters do not exist. We are in a theatre, as you well know, and we see no need to hide it.' (*AR*, 3) This is important as again it points to the constructed nature of the narrative and issues.

Osofisan punctuates naturalistic interaction and the unfolding of events with the overtly fantastic forms. Act One overtly references the construction of the fictive in the explanation that the stage is the sea, the mats are the raft and the actors 'are not the people they are pretending to be.' (*AR*, 3) As does the invitation toward the end of this first act for the audience to ask about anything they may not understand. This signals Osofisan's interest in his audience's conscious and critical engagement with the action, and the importance of this beyond entertainment. The act ends with the statement: 'For, remember, it is the fate of our nation that is at stake' (*AR*, 4).

This same juxtaposition of the overtly fictive and critical is again evident in Act Four, the middle of the play, which takes the form of a traditional masque. Sea-sprites who are obviously black men dressed as white females appear, 'but conspicuously and grotesquely, as in agbegijo masque.' (*AR*, 34). In Yoruba and English they sing of rowing the story like a boat, 'words are paddles on the tongue... Boat of fable, raft of song'. The three Yemosa emerge from among the sprites and introduce themselves as creatures of fantasy that do not exist. They insist that:

Yemosa Two: We're merely the figures of fantasy.

Yemosa Three: Actors made up. Dream images.

Yemosa One: Made real only in the minds of

These men on the raft.

Yemosa two: And in all the minds.

Where such things as goddesses still exist.

Yemosa Three: Minds such as yours – perhaps?

Yemosa One: In fact, when the Director

First called us this morning, to play the role,

We didn't know how to proceed. (*AR*, 35)

They go on to explore the implications of each man having a different Goddess in their mind, and thus the Costume Designer having had to create a compromise. The implications of this are that the religious or spiritual beliefs of the audience are likewise constructions and projections of personal need. This is a preparatory step towards the play's final ideological trajectory.

The masque then shifts to the first of two fables that move the play towards its resolution where the audience is invited to make an active choice for a resolution at the end of the play. This first fable is the story told by a skull of how it came to be there to a Hunter who then recounts the tale without pausing to consider the meaning of the answer to his initial question. He thus repeats the skull's mistake and ends in the same dire situation, as a Skull. A song both opens and closes the Act. Again Osofisan uses a very simple traditional oral storytelling mode to covertly demand active engagement with a clearly didactic message that is nonetheless entertaining.

The second fable comes in Act 6, again in a Masque that parallels Act Four, where by moonlight water-sprites dance and sing around the raft, and tell the story of a king and his three sons. He is unsure to whom to leave his kingdom, so he asks them each to go, and return after three months: 'And the one that brings back a proof / Of his love and devotion, which surpasses that / Of the others, shall inherit [the] throne' (*AR*, 73). The first son brought 'See-far' with which he 'could see to the very ends of the earth'. The second brought Fly-fast, with which the farthest distance vanishes in a mere second of thought; and the third son brought 'Heal-at-once', with the power to cure death itself. Together, with these three gifts they prevent their father's death. However, he is unable to choose between them, and the act ends with by inquiring of the audience: which of the three sons deserves the crown? Which is the most loving, the truest friend? The best answer shall receive a 'handsome prize' at the end of the play (*AR*, 74). This story again demands active engagement from the audience who must evaluate the criteria for good governance, and compare values about what constitutes a worthy contribution to a society.

This signals the final Act, with the remaining characters on the shredded remains of the raft, heading for a whirlpool. They see flying fish and hear voices from a town. Oge suggests that if they row together with the paddles he made in the night, they have a chance of survival. He teaches them to row. (*AR*, 80) Slowly the raft turns, then stops. Orousi then encourages Oge and says that the goddess will help (*AR*, 81), and Oge agrees that they must fight the sea and win (*AR*, 82). At this point the Yemosa return, and the real and the fantastic aspects of the play intersect as the Yemosa reintroduce the question of the story and which of the three sons is most suited to rule. Reore shouts that he knows the answer: 'We're saved!' and Orousi agrees: none or 'rather, all of them together!' Reore: 'All of us! That's the answer to the riddle!' (*AR*, 82)

This then raises the question of the status of these fantastic creatures. When the men ask whether they were sent by the goddess to help, the Hyacinths reply that they 'Breed in the minds of men' who 'invest us / with all kinds of extraordinary powers / But all such powers as we have / are made only by your will/ our force is your fear…' The warning here is that, like Hyacinths, if left to the caprice of man, the embodiments of men's beliefs can drift with the currents and 'choke up the fresh springs and waterways of man's lives' (*AR*, 83). Yemosa two suggests that they harness their hyacinths of belief 'with science, which is / the supreme will of man', and to 'command the winds / and the currents / by the force of their own insights / and the music of their muscles… Not wasting energy on 'conflicts and recriminations / fighting their own brothers / and sisters'(*AR*, 84). With this they 'recover their will' and Reore says: Yes! We make and unmake our destiny, we're human beings! This then raises the issue of mankind's voluntary enslavement to religious and political ideologies that create conflict, highlight difference and disempower the people themselves. The answer is not to deny the supernatural, but to look to themselves first to define their course and destiny, rather than being passive victims of others' decisions.

> The Yemosa then strip their costumes and as men begin to row, and the raft turns around. They then combine forces and take turns to call 'I am Fly-fast... Heal-at-once... See-Far... Heal-at-Once...' and the play ends on their rowing and singing.

The Masque and fable forms traditionally offer no resolution. In these forms, to which Richards adds the dilemma tale, moral definitions are seen to be contextual, rather than absolute, and the audience is offered a choice of alternatives designed to elicit spirited debate among those assembled (Richards 1996:82). One can see why Osofisan favours these forms as they develop reasoning skills and offer various viewpoints. He intensifies this aspect of the play by often insisting on the active interplay between audience and narrator. This not only includes the audience in the action of the play, but demonstrates their ability to think and act and thus builds their confidence and potential advocacy.

This empowerment of his audience directly relates to how Osofisan constructs and deconstructs himself as *auteur*. Hew does this primarily by exposing the constructed nature of presented realities and narratives of his play, and by implication the world itself. Osofisan's primary means for accomplishing this in this play is through his use of the Yemosa, and by the overt deconstruction of the metaphysical, which is depicted as being driven by material concerns, rather than fatalistic or supernatural forces. Although the frame is fantastic, as we have said, he is careful to set the play within recognisable and specific socio-political realities of contemporary Nigeria. He also carefully situates the debates among a group of people likely to differ in their responses to himself. Through the Brechtian-like commentary of the Yemosa Osofisan constantly thwarts any tendency towards emotional involvement with the characters' crises by means of shifting roles, songs that evaluate the events, and direct reference to the mechanisms whereby the actors create illusion, with points of rupture and movements between realism and the fantastic. All of this serves to highlight the dramatic, fictive nature of the work, simultaneously engaging the audience in exploring how stories, symbolic and social systems, indeed, all hegemonic realities are constructed and presented as essential, natural. Such understanding may point to processes by which such oppressive realities may be overturned and replaced by other, similarly constructed fictions.

For example he looks at how religious pronouncements and rituals are not without their pragmatic, material determinants.[4] He thus highlights the

---

[4] This is comparable to the Most Handsome Stranger parable in *Farewell to a Cannibal Rage*.

extension of colonialism by religious figures, civil servants and village elders. Economic gain is revealed as the motive driving symbolic systems and figures set up in the post-colonial context, often in the name of tradition, but in reality revealed as functioning in the service of material gain. At the end of *Another Raft* the characters realise that the Goddesses or Yemosa upon whom they have depended throughout are simple manifestations of their own minds, and Reore concludes: 'There's no goddess but our muscles! The strength of our forces combined! Rowing together, working together!' (1988: 85)

What is of note here is the repetition of the importance of self-determination. Osofisan develops this idea, and its relation to history explicitly in *Another Raft* where 'the sea is history' (*AR*, 69) upon which all are rowing, and trying to navigate a path. His final position is that the characters' only hope of survival is rowing together against the current (*AR*, 85). This emphasises the individual's free will, and the need to take responsibility for one's own self and destiny and not rely on others or the gods, who Osofisan chooses to represent ambivalently as metaphoric, more than real. In challenging the relationship between power and being determined externally for those on the raft to defining and relying on themselves, he suggests that the position of the individual in society can also shift from helpless, potentially tragic victim to that of an empowered individual who has choice and is capable of action.

Other issues raised in the play include loyalty to kinsmen and the sanctity of life and blood, which suggest the importance of a sense of a common humanity over a specifically ideological cause. These are important issues in an African history torn by ethnic and other genocide. For example, in *Another Raft*, Gbebe compares Africa to 'the black man's graveyard', in which 'each of you is the black race, each is a son of a shark, to be eaten by other sharks. Our future is – death' (*AR*, 69). This is an interesting echo of the Warrior in *A Dance of the Forests* who sees the future in terms of cannibalism. Although the leaders are exposed for greed, the workers do not stand together either.

Richards argues that: 'In contrast to his contemporaries, Osofisan critically dramatizes processes whereby history and art function hegemonically to reinforce the power of the ruling elite.' (1996: 93) Osofisan achieves this by overtly signalling the fictional frame and aesthetic forms in which the arguments are being made. Using the various forms of contemporary and traditional Nigerian performance forms, including of elements of story-telling, masquerade, the folk-tale, Yoruba song and popular rhythms and proverbs, and the repetition of scenes other stories, and even plays within his play; and then disrupting them allows him to expose the way they are formed and suggest how they work for his audience. However, finally in the way he constructs and deconstructs his own position in the text Osofisan challenges the way narratives are constructed and thereby encourages his audience to engage with how they receive ideological narratives and in turn respond to these when making decisions. In this way he uses history to suggest how Nigerians can realise their own power and agency, and thereby negotiate their own active future.

Bibliography

Awodiya, M. P. 1992. 'Oral Literature & Modern Nigerian Drama: The example of Femi Osofisan'. *African Literature Today*, No. 18, 105-114.

Cesaire. A. 1969. *Return to my Native Land*. J. Berger & A. Bostock (trans.) (Harmondsworth: Penguin Books).

Clark-Bekederemo, J.P. 1964. *The Raft* in *Three Plays* (Oxford: Oxford University Press).

Dunton, C. 1992. *Make Man Talk True: Nigerian drama in English since 1970* (London / Melbourne / Munich / New York: Hans Zell Publishers).

Enekwe, O. 1980. 'Interview with Femi Osofisan'. *The Greenfield Review*, 8, 1/2, 76-80.

Enekwe, O. 1981. 'Myth, ritual and drama in Igboland', in Y. Ogunbiyi (ed.). *Drama and Theatre in Nigeria: A Critical Source Book* (Lagos: Nigeria Magazine).

Hutchison, Y. 2000. 'The seductive dance between history and literature: The Moremi legend by the historian Samuel Johnson and playwrights Duro Ladipo and Femi Osofisan', in *History and Theatre in Africa*. Y. Hutchison & E. Breitinger (eds.) (Bayreuth: Bayreuth African Studies 50/ SATJ 13, pp. 31-47).

Jeyifo, B. 1985. 'Tragedy, History and Ideology: Soyinka's *Death and the King's Horseman* and Ebrahim Hussein's *Kinjeketile*', in *Marxism and African Literature*. G.M. Gugelberger (ed.), (London: James Currey Ltd, pp. 94-109).

Johnson, S. 1973. *The History of the Yorubas* (Lagos: C. S. S. Bookshops (first published in 1921)).

Kapteijns, L. 1977. *African Historiography Written by Africans 1955-1973: the Nigerian case* (Leiden: Afrika-Studiencentrum).

Obafemi, O. 1982. 'Revolutionary Aesthetics in Recent Nigerian Theatre'. *African Literature Today*, No. 12, pp. 118-125.

Obafemi, O. 1996. *Contemporary Nigerian Theatre* (Bayreuth: Bayreuth African Studies 40).

Ogunbiyi, Y., ed. 1981. *Drama and Theatre in Nigeria: A Critical Source Book* (Lagos: Nigeria Magazine).

Olaniyan, T. 1995. *Scars of Conquest/ Masks of Resistance: The Invention of Cultural Identities in African, African-American, and Caribbean Drama* (New York/ Oxford: OUP).

Olaniyan, T. 1999. 'Femi Osofisan: The Form of Uncommon Sense'. *Research in African Literatures*, 30:4, 74-91.

Osofisan, F. 1982. *Morountodun*, in *Morountodun and other plays* (Ibadan: Longman Nigeria Ltd.).

Osofisan, F. 1983. 'Drama and the new exotic – The paradox of form in modern African Theatre'. *African Theatre Review*, 1:1, April, 76-85.

Osofisan, F. 1988. *Another Raft* (Lagos: Malthouse Press Ltd).

Osofisan, F. 1999. 'Theater and the Rites of "Post-Negritude" Remembering'. *Research in African Literatures*, 30:1, Spring, 1-11.

Oyewese, S. 1988. 'The value and limitations of Early Arabic Acconts in the Reconstruction of Nigerian History'. *Islamic Culture*, 62:1, 12-23.

Richards, S. 1996. *Ancient Songs set Ablaze: The Theatre of Femi Osofisan* (Washington D.C.: Howard University Press).

Tamano, T.N. 1973. *History and History-Makers in Modern Nigeria.* Inaugural lecture delivered at University of Ibadan, 25 October 1973 (Ibadan: Ibadan University Press).

Temu, A. & Swai, B. 1981. *Historians and Africanist History: A Critique - Post-Colonial Historiography Examined* (London: Zed Publishers)

THE POETICS OF POSSIBILITY: A STUDY OF FEMI OSOFISAN'S *THE CHATTERING AND THE SONG* AND *MOROUNTODUN**

HARRY GARUBA

I

Criticism and by extension critical theory defines our mode of access to artistic experience. It should be obvious to everyone that the kinds of questions that we ask of a text or of any work of art relate profoundly to particular kinds of cultural-ideological formations operating upon our consciousness thereby controlling the directions of our perceptions and analysis.

There has, however, developed a peculiar dependency syndrome in the criticism of African literature that has led to a situation whereby critical theories and precepts are not historically related to or developed from the native soil, so to speak, but are 'inherited' from other societies. Among the many problems of the dependency syndrome is that critical issues and debates often relate more to a cultural tradition outside the continent than within it. The issue of commitment, for instance, has been one such problem examined against the backdrop of European intellectual history and the art for art's sake movement rather than within the context of a different cultural history.

An epistemological urge has always been part of that primal aesthetics desire which is the basis of art, and that urge may have created the necessity for criticism itself. This makes the question of commitment a pertinent one in any circumstance. But in approaching this issue, it seems to me important that we begin historically and theoretically from Africa, using its cultural tradition as a 'base' and also deriving our models of analysis from it. Femi Osofisan's plays provide an avenue where these perspectives can be profitably applied.

---

* This paper was first presented at the University of Ibadan English Department Seminar Series of the 1984/85 academic year. Accepted for publication in two Nigerian journals that died premature deaths before print, the paper has thus circulated – in true oral fashion – by word-of-mouth information and from hand to hand. Apart from a few minor corrections here and there, I have not attempted to update or revise it, first, because it has been so extensively quoted in essays and dissertations on Femi Osofisan. But beyond this, I believe that on an occasion such as this – that pays tribute to Femi Osofisan – presenting the essay in its original form gives a more appropriate record of the intellectual climate of those days and the major debates that animated the space of literary and cultural production.

A casual reading of Osofisan's criticism reveals a curious vulgarity; obtuse theoretical formulations are smuggled into a decadent, empiricist sociology of literature which equates content with message and vice versa. The problem, one finds, is pervasive in African criticism – due to the dependency syndrome, the critic often unaware of the historical subtext of his critical method ends up in a series of theoretical confusions. One of the enduring confusions of 'committed' sociological readings of African literature is this equation of content and message. This is not only a problem of superficiality but the more serious one of the dependency syndrome which makes the critic completely ignore the cultural context that informs the history of artistic/meaning production in particular communities within the African context.

There are certain cultural modes of expression to which not only the artist but also the community as a whole share collective inheritance and it is the artist's relationship to this which often determines his vision and therefore relevance. The critic who ignores this and gives the artist a convenient label before attempting to define this relationship is guilty of condescension and arrogance and may, at the worst, be involved in an act of undiluted fraud. Enticing phrases such as 'radical and prescriptive'[1] and even sometimes more puzzling theoretical words such as 'Marxist' have been attributed to Femi Osofisan's plays. This paper intends to look into two of his plays, *The Chattering and the Song* and *Morountodun*, and by examining their pattern of dramatic organisation elicit from them, perhaps, a certain vision of man, society and the world.

II

In a paper presented at the Conference of the Association of African Literary Critics at the then University of Ife in December 1975, titled 'Criticism and the Sixteen Palm Nuts: The Role of the Critic in an Age of Illiteracy'[2], Femi Osofisan made a passionate almost hysterical appeal to the assembled critics to come to a proper realisation of their function. In it, he defines the role of the critic, using a ritual metaphor, in this manner:

> The true critic is the channel between, the gateman who knows the right doors leading to full communion with the ritual. He knows the magic

---

[1] See Chris Dunton's review of *Morountodun and Other Plays* in *West Africa* 28 May, 1984, p. 1122.

[2] Now published in Femi Osofisan, *The Nostalgic Drum: Essays on Literature, Drama and Culture*, Trenton, N.J. and Asmara, Eritrea: Africa World Press, 2001, pp. 121 – 134 – Ed.

formula, the *sesame*: he can unlock the cryptic passages of the event, teach the hard steps of the dance... To function totally, one of his amulets is called humility. Perhaps that is what the critic needs most, that amulet, before he loses himself wandering in the infinite maze of the arts technology (Osofisan 2001: 127).

This amulet, I must add, will lead the critic first to an understanding of the cultural tradition within which the writer places himself, and then, ultimately, to which specific paradigm or metaphor of expression he relates most to within that tradition.

Femi Osofisan gives away this 'magic formula' in another paper 'Ritual and the Revolutionary Ethos'. This little known paper as brilliant and tendentious as others of its kind, can, unreservedly, be called his artistic manifesto. This paper presented at the First Ibadan Annual Literature Conference in 1976 was for so long almost inaccessibly tucked away in the unpublished files of the Conference proceedings until it was finally published in a collection of Femi Osofisan's essays in 2001. I shall take the liberty of summarising and quoting extensively from it.

Osofisan begins with a very unambiguous statement of his social concerns: 'Chaos and incoherence define the modern State' (Osofisan, 2001: 91). How then does the dramatist concerned with this state of anomy evolve the artistic tools for exploring and dealing with this phenomenon without compromising his vision through the medium of his art?

> The dramatic heritage available to us has simply proved to be inadequate. And it is not only that the machinery provided by the old society for dealing with chaos has lost its capacity for total effect, it is also that the very metaphysical *raison d'etre* of that machinery has been eroded with the advent of a new sociopolitical philosophy (Osofisan, 2001: 92)

The question now is, does the artist therefore abandon his heritage or can he develop it? 'Nevertheless', Osofisan continues, 'to claim that ritual dilutes the revolutionary ethos is to oversimplify, to engage in a narrow definition of ritual experience or to identify the dramatic apparatus with its thematic content' (Osofisan, 2001: 94). The possibility exists then, it is implied, of appropriating the apparatus and by an act of *mediation* and *re-interpretation* adjusting it to his own requirements. 'As long as the Archetype remains on the objective level of historical symbol rather than eternal paradigm, the wedding of ritual form and the revolutionary ethos should be possible' (Osofisan, 2001: 98). What Archetype then does he choose within his historical circumstance to deify (?) his revolutionary vision?

I believe that the mythic personage who incarnates this tension between the existing and the visionary, between the past, the present and the future, not as deity but metaphor, is the god Orunmila. *For it is obvious that we shall never have the truth completely within our grasp, but only as an aspiration.* Art after all is a wager, "a wager on the capacity of human beings to invent new relationships and to experience hitherto unknown emotions. For we are as much what we have been and what we are able to imagine."[3] It is why *Orunmila continuously enters my work, why he is the presiding spirit of my play, The Chattering and the Song* (Osofisan, 2001: 99, emphasis mine).

Just as it is impossible to fully understand James Joyce's *Ulysses* without a little knowledge of the original, it is inconceivable that one can arrive at a complete understanding of Femi Osofisan's *The Chattering and the Song* and *Morountodun* without an understanding of the full import of this statement.

III

After the works of William Bascom, Wande Abimbola and other scholars on the Ifa divination system, this paper cannot even pretend to be an exegesis of the Ifa Oracular system, and that endeavour is indeed outside its scope. As Femi Osofisan himself has pointed out, it is not the thematic content that interests him but the dramatic apparatus. However, a word or two before going into the plays will not be completely unnecessary. Orunmila or Ifa (the names are used here synonymously) is believed in Yoruba mythology to be one of the deities who descended from heaven to earth (at this point, Ile-Ife). He later settled at Ado where he raised eight children who went on to become important Kings in other parts of Yorubaland. Much later, on an insult from his last son who refused to pay him traditional homage, he returned to heaven. Since he had been the embodiment of wisdom and order on earth, his departure occasioned chaos.[4] His children on realising what the loss of his guiding wisdom meant went to appeal to him to return, but he refused and instead gave them the sixteen sacred palm nuts which became the embodiment of Orunmila on earth and the core of the divination system.

---

[3] Osofisan quotes here Jean Duvignaud, *The Sociology of Art*, London: Paladin, 1972, pp. 134, 145.

[4] Remember 'Chaos and Incoherence define the modern State.'

The interest of Ifa, for Femi Osofisan, goes beyond the mathematical computations of the divination process into its very essence as a mode of conflict resolution. The aim within the traditional system was to restore order and continuity by an elaborate system of sacrifice and appeasement but Femi Osofisan goes beyond that to impose upon it a historical dialectic that focuses on possibility and change. Since its structural pattern symbolises for him 'the tension between the existing and the visionary', it becomes the nodal point within the historical process which points in the direction of protean possibilities and alternatives, not continuity as this will be negation, in terms of our own society and historical circumstance, of the revolutionary ethos and endorse a continuation of chaos. Truth, he has already told us, is, and remains, for him, only an aspiration.

IV

To anyone completely unfamiliar with the Ifa Oracle, its system of divination must look like an elaborate game designed perhaps for entertainment or to serve the whims of a community made up of greedy shamans and a pretentious public. Femi Osofisan's *The Chattering and the Song*, at a first glance, appears like a series of unending humorous games lacking in focus but merely designed to elicit laughter from the audience and swell the pockets of a few performers. Further inquiry however reveals that the *game* is used in this play not only as dramatic metaphor but as the very *medium* of exploration. The entire play is built around a series of games and through the games the past is re-enacted and re-created, the tensions of the present are explored and the future is hinted at. The jokes and games are the means through which in one day in lives of the characters a whole historical canvas is created with antennae that stretch into the future. The games seem to lead to the original conception of the play as *play*, and as the *play* progresses it begins to take on oracular resonances that indicate the seriousness of the events dramatised.

At the beginning Sontri, Yajin and Mokan re-enact, through a game built around the *Iwori Otura* motif (a compounding of two *Odu* which is meant to wish the lovers good luck),[5] a serious event in their past. This prologue occurs in memory, and its enactment becomes a formalised dance of betrayal and courtship. The prologue outlines the origins of the real event of the play, namely

---

5 See Olu Obafemi, 'Revolutionary Aesthetics in Recent Nigerian Theatre.' ALT 12, p. 128, and Jide Ogungbade, 'Vision and the Artist: The Dramaturgy of Femi Osofisan', Unpublished MA Thesis, English Department, University of Ibadan, 1982, p. 24.

the preparations for the wedding ceremony between Sontri and Yajin. It is the advent of what Sontri calls the bigger riddle which is the play. We come to realise that the riddling contest is larger than just a game. Sontri says:

> We buy our life with a riddle, and then afterwards... we have to live it...[and] A bigger riddle begins. (Osofisan, *Chattering,* p.3)

Their lives are conceived of, within the play, in terms of riddles. The bigger riddle, which always begins after the priest has chanted the relevant Odu to you, is what this play is about. Put simply, in this case, it is the possibility of sustaining love (not just romantic love) in an environment of hate. This first game conceived and choreographed as a predator-prey dance therefore assumes more significance with the context of the play.

This dance which is formulaic re-enactment of the past was actually meant for Funlola, to dramatically narrate to her the incidents leading to her friend Yajin's engagement to Sontri. The dance sets the background of the play both for Funlola, a character in it, and the audience. Funlola then begins to ask more questions about Sontri and through Yajin's answers we are given character portraits of Mokan and Sontri, the two friends who have been involved in her life. Mokan comes across as an all-forgiving, cool-headed, intelligent man while Sontri, described in elemental terms, seems to be a life force simultaneously capable of genuine love and vulcanic fits of temper. The description goes on and Mokan and Sontri are physically introduced on stage. Mokan comes in playing the clown and Sontri almost literally erupts onto the stage in a fit of temper over the escape of his weaverbirds. In this humorous first act is incorporated a whole package of satirical swipes which serve to provide the social context of the play.

A lot of dramatic symbols are employed in this act. Sontri's weaverbirds, the symbol of the captive country and his caged anger are released by Funlola. Their chattering which Sontri calls a song, she sees as just noise. For Sontri the chatter of the weaverbirds represents the nation in restive captivity and Funlola's ignorance of this shows her innocence. Innocence is equated with virginity and virginity, in this situation, is a crime, a refusal to acknowledge the state of affairs, a romantic retreat into illusion and make-believe. In the mock trial for virginity she is sentenced to rape by a squad of lechers. (It is interesting to note that this use of the image of virginity can also be seen in John Osborne's *Look Back in Anger* with which this play shares several affinities).

Leje and Mokan play a game replete with symbols and omens. Their card game is the repository of much of the latent symbolism in the play.

LEJE: (*whistling*): Phew! Then I declare the gamble worth it. (*To Mokan*) Your card, sir.

MOKAN: (*reluctantly*): Well, circles? (*Runs round Leje*) Play.

LEJE: Circles? There must be an end to running. How about...? (*Builds a cross with his arms*)

MOKAN: A cross? Good for crucifixion. (*"Cruficies"* (sic) *himself of Leje's extended arms*). Last card.

YAJIN: Good for me too, Mokan?

MOKAN: I said, last card. Play, sir.

FUNLOLA: Pay no attention to their babbling, Yajin. You see they've had too much already.

YAJIN (*insistent, to Mokan*): What if I held the master card? The power to bang the game down (*hits their arms*) crying: Check!

LEJE: Check!

MOKAN: (*falling, with his neck out like a sacrificial offering*): Eloi... eloi...

LEJE: ...lama sabaktani (*Cuts the offered neck*)

MOKAN: (*Screaming*) Yeaah...!

LEJE: (*blessing the sacrifice*): A-a-amen!

MOKAN: (*looking up at last*): But do you have the master card? (Osofisan, *Chattering*, p.23)

The very dramatic irony of this situation is that the underlying symbolism of this game is completely lost on Yajin who interprets it her own way. Leje however begins to smell something in the air and knows that the stake in this seemingly innocuous game is really high. But Yajin, unaware of the consequences plays into Mokan's hands by inviting them to a game. This time the game takes the form of a historical play that centres around the conflict between Latoye and Alafin Abiodun.

In the second act, Mokan and Leje keep at their games while the preparations for their wedding continue. The crucifixion imagery introduced during the game in the first act is again extended. When Leje wins by dropping a master-card and asking for crosses Mokan simply says, 'Someone's definitely going to be crucified tonight' (Osofisan, *Chattering*, p. 31). There will no longer be any running around in circles. While still at their games Yajin interrupts and reminds them of the play. Preparations for the play begin and when the costumes and props are ready the play-within-the-play begins. Here again the cards are used as the device of transition. In this more ancient form of the card game which the Alafin plays with his wife he always wins. Victory has, for him, become routine. The game-symbolism runs deep in the play. The games which are supposed to be for amusement become rituals and their symbolism have a direct bearing on the fate of the characters. The cards, in this sense are as ominous as Madame Sosotris' cards in T. S. Eliot's *The Wasteland*, and their significance in the play being both thematic and structural can also be compared with the same poem or Elder's *Ceremonies in Dark Old Men*.

The play-within-the-play which is Femi Osofisan's re-interpretation of Yorùbá history is important not only within the context of the message of this play – a point much harped upon by critics – but also, and more importantly, because it signals the use of a dramatic technique which reverses the wisdom (thematic context) of the traditional system while retaining its form. Yajin's scenario, metaphorically speaking, is an Ifa Odu the meaning of which the playwright subverts by a subtle process of re-interpretation. The good luck love chant of the beginning does not integrate the lovers into the social system nor does it solve their problems, rather another Odu, a historical not mythic one, becomes more operative in their lives and the bigger riddle begins. The riddle extends beyond their personal lives to encompass that of the community as a whole. Mokan and his secret police succeed, but only temporarily. The lovers will be released and will learn some lessons in the process. Sontri may harness his ecstatic rage and his romantic carrier psychology into the channels of organisation and Yajin may grow in the spirit of commitment. Meanwhile, Leje and Funlola set off on their own hazardous dance at the close of the play (the playwright insists that the play does not end). The lovers' dance is not a predator-prey dance but a constructive one that looks into the future with hope.

V

The interaction between play and play, i.e. the *reality* of the play (*Chattering*) and the *act* of the play (the Abiodun/Latoye scenario) is one important element of the second act of *The Chattering and the Song*. The transition from reality to illusion and back again becomes the major dramatic technique of *Morountodun*. The very first scene of the play brings the director on the stage. He tells us the progress of his travelling troupe so far, the incidents that they have encountered, the disturbances and riots that have dogged their path. Tonight, however, he expects, despite the anxiety of the actors, will be different. As he goes ahead to provide the background of the play, a group of placard carrying demonstrators invade the stage and History or Chance or Fortune takes over. The *play* really begins.

Titubi, the spoilt daughter of Alhaja Kubirat, erstwhile leader of the demonstrators suddenly feels a heroic stir and decides to play Moremi, this time to save the rich from the fury of the revolting peasants. The contemporary and the historical are immediately linked and the shuttle from past to present which becomes a major element later in the re-enactment of the Moremi story is pre-indicated.

Determined to save her clan from the farmers, she first leads a protest march to stop a play about the farmers' uprising, but realising that the play is not really the problem, volunteers to infiltrate the enemy camp, find out their strategies and help bring their leader to justice. In this bid she willingly allows herself to be locked up in prison so that when the peasants invade the prison she will also be taken along with the freed prisoners. The Police Superintendent gives her a story of woe to tell to the peasants to win their sympathy.

Alhaja Kubirat, Titubi's influential mother hears that her daughter has been locked up. She bribes her way into the maximum security prison and wants to physically carry her daughter away. Titubi reveals the plans to her and after some initial objections she finally agrees to go along with it. At this point, Titubi begins to doubt her ability to carry out this mission but she manages to draw strength from the Moremi myth. Looking at the Moremi necklace she wears, she goes into a reverie and during this the Moremi story is dramatically re-enacted on stage. The temptations and doubts she had had to go through are presented. This re-enactment serves as a humanising factor; it places the myth within a human context with all the vanity and ulterior motives which had propelled Moremi towards her heroic act. Her intentions appear to have been not much nobler than Titubi's, who is also moved by a combination of vanity, caprice and her exposition to theatre and folklore. Titubi's mythic compulsion and Moremi's heroic endeavour are thus theatrically related through the flashback technique or what may be called the montage.

The cinematic montage technique as used by Femi Osofisan in this play is really an extension of the traditional tabloid form of theatrical representation where action is presented as dramatic sketches almost in the form of *tableau vivants* symbolically (not causally) linked. The fade and dissolve of the film is done here by way of a physical symbol becoming the transitional link between the present and the past. The movement from Titubi to Moremi is done, so to speak, by necklace just as the movement from the drunken pair to Alafin Abiodun in

The Chattering and the Song had been through the cards. The symbolic rather than causal link is an important element of the form of the play.

Everything goes according to schedule. The farmers strike and free Titubi. She goes with them, lives among them, finds out who their leader is, and brings him to the Police Superintendent but this time not as Moremi. Having lived among the forest folk and seen their pain and anguish, she realises that they are in the right and fighting a just war against the brutality of the state. Moremi had been on the side of the state and so she has to kill the Moremi ghost in her to truly be on the side of the poor and oppressed. Through flashbacks she tells her mother and the Superintendent the story of her life among the farmers and how she arrived at her decision. Her decision is a kind of class suicide. So instead of handing Marshal over to the state she falls in love with him. Marshal barely finds the time to get married to her and name her Morountodun before he goes off to die in another battle. What had started out for Titubi as a vain romantic longing for glory turns out to be a quest for self, a soul journey of self-discovery that begins from the mythic and moves through the historical to the personal and social.

Morountodun is therefore not only an epic struggle in the historic sense of the farmers' collective confrontation with the state but also on the personal level in Titubi's battle with the mythical and socio-historical forces that have fashioned her. This battle, some might argue, has not been given its proper place in the play because Titubi's decisions seem to be capriciously arrived at and often seem not properly thought out, but this, we must insist, has to do with the form of the play. Having been weaned on the Western theatrical tradition where causality and the process of motivation and action are meticulously documented we often ignore the fact that the traditional theatrical practice did not lay too much of an emphasis on motivation since the representational mode was much closer to the *symbolic* than the *mimetic*. *Morountodun* relies much on this tradition and what looks like an omission in this play is really a carry over from the traditional technique of dramatic elision.

Morountodun is divided into sixteen parts and these episodes, need one say, represent the sixteen palm nuts which are Orunmila's repository of wisdom. What meaning does one then extract from Femi Osofisan's arrangement of these nuts of knowledge? It is obvious from the betrayal that it is the Esu element that is given dominance in this play. Esu, the capricious trickster god, is in reality a central figure in the Ifa divination system. Titubi by subverting the intentions of the state and her mythic mission is also by metaphoric extension subverting the repetitive form of the traditional system by introducing change into it.

VI

A questioning spirit pervades all of Femi Osofisan's plays, the questioning is not just a thematic concern with inverting attitudes to myth as in *Morountodun* or history as in *The Chattering and the Song* or even stereotypes as in *Once Upon Four Robbers* but it is also a structural or formal concern having to do with dramatic conventions and modes of theatrical organisation. In the premiere of *The Chattering and the Song* for instance, actors were made to come on stage with boards announcing the scene and its setting in space and time before the action began. The role of the director in *Morountodun* is not much different from that. This perhaps is why Brecht is invoked in a lot of critical essays and reviews of Femi Osofisan's works, and the playwright himself has said that his kind of theatre is closer to Brecht's than Artaud's.[6] These attempts at making the audience continually aware of the fact that they are watching a play are, like Brecht's alienation effect, designed to reduce empathy and sharpen critical perception.

In these plays also there is a certain protean conception of character not so much as personality limited within an ambit of psychological drives and subconscious motivations but as a role within the nexus of socio-aesthetic relations which the play presents. Characterisation in this sense is largely a matter of possibility. This means that characters are not so much presented as *people* but as *actors*. This should not appear strange given the fact that Femi Osofisan's historical message has been emphasised by critic after critic, this is only an attempt to indicate the working of the historical imagination behind that message. Titubi thus carries within her the possibility of Moremi, Titubi the Alhaja's daughter, and Morountodun the peasants jewel of hope whose 'battlefield [is] among the wounded and the stricken' (Osofisan, *Morountodun*, p. 75) and Mokan can play Latoye and subvert his revolutionary role.

VII

What finally can one say is Femi Osofisan's vision as it comes through in these two plays? There is of course no doubt from the plays and our argument that he has been able to wed his revolutionary perspective with the ritual form, but what

---

6 Femi Osofisan, 'Radical Playwright in An Ancient Feudal Town', in *The Nostalgic Drum*, 2001, (207 – 217) p. 209.

exactly is this perspective, what *epistem*, in other words, can one arrive at by way of his theatrical practice rather than pronouncements?

Traditional wisdom emphasises the repetitive nature of the world and human experience and this, simply stated, is the very metaphysical *raison d'etre* or the epistemological logic which is the basis of the Ifa oracular system. For solution to crisis, the only way to go forward is to go back to those nuts of experience left by the ancestors, which when cracked and properly interpreted gives the clues to regeneration. The Ifa system is only a more formalised aspect of this logic which is contained in a lot of proverbs, idioms and traditional adages and sayings. This is in fact the core of the communal tragedy contained in the last part of Chinua Achebe's *Arrow of God*. When every yam harvested is now done in the name of the son, the reversal of an entire way of life is implied. One of the common denominators among African cultures is ancestor worship and for a society of this nature it is an unmitigated tragedy to find that the Christian doctrine of salvation through the son has invaded its fabric.

In Femi Osofisan's plays we discover that there is a concern with the corpus of traditional knowledge but it is a concern that seems to question the repetitive basis of its wisdom. He seems to insist, if we must use his own metaphoric machinery, that since Esu is always a central figure on the divination board, there is therefore a way in which we can look into the past with the eyes of the present and modify or change the meaning it held for our ancestors. Betrayal then becomes a central element in his re-interpretation of the past and its impact on the course of present events (cf. Mokan and Titubi) and one of the characteristics of Esu, our trickster god, is betrayal. So while it is true, as the playwright himself has said, that Orunmila is the presiding spirit of his play we must also emphasise Esu's dominance as the secret key to finally unlocking the vaults of knowledge, and Esu here functions most in his trickster aspect not as custodian of the traditional interpretation. As Henry Louis Gates tells us, 'Ifa is the god of determinate meanings, but his meaning must be rendered by analogy. Esu, god of indeterminacy, rules this interpretive process; he is the god of interpretation because he embodies the ambiguity of figurative language' (1988: 21).

At this point, I think, we can safely conclude that what we have tried to argue, in the main, is that Femi Osofisan in his plays strives at a subtle balance of traditional wisdom which stresses the repetitive nature of human experience and the historical dialectic of change, or put paradoxically, he emphasises change in recurrence. This is what is worked out in his plays and it is this emphasis on pattern and possibility that we refer to as the poetics of possibility. Perhaps because of his self proclaimed bias on the side of the oppressed and his infectious optimism in the future he had earned himself the appellation 'Marxist'. Though undoubtedly a playwright of the left, Femi Osofisan's 'Marxism', I believe, should be left for another day when theoretical arguments are properly conducted and raised beyond the level of sentiments and slogans.

Works Cited

Gates, H. L.. 1988. *The Signifying Monkey: A Theory of Afro-American Literary Criticism*, New York, Oxford: Oxford University Press.

Obafemi, O. 'Revolutionary Aesthetics in Recent Nigerian Theatre', in Eldred Jones & Eustace Palmer (eds.), African Literature Today 12 (1981), p. 128.

Ogungbade, J. 1982. 'Vision and the Artist: The Dramaturgy of Femi Osofisan'. Unpublished MA Thesis, English Department, University of Ibadan, p. 24

Osofisan, F. 1977. *The Chattering and the Song*, Ibadan: Ibadan University Press.

Osofisan, F. 1982 (1999 rpt). *Morountodun* in *Morountodun and other plays*, Lagos: Longman Nigeria

Osofisan, F. 2001. *The Nostalgic Drum: Essays on Literature, Drama and Culture*. Trenton, NJ and Asmara, Eritrea: African World Press

RHETORICAL STRATEGIES IN OKINBA LAUNKO'S *MINTED COINS*

AMEN UHUNMWANGBO

Introduction

There is undoubtedly the assumption that understanding discourse presupposes vast amounts of general knowledge of the world. In this dimension, 'theories and methods must be essentially communicable, learnable and applicable. If not, they have no critical, let alone, revolutionary potential' (Van Dijk 1987: 12). Because nothing escapes textuality, we shall propose in this study that in addition to its literary roles, rhetoric is an instrument in socio-political struggles, which is no less intense in the field of literary criticism. Grammar and rhetoric are two important tools of the literary artist beware both play complimentary roles in literary discourse. This paper examines the meaning and scope of rhetorical analysis and the strategies it adopts. It explicates the use of rhetoric in Okinba Launko's *Minted Coins*. As Paul de Man (1973: 28) points out, it is a peculiarly modern idea that one can 'pass from grammatical to rhetorical structures without difficulty or interruption'. The two disciplines, he notes, cover the linguistic field, but with different epistemologies behind them.

The origin of 'rhetoric' dates back to classical antiquity. An attempt to look at it will take us back to the period of the Greek City states and the Great Roman Empire-two primordial forerunners of modern civilization. The dictionary definition offers that 'rhetoric is the act of speaking or writing so as to persuade people effectively' (Procter 1978). This definition dovetails significantly into the definition of the ancients who saw rhetoric 'as primarily intellectual, a progress from idea to idea determined logically' (Baldwin 1959: 3). Naturally, people are pleased when a speaker / writer hits on a wide general statement of opinions that they hold in some partial or fragmentary form. Thus, the theory of rhetoric as the energizing of knowledge and the humanizing of truth is explicitly the philosophy of Aristotle and implicitly that of Cicero, Tacitus and Quintillian.

As a forerunner to applied linguistics, rhetoric is interesting because (a) it deals with language as real discourse, (b) it isolates categories and criteria for effective communication, and (c) it provides practical guideline for one group of language user, the public speaker. As observed by Christensen, 'grammar and rhetoric are complementary in that grammar maps out the possible; rhetoric narrows the possible down to the desirable' (1967: 39).

Rhetoric as Discourse

In any analysis like the one we have embarked on, meaning of representation takes two forms. First a semantic memory representation is established of text itself. At the same time, readers build a so-called 'model' of the situation (action, event, state of affairs) referred to by the text. This model is the ultimate goal of comprehension. Identifying rhetoric as discourse, Jonathan Culler is extensive in his description:

> Discourse has the power to produce events: events of persuasion, understanding, revelation, etc. If rhetoric is the art of producing events through discourse, then rhetorical analysis attempts to account for these events and it does so by identifying structures, patterns, figures, which then constitute rhetoric... The relationship between structure and event is incalculable, which is why rhetoric is fated, as the name of this incalculable textuality, to be simultaneously and alternatively a discourse of structure and event (1978: 608).

There is no gainsaying the fact that rhetoric in discourse is of high communicative value if patterned well. An absurdity may gain its point through ironic interpretation while parallelism may be for linguistic reinforcement. The constant theme in dramatic literature or literature with dramatic elements is motivation, the bringing out of character through the movement of plot, and the dramatic management of persons through interaction.

In our analysis, we shall rely on the general features of rhetorical structures in addition to what Mann and Thompson (1988) call Rhetorical Structure Theory (RST). According to them, RST is a descriptive theory of a major aspect of the organization of natural texts. It is a linguistically useful method for describing any natural text, characterizing their structure primarily in terms of relations that hold between parts of the text.

Analysis of Rhetorical Strategies

Narrative discourse often employs the first or third person form of expression. First person accounts tend to be more informal, third person accounts, on the other hand, tend to be more formal. Traditional African poetry (the progeny of modern African poetry) 'speaks a public language' (Chinweizu et al. 1980: 188). This is in consonance with Maduka that 'an ideal poem should use words in a simple, clear, precise way so that it can be made accessible to a majority of readers' (1988: 197). Okinba Launko is aware that political crisis is the most acute today and has, therefore, made it his canvass. The inescapable lesson from the status of politics, it seems, is that even if we ignore politics, politics will not ignore us. Narrative, dramatic and satiric poetry are generalized concepts which involve the substitution of verse for prose in the telling of a story, the presentation of dramatic dialogue, or the formation of moral commentary. Broadly, a pragmatic analysis of discourse is concerned primarily with dimension of action in which a discourse is taken as some conventional form of social action. In our analysis of the rhetorical strategies in Okinba Launko's *Minted Coins* (1987), we shall start with the strategy of figures of speech.

Figures of Speech

Language, literature and art, work by codes, that internally self-consistent systems of signs, from which meaning is created by the differences between the elements making up the code. These signs themselves are meaningful solely because they are familiar to us as part of a code which we already know, or are used in a context that makes them clear. The traditional figures of speech are often thought of as features of meaning and expression which are exceptional in ordinary language, but normal in literature, according to Leech et al, (1988: 160), 'for their special communicative power and values'. Davies and Abdelali (1989) have demonstrated that the interpretation of a metaphor should evoke such notions as similarity, silence and relevance in order to explain the relationship that holds in figurative interpretations. The metaphor of love duplicating as <u>life</u> and <u>death</u> runs through the seven movements of *Minted Coins*. In the prologue page, we have

(1)   Love's always the <u>starting point</u>

Till the season insists on <u>corpses</u>

What this dual nature of survival and death recreates is that our quest for love remains in vain because by and large,

'the stories we tell

of our meeting, and parting,

and returning

are minted coins...'

The poet also relies on the metaphor of 'dream – in essence, life, aspirations and all that are ancillary to them – to state the ideological path he would want sane humanity to take in times of tribulations like those described here. In 'Awakening' he states plainly but potently:

(2)   Take your <u>dream</u> to the end of the street.

Then stretch the street.

Take <u>it</u> to the end of your <u>dream</u>. (p. 2)

In 'So I went seeking,' there are series of metaphoric expressions of a dream conditioned by disappointment which does not provide anchorage to the quester. In painting this unfulfilled hope from a society made up of the greedy, the voracious, the cunning and the cannibal, the poet ruminates morally:

(3)   So I went seeking

in the forest of the world

> I went to the <u>lion</u> who roared and said
>
> Come closer now, I'm hungry
>
> I asked the <u>elephant</u>
>
> Who
>
> picked me with his
>
> trunk, and dropped me in a
>
> nowhere land...
>
> The <u>tortoise</u> kindly left word
>
> That he'd gone to a feast
>
> With his brother the politician out of jail (p. 11)

The imagery of the *lion, elephant* and *tortoise* is famous enough in our traditional fables and expressions that when the poet gives attributes to these animals, we recognize them as the 'cannibals', 'oppressors' and 'cheats' in our society.

Demonstrating the changes characterized by changelessness that have taken place in our landscape and life, he employs the powerful metaphor of a vicious circle that comes and goes endlessly. This is the pivot of 'When the Drums Beat'. He illustrates:

> (4) ...And the cycles
>
> they are ever returning...
>
> Cycles ago I met you: we danced
>
> the dance that will yet be starting
>
> tomorrow, if the weather holds (p. 16).

As sure as the next day would come, this dance will continue. The point about the above examples is that apart from intensifying meaning, metaphor is the most important element in expressive language which is the meat of creative writing.

Another level of figurative language replete in this text is linguistic irony which demonstrates human disposition to adopt a pose, or to put on a mask. What is concealed here is meant to be found out. This is because 'the structure of a piece of writing and whatever it communicates are under the direct control of the author's manipulation of language, and concomitantly, of the reader's recreative sympathy, his desire and ability to realize and release the technique from verbal clues deposited by the author' (Fowler, 1977: 3). In out text, it is possible to conceive the entire exposition as an expanded irony of life. This is because as love is what the world cannot live without, this same love is the bane of the world's progress. In lamenting the progress we have made so far, the poet stylishly welcomes two journalists[1] from jail painting our 'significant' march toward progress in striking irony.

'According to him:

(5)   You will find the streets

clean, but empty of hope and dance;

the beggars gone, replaced

by the well-dressed unemployed;

& where the old hawkers used to stand,

loud with their wares

shoving imported plastics in your face,

You will arrive to find

new hawkers – women with wailing infants

on their backs...(p. 40)

The irony inherent in the expression above is that people who go to jail not as criminals but as defenders of society's rights and advocates of such societies often hope on release from incarceration to meet exuberant crowd of well-wishers acknowledging their stand, a sign of preparedness to face the challenges ahead. But here, the expectation of the crusaders is assaulted by the unexpected turn of events. Herein lies the irony of our progress. In 'Animosity', we get the message of how the lust for power has ironically thrown spanners in the otherwise smooth friendship between three friends in our recent history.

(6)   Take the three generals

the rivals in our story:

One is President over a vast country

One is in detention

and the third has gone to the firing-squad (p. 60)

The three generals mentioned above are significant in our immediate past history. Generals Muhammad Buhari, Mamman Vatsa and Ibrahim Babangida are said to have joined the Nigerian Army the same day. They also rose through the ranks to become generals, and were notable friends who also toppled our second republic with Buhari assuming leadership of the 'vast country'. But because of love for earthly desires, animosity crept in and the three friends embraced separate destinies. While one had his enviable office taken from him through a coup d'etat (an act fuelled by 'love' for power), this same friend sent

---

[1] Nduka Irabor and Tunde Thompson were jailed by the military junta in 1986 for publishing reports that were not sanctioned by the government, as expected under the then Military Decree 4.

the third general to death because of the latter's love ironically for the same power the former general stole in the night. The irony here depicts a dog-eat-dog world, a world of deceit, betrayal and the consequences of such.

Hyperbole falls within figures of speech which Leech (1969) calls 'honest deception devise'. Traditionally known as an 'overstatement', its exaggeration is often incredible because what is assumed is at variance with a known fact. In rhetorical expressions or speech generally, it is not for deception but for emphasis. In *Minted Coins*, we have a lot of hyperbolic expressions starting with the one in 'Awakening' in which it is said graphically:

> Take your dream to the end of the street. (p. 2)

This is impossible, for *dreams* are intangible things that cannot select *'street'* which is concrete. A componential analysis of the two words will show the following features:

(8)   dream   street

   (+ Noun)   (+ Noun)

   (+ Abstract)   (+ Concrete)

   (- Concrete)   (- Abstract)

Though this breaks our selectional restriction rule of transformational generative grammar (Chomsky, 1965), we can find accommodation for its interpretation when we look at language in the sense of communicative competence. Quite ambitious in its construction, it sets off to explain our call to duty. Our call to declare for a mass-orientated movement that would make us realise our true humanity. In a world full of obstacles, the only way to vanquish these obstacles is to take up our destinies in our own hands. This is what the poet is emphasizing in a poem like 'love beginning' where we have:

(9)   Children's voices are sweet...

   A minstrel's voice is sweeter:...

   Sweetest

   (to those who can hear)

   Is the voice of a love beginning. (p. 12)

In the above, voice is described in graduated superlatives in terms of taste. It is humanly impossible to give tactile attributes to a sense we perceive only through our auditory organs. We easily know that it is the voice quality that is sweet, sweeter and sweetest in that order to give expression to the poet's quest for justice.

The use of litotes represents another 'honest deception' devise, which is the use of rhetorical 'understatement' that depends a great deal on what we know of the situation. This thrives on a negative expression where a positive would have been appropriate. In the moral lesson aptly delivered in 'Blessing', we have

(10)   Son, the best route

to anywhere

is not always the <u>shortest route</u> (p. 7)

which is an understatement. In geometry, we know that a straight line is the shortest distance between two points. But here, we are admonished to beware of the shortest route for it is not always the best route.

Pictorial Rhetoric

According to Stanley Meltzoff (1978: 577), 'language, semiotic codes, and the rhetorical inflection of each separately and in comparison with the others, lead us to our judgement of the speaker's meaning, his intended meaning, and his unintentional meaning'. When we are shown a picture, he continues, we use linguistics to analyze the words which come with the picture. In this dimension we shall be concerned only with 'iconicity' used loosely as what is conveyed by the image of a picture painted before us. In *Minted Coins*, we have five pictures with the first depicting prayers as performed by an African traditional priest giving more power to the words of the poem, 'blessing'. The second picture shows a bachelor in his sleep with his dream fully occupied by his loved lady. This natural love can only illustrate our collective love and dream which is the central theme in the collection. The love and dream for a better country.

The third picture is that of a water mermaid (Olokun) a strong belief system in Western and Southern Nigeria. Perhaps the graphic representation of Tunde Thompson and Nduka Irabor in chains epitomizes the state of journalism in Nigeria and most third world states under military or civilian dictatorship. The poem that this picture illustrates speaks volume of the travails of journalism in Africa. The pall hanging around the neck of the press is what is painted with pungent blows on page 39. The last picture is that of execution. Two lifeless bodies hang precariously from the stakes after another round of barbaric display of the bodies of military officers executed on 5th March 1986 for an alleged coup attempt. Among those silenced was General Mamman Vatsa, Minister of the Federal Capital Territory and former friend and colleague of General Ibrahim Babangida. These pictures are of effect since they combine in driving home the message of the poet. The pictures can be said to be performing the role of intensifiers. A poet's use of imagery from his environment is in the view of Tayo Olafioye (1984), an attempt to gain vitality, freshness, and excitement and also to suit his indigenous sensibility. The use of local imagery is also to 'meet the emotional response of the people/audience' and to inspire the readers for better understanding and thus to make African realities more concrete and factual. This is a claim reading this text would clearly validate because 'in standard reference works in literature, it is assumed that one important response to text is the construction of images of the information described by the text' (Brewer, 1988).

Sound and Sense: Phonological Features Analysis

Human beings respond to sound favourably or otherwise depending on the nature of the sound. On the status of sound in poetry, we want to assume that it is a well-known fact that unlike other genres of literature, poetry is the one most closely related to sound. Originally meant to be sung, poetry in modern times has not lost its appeal to sound. On this claim, Anthony Easthope (1983) says:

> Most poetry in most epochs has been linked intimately with music and dancing…There seem good grounds to suppose that poetic discourse will live on, especially if it is reunited with music and even with dancing as well (160-162).

This pleasure probably informed the great psychoanalyst, Sigmund Freud (1976: 170) to assert that 'it is generally acknowledge that rhymes, alliterations, refrains and other forms of repeating similar sound which occur in verse, make use of the same source of pleasure-the rediscovery of something familiar'.

Alliteration

One prominent feature of sound is alliteration. This is the repetition of the same consonant sound through the lines of a poem. It can be within a line or horizontal alliteration and alliteration from one line to another better known as vertical alliteration. A few examples of the former are:

(11)   Take your dream to the end of the street

then stretch the street (p. 2)

(12)   & so, with

coins from the embrace of prayers

rub your forehead:

moist like the lions of love (p. 8)

The horizontal alliterative sounds in the examples above in (11) are stop /d/ in line 1 and sibilant /s/ in line 2. In (12) we have a cluster of the lateral sound to the beat of the poem, which foregrounds the emotion of seriousness the poem is drawing attention to. Whether it is a call to revolt (ideological battle) or a performance of African ritual, the action is serious. It is this seriousness our poet has captured in sound. Vertical alliteration is also used for reinforcement of meanings where necessary as shown below:

(13)   Children's voice are sweet

in the flesh of noon

are

dimples on dumples of seaside –

a minstrel's voice is sweeter (p. 12).

In (13), the same sibilant sound /s/ is repeated purposely at the end of the lines for this emphasis. Note that in this vertical system, there is an attempt to play on superlatives. Here, an atmosphere of dance is foregrounded.

Repetition

Repetition, in its primary mode, is to intensity the message being communicated. In 'Blessings', a parable is repeated in 'part iv' to intensify the fact that the shortest route is not always the best route. It says:

(14)   (i)   Learn from those who have gone before...

       (ii)   words from those who have gone before...

(15)   And the stories we tell,

      of our meeting, and parting,

      and returning,

      are

      minted coins...(p.vii)

(16)   ...And the stories never rust

      of our meeting and parting

      and returning, like minted coins, (p. 72).

In the case of (15) and (16), we posit that these lines with cataphoric closings and repetition in the end with anaphoric and conclusive marker is a cohesive devise neatly employed to tailor the poems in the entire collection into a unified text.

Onomatopoeia

This is a kind of reinforcement which takes the form of a resemblance between what a piece of language sounds like, and what it refers to. This has been found to be of universal applicability as far as naming is concerned. A good example is:

(17)   I do not know how to express you

      whether as liberation, a flag of

      freedom flung to the air:

      or as a dungeon into which I

      tumbled, splashing for air (p. 21)

Tumbled and splashing, by their collocation is directional and demonstrative at the same time. This imitation sound gives us the mode and manner of the fall.

239

On a meaning level, this is a description of our kind of independence. It is a flag independence without economic base which is to say the least, a sham.

Graphological Analysis

Graphology is the graphic representation of language on paper. Crystal (1983: 143) says it is a 'term used by some linguists to refer to the writing 'system of a language'. A 'graphological' analysis would be concerned with establishing the minimal contrastive units of visual language. Thus, a written discourse will have several features which speech lacks, including punctuation, paragraphing and capitalization of letters. A starting point for the analysis of graphology in *Minted Coins* is to mention that it is structurally divided into seven (7) sections; 'awakening', 'initiation', 'love's always the starting point', 'till the season insists on corpses', 'on memories of the dead', 'but life re-affirms itself in new beginning', and 'suddenly, it is morning again'. A graphological structure of this text is summarized in the table below:

Table 1

Title of Poem	Awakening and initiation	Love's always the staring point	Till the season insists on corpses	On memories of the dead	But life reaffirms itself in new beginning	And suddenly, it is morning again!.
Number of poems	3	16	9	7	4	1-2
Number of stanzas	26	117	48	20	28	3-4
Number of sentences	13-15	56-60	23-30	47-49	16-18	1-2
Number of lines	107	477	365	188	112	8-11

There is a deliberate neglect of the norms of capitalization and punctuation in instances too numerous to mention here. An important feature of graphology observed is the use of the graphical sign /&/ to represent the coordinator and as in

(18)   & the lion roars, the

cub strolls

but always regain the den (p. 7).

This is of stylistic effect and novel in modern African poetry. Perhaps it should be noted that all the features focused on in this section contribute to extol the rhetorical strategies in *Minted Coins*. The crucial point about rhetorical underpinnings is that the author or narrator (in case of literature oral or written) does not want you to miss the important point of the story so he takes a few extra words to tell it. Whatever style he may employ is only to ensure that the reader does not miss the point.

But rather than simply being phonological or linguistic units, the components comprising the system we have examined are distinctive integrations of – minimally – dialect, mode of speech, preoccupation and demeanour, which crosscut communicative and behavioural modalities and integrate them thematically (Irvine 2001: 23, Coupland 2001: 348 and Rampton 2003: 73).

Conclusion

The strategies we have discussed in this study are merely those we could simulate as far as the tenets of rhetoric can yield in the analysis of poetic language. Among other things we can identify two crucial points from our study. One is that, in pursuing development, artists have foregrounded aspects of our culture that have limited our growth as a people. It would seem that we need aspects of world culture that would make us feel more at home and selectively developed and introduced into what is displayed in the West (Ikpe, 1999: 8). Another point is that the legacy of politics, civilian or military, in Nigeria since independence, has been that of material and moral depression. The reversal of this legacy requires new initiatives in thinking and action of all intellectuals, be they academics, writers, artists or politicians as Olusegun Oladipo (1999) recently articulated. We can only say we are gratified that Okinba Launko (pseudonym for Femi Osofisan) has responded to this call in his collection aptly entitled, *Minted Coins*. Afterall, history is a discourse in which accounts of events are set and interpreted in relation to time frames.

References

Baldwin, C.S. 1959. *Ancient Rhetoric and Poetic* (Gloucester, Mass: Peter Smith).

Brewer, W.F. 1988. 'Postscript: Imagery and text genre' *Text* 8/4.

Chinweizu, O. Jemie and I. Madubuike. 1980. *Towards the Decolonization of African Literature Vol. 1* (Enugu, Nigeria: Fourth Dimension Publishing Co.).

Chomsky, N. 1965. *Aspects of the Theory of Syntax* (Cambridge: Massachusetts Institute of Technology Press).

Christensen, F. 1967. *Notes Toward a New Rhetoric* (New York: Harper and Row).

Coupland, N. 2001. 'Dialect Stylisation in radiotalk' *Language and Society* 30/3 (345-76).

Crystal, D. 1985. *A Dictionary of Linguistics and Phonetics* (Oxford: Basil Blackwell).

Culler, J. 1978. 'On Trope and Persuasion' *New Literary History* vol. Ix No.3.

Davies, E. E. & B. Abdelali. 1989. 'Familiar and less familiar Metaphors: An Analysis of Interpretation in two languages', *Language & Communication* vol. 9, No.1 (49-68).

De Man, P. 1973. 'Semiology and Rhetoric' *Diacritics* 3, 22-33.

Easthope, A. 1983. *Poetry as Discourse*. (London: Methuen).

Fowler, R. 1977. *Linguistics and the Novel* (London: Methuen).

Freud, S. 1976. *Jokes and their relation to the Unconscious* (translated by Strachey, J) (Harmondsworth: Penguin Books).

Ikpe, I. 1999. 'The culture of development and the development of culture' *Viewpoint: A Critical Review of Culture and Society* Vol. 1. No. 1 & 2.

Irvine, J .2001. 'Style' as distinctiveness: The culture and ideology of linguistic differentiation. In P. Ecker & J. Rickford (eds) *Style and Sociolinguistic Variation* (Cambridge: CUP).

Launko, O. 1987. *Minted Coins* (Ibadan: Heinemann).

Leech, G.N. 1969. *A Linguistic Guide to English Poetry* (London: Longman).

Mann, William.C. and Sandra Thompson (1988) 'Rhetorical Structure Theory: Toward a functional theory of text organisation' *Text* vol. 8/3.

Meltzoff, S. 1978. 'Rhetoric, semiotic and linguistic look at the 'Strolling Actress of Hgarth', *New Literary History*, Vol. IX. No.3.

Oladipo, O. 1999. 'Intellectuals and social change in an African context' *Viewpoint A critical Review of Culture and Society,* vol. 1 Nos. 1 & 2.

Olafioye, T. 1984. *Politics in African Poetry* (Martinez C.A: Pacific Coast Africanist Association).

Procter, P. 1978. *Longmans Dictionary of Contemporary English* (London: Longmans Publishers).

Rampton, B. 2003. 'Hegemony, social class and stylisation' *Pragmatics* 13/1 (49-83).

Van Dijk, T.A. 1987. 'Episodic Models in Discourse Processing'. *Comprehensive Oral and Written Language* (New York: Academic Press).

OSOFISAN'S THEATRE AND THE EMERGING-*EMERGENT* CONTROVERSY WITHIN THE RE-CREATIVE THEATRE TRADITION IN NIGERIA

SUNDAY ENESSI ODODO

Introduction

Theatre practice is an artistic medium that has shown a lot of eclectic and boisterous transformation since the concept emerged, dating back to the after-work entertainment engagement of the early man through religious rituals shaped by the Greek's theatre experience. These early manifestations of the consciousness to continually refurbish theatre practice with fresh performative and staging ideas brought exciting and outstanding innovations and conventions to theatre practice within the last two centuries. The theatre thrives on the reflections of human experiences and can therefore not afford to be static because human nature is a pendulum constantly undergoing a dynamic motion. One can therefore appreciate the enormity of experimentation in staging theories, conventions and concepts that the theatre has witnessed since the 'three unities' popularised by the Greek Theatre. Some of the notable ones out of several historical conventions of theatre include Naturalism, Realism (popularised by Henrick Ibsen), Richard Wagner's *Gesamtkunstwerk*, Brecht's Epic Theatre (and the *verfremdungseffekt*), the Avant-garde, Tairov's Synthetic Theatre, Artaud's Theatre of Cruelty, Okhlopkov's Theatre of Ecstasy, Puppet Theatre and Grotowski's Poor Theatre.[1] There are also stage types such as the Proscenium, the Thrust, the Transverse, and the Arena (theatre-in-the-round). A close and critical study of all these forms and conventions reveal a preponderance of shared elements. In other words, the newness of any 'new' theatre form is to be assessed and appreciated by its own unique aesthetic priority, style and techniques.

The dominance of some of these theatre forms and conventions on African theatre has been so pronounced in the theatre world to the extent that they were perceived and interpreted as amounting to aesthetic colonialism. This became the rationale for the decolonisation of African Theatre. Clark, for instance, describes this perception by asserting that literary drama 'has its heart right at home in Nigeria and its head deep in the wings of American and European theatre' (1981: 65-66). Ukala similarly contends that 'much of African literature has remained tied to the apron strings of Western literature, especially in terms of aesthetics, language and, to some extent, worldview' (2001: 33-39). Serious

---

[1] For further appreciation, please read the following exciting studies: Ogunba 1978, Uka 1977: 177-187, Ogunbiyi 1981, Jeyifo 1984, Obafemi 1996 or 2001.

experimentation in performance aesthetics thus began to retrieve African Theatre from the clutches of Western aesthetics and to foist an African identity on African Theatre based on its own traditional and indigenous performance models and cultural artistry. Scholars and practitioners of African Theatre as well as playwrights lent their voices to this search for an authentic African Theatre.

From the beginning, so much effort was expended to defend African rituals and festivals as theatre under very fierce discursive atmosphere. Major contenders of this ritual theatre dialectics include Mahood 1966, Kirby 1974, Ottenberg 1975a and 1975b, Amankulor 1977 and 1982, Ogunba 1978, Adedeji 1978, Clark 1981 and Rotimi 1981. Others are Echeruo 1981, Horn 1981, Obafemi 1981, Drewal and Drewal 1983, Nunley 1987, Hagher 1987, Kofoworola and Lateef 1987, Drewal 1992 and Ibitokun 1993 and 1995. The scholarly contention over ritual or festival as the constituents of African Theatre engaged the critical attention of Etherton 1982. Etherton's summation is that the form of African drama needs to evolve in the same way as the content, and that the proponents should regard it as a dynamic process. This is a useful comment that suggests direction and focus to the search for African theatre identity. It is not the intention of this essay to further rehash and reposition claims and counter-claims on what constitute African Theatre. However, it is pertinent to observe that most of these works are painstaking scholarly efforts that try to isolate the internal aesthetic valve that characterises and defines the indigenous performances that they examined. By doing so, cultural conventions are positioned within their own inner logic, thereby avoid drawing undue parallels between two culturally divergent performance forms in order to gain foreign acceptability. The ritual and restorative theatres of Wole Soyinka and Ola Rotimi respectively, are explorative experiments in this direction. While the former is essentially informed by the general notion of self and communal renewal which is an accepted law of nature, the latter interrogates the cultural nuances of the people in a more reachable fashion to achieve an audience-centred theatre.

Another phase of theatre experimentation emerged with materialist vision championed by, in the forefront, Femi Osofisan, Bode Sowande, Olu Obafemi, Biodun Jeyifo, Kole Omotoso and Tunde Fatunde. This is an experiment that has attracted several appellations and commentaries. These commentaries are mostly coined to reflect the dialectical and social contents of the dramatic out-put of this theatre without due regards for the mode of production. Recently, this type of theatre has been referred to as 'dialectical theatrical tradition' (Obafemi and Yerima 2004: 5) and 'theatre of ideology and politics' because of its commitment to 'social and historical reconstruction through class struggle and a proletarian consciousness' (Adelugba and Obafemi 2004: 153) due to its Marxist aestheticism and its radical departure from the prevailing conservative theatre approaches of the time. Akinwale tags it 'Protest theatre' because its 'content shows a lot of agitation and protest against the status quo' with 'sharp and biting comments on the socio-political and economic systems of the country' (1993:

17). Gbilekaa conceptualises this form as 'Radical Theatre' because the main goal of the experiment is for 'radical transformation of society' (1997: 214). This same theatre form has also earned names like 'Theatre of revolt', 'Agitational Theatre' and 'Ideological Theatre'. However, when one takes a closer examination of all these labels and descriptions, one finds an attempt to describe different exciting colours of the same object. Essentially, the theatre uses Marx and Engels' dialectical materialist theory to propose new poetics for the Nigerian theatre. The thrust of this proposition is to dismantle social decadence and oppression in society through determined collective action. It is a theatre of urgent social action aimed at addressing injustice, insecurity, corruption, poverty, violence, disease and other societal ills.

Given the social relevance this theatre seeks in society and the radical approach adopted to achieve this, the practitioners have also had to contend with matching their life styles with the ideological and social issues raised in their works. This was why it became fashionable for most of the proponents of this theatre in the early seventies down to the early nineties, to make controversial comments on urgent topical issues, even at the risk of being hounded by the authorities. Many of them also adopted a low profile life style in furtherance of their social creative vision. The aim being to identify with the masses and proletariat, whose living condition they seek to improve by organising them to stand and defend their rights.[2]

In our attempt to capture the theory and practice of this theatre form, we propose the notion of Re-creative Theatre. It is re-creative in the sense that the practitioners of this theatre genre have engaged in bold experimentation of skilful reconstruction of ancestral and cultural myths and legends into radical concepts. The socialist dialectics that inform the practice of this theatre is thus recreated with a sense of immediacy that urges its audience into critical and urgent action of social change. Femi Osofisan for instance, has creatively demystified some of the major gods of the Yoruba pantheon (Orunmila, Sango, Esu, Yemoja, Ogun, Sopana, etc.) through a reinterpretation of their mythic origins and static conservative status into social relevance. Examples of this can be found in Osofisan's plays like *Esu and the Vagabond Minstrels*, *Another Raft*, *Twinge Twangle*, *A-Twyning Tayle* and *Many Colours Make the Thunder-King*. The recreation is further extended to rendering some source texts to meta-textual creation. This is a creative adventure that takes a re-interpretative look at some play-texts that espouse metaphysical and elitist consciousness. Some of these are mere evocation of African pantheon and spirits as can be seen in some of Soyinka's plays, especially *The Road* and *Death and the King Horseman*. Through Osofisan, meta-texts like *No More the Wasted Breed* (a response to Wole Soyinka's *The Strong Breed*), *Another Raft* (another response, to J.P.

---

[2] Bewildering beards were left untrimmed, cheap fabrics like *adire* or *kampala* were used for dresses in less fashionable styles. Sandals were the common footwear adopted.

Clark's *The Raft*), *Tegonni, an African Antigone* (an adaptation of Sophocles' *Antigone*), have been created. Beyond these, it is a theatre that is amenable to any staging process and condition. It has the capacity to be realised with rich deployment of stage iconography or its sparse utilisation while retaining its organic strength in contextual meaning and communication. The flexibility of this theatre form can be measured by the fact that its innovative dramatic resourcefulness and staging attributes transcend earlier and new or newly proposed theatre forms. In an earlier experimental phase for instance, Clark (1981: 67) notes that his *Ozidi*, Soyinka's *Kongi's Harvest* and Aig-Imoukhuede's *Ikeke* utilised the composite art of the folk theatre. Folkish elements (folktale narrative, incantations, chants, proverbs, riddle, aphorisms, poetry, dance, mime, music and so on) are manifested with great artistic efficiency in the re-creative theatre. Osofisan for instance,

> radically scrutinizes tradition, mining its lore and philosophy in order to critique its material foundations and question its relationship to present conditions. In so doing, he fashions a dramaturgy seemingly more equipped to meet his society's challenges (Richards 1987: 224).

This further confirms the flexibility inherent in the re-creative theatre. The rigid creative process that traditional materials are subjected to in ritual theatre for instance is non-existent here. It is the totality of the reconstructive essence of these folk elements in distilling new social vision of a revolutionary kind that Obafemi (2001: 21) refers to as the 'fabulist aesthetics' of Osofisan's theatre.[3] It is the skilful re-invention of these same folkish elements that has also informed Sam Ukala's proposition of the emerging concept of 'folkism' in the Nigerian theatre. It suffices here to state that the core distinguishing element between 'folkish' and 'folkism' is the re-inventive ingenuity that turns the source elements of folktales (folkish) into new functional reality of fabulism. 'Folkish' is a folktale heritage propelled with creative imagination and passed from one generation to another, while 'folkism' and 'fabulism' are re-creative products of that initial heritage, using contemporary reality to spell out new literary dialectics with boisterous social commitment and compelling instructional values.

The Emerging-Emergent Controversy

One of the controversies surrounding the relevance of these dramatists borders on the conceptual theorising by Obafemi in 1981, who describes them as 'Emergent Dramatists'. There has been subtle questioning of the correctness of this term in present usage. The argument being that if the dramatist were

---

[3] The paper was originally presented at the International Symposium on Black and African Cultures and the Challenges of Globalisation organised by CBAAC and held on August 20 and 21, 2001.

'emerging' in 1981 by now (2006) they must have long emerged to make the term 'emergent' irrelevant. Chris Dunton brings this argument to the fore stage in 1997 while reviewing Obafemi's *Contemporary Nigeria Theatre: Cultural Heritage and Social Vision[4]*. Dunton 1997: 693 questions the appropriateness of the term 'emergent dramatists' in describing Femi Osofisan, Kole Omotoso and Bode Sowande at that time.

This argument stems from the root word – 'emerge', and the distinction lies between 'emerging' and 'emergent'. This distinction forms the basis of the clarification offered by Bodunde (2000). Citing Obafemi's claim that Osofisan 'has developed quite rapidly from an emerging dramatist to become the leading proponent of the emergent alternative dramatic tradition in Nigeria and Africa' (1996: 272), Bodunde underscores the 'deliberate separation of what is 'emerging' from that which is 'emergent', adding that 'what needs to be apprehended is the materialist sense of the term' (2000: 76). Relying on authorities like Williams (1978) and O'Connor (1989) Bodunde explains that the value of the emergent tradition is to be understood as alternative or *oppositional* elements to the dominant culture. That is, it is conceived 'to negate the dominative culture which has been built to protect the propertied class' (2000: 76).

What can be inferred from Bodunde's submission is that the 'emergent' concept derives from a cultural materialist vision (of Raymond Williams) but adapted to the Nigerian context by Obafemi to position aspects of the development of the literary dramatic activities in the country. One can therefore conclude that it is ideological, while 'emerging' is conventional. This conceptual distinctive deduction is further boosted by Javed Malick's description of the radical theatre in the West in the late 60s:

> The infusion of revolutionary ideas and ideals energized the theatre by effecting a radical alternative in both its concept and its practice... There was an exciting intermingling of the twin concepts of political action as performance and performance as political action. As a result, theatre became bolder, more innovative, more flexible, more portable, more community based, and, above all, more directly involved with the material and emotional life of its audience. Theatrical activity itself broke out of the conventional, architecturally enclosed space and relocated itself in the socially (as well as physically) more open spaces of streets, neighbourhood shop floors, fairgrounds, parks, and marketplaces (Malick 1995: 146).

The above are the main features that inform the dramatic construct and the staging of the theatre of the 'emergent'. But over the years it is the ideological content of this drama that has attracted more critical attention than its practice as theatre. For instance, major works that pay some significant attention to this

---

[4] The book being a reworking of Obafemi's doctoral thesis at the University of Leeds in 1981 (before its first publication in 1997 with minimal updating).

ideological theatre form engage more in analytical foray of the dramaturgy than the theatrical potentials. In this category are works like Chris Dunton's *Make Man Talk True: Nigerian Drama in English since 1970* (1992), *Nigerian Drama in English* (1998); Martin Banham's *Dances in the Forest: Five West African Playwrights* (1998); Sandra Richard's *Ancient Songs Set Ablaze: The Theatre of Femi Osofisan* (1996) and Muyiwa P. Awodiya's *The Drama of Femi Osofisan: A Critical Perspective* (1995). However, the last two give some consideration to the theatrical possibilities of the dramatic form using the works of Femi Osofisan, the major proponent of this form.

It is against this background that this essay seeks to look at the creative philosophy of Osofisan's theatre within the re-creative theatre tradition in Nigeria. To achieve this, we shall rely mainly on a personal interview we had with him, our experience with his theatre as well as the production of his plays by other directors, and other available literature on his theatre.

The Creative Philosophy of Osofisan's Theatre

Osofisan's first major creative assignment emerged when his friends at an annual students' week in Akure asked him for a play. His response to the challenge resulted in the birth of *A Restless Run of Locusts* in 1968 but published later in 1975. This was the beginning of a long theatrical/literary journey that Osofisan has perfected today. As a creative writer he has virtually touched all the areas of the arts – prose, poetry and drama. But it is in drama that his fame is located.

Osofisan's dramatic development is directly linked to the boisterous literary and theatrical activities of the 1960s in Nigeria engendered by Wole Soyinka. Even though the playwrights Henshaw, Clark-Bekederemo and Nwankwo wrote at the same time, Soyinka's thorough grounding in the mechanics of theatre practice elevated him above his contemporaries. Osofisan was one of those who worked closely with him during those early days, especially during the Mbari[5] days. Even before this artistic association his works had made some strong impressions on the young mind of Osofisan. Going down memory lane Osofisan recalls that:

> His example has always influenced me, so even before I began to write at all I was already under his influence as somebody who deserves to be emulated. I'm still very much influenced by him (Interview with Ododo 1988).

He quickly adds that being influenced by him

> doesn't mean that I've been enslaved by him. I'm influenced by him but I've also developed as an artiste and I hope as an original voice too. But

---

[5] Mbari Club in Ibadan was founded by a group of artists and intellectuals as a centre for artistic minds and exhibitions. Wole Soyinka was one of the key founders.

I've been influenced too by so many other theatres and playwrights, it's not only him (Ododo 1988).

As the pioneering efforts of Soyinka in the Nigerian literary theatre inspired some young dramatists, so it also towered above their emerging efforts, shielding them from due recognition. It was from this seeming impregnable dominance that Osofisan took his creative bearing. Drawing from his experience with Soyinka's theatre, he concluded that one of the major problems with Soyinka's plays – not really faults – is that they require talented and gifted actors, and a sophisticated theatre, to realise. If all these requirements are adequately satisfied, the elliptical nature of his plays would be more clarified. To illustrate, Osofisan claims that when *Madmen and Specialists* was staged with tested actors like Femi Johnson, Tunji Oyelana, Wale Ogunyemi and Dapo Adelugba, the difference was glaring:

> But when I was starting, whereas the gifted actors were willing to work with him, they were not willing to work with small price like us; which meant that we had to write for people who are gifted actors but not as talented as those with Soyinka. We had to write for amateurs. So I have developed working with amateurs. Working with people who have not really had much experience and I had to face the challenge of building them up... (Ododo 1988).

He adds that,

> Since I never had the use of these theatres except through some clandestine manipulations, I had to write for other places other than that – small plays that we could rehearse in small rooms (Ododo 1988).

The nature of Osofisan's theatre is hinged on experimentation with forms, which is further propelled by the growing search for an authentic African Theatre idiom. The ultimate aim is to enhance audience-stage relationship and de-emphasise heavy reliance on theatre equipment in production, which also in effect means drastic production cost reduction. Like Ola Rotimi before him, Osofisan experiments within the presentational mode of production. To vitiate this observation, unlike some of his earliest plays like *A Restless Run of Locusts* and *Who's Afraid of Solarin?* that are more attuned to proscenium staging, the later ones are bold experiments in space utility, effective stage iconography and social rendering of cultural poetics. The abiding wide range use of space that is worked into the dramatic construct of *Once upon Four Robbers, Another Raft, Esu and the Vagabond Minstrels. Twingle –Twangle, A-Twynning Tayle, Yungba Yungba and the Dance Contest* and more recently *One Legend Many Seasons* are good examples.

In most of his plays, staging forms are originally conceived and their essences are production-driven, and are almost mandatory on the producing director. In *Farewell to a Cannibal Rage* for instance, the scenography is suggested to be achieved by the actors' bodies[6], *The Chattering and the Song* uses the play–within–play technique in which the actors transform roles by changing costume in the full view of the audience; in *Another Raft* the stage becomes a Lagoon; in *Esu* the use of costumes and props are expressly made optional. As Awodiya observes,

> What is considered Osofisan's greatest contribution to Nigerian theatre is his extra-ordinary theatrical fertility of forms. For long, he has been exploring new forms, searching for new ways of saying the same thing but using the same stage (1988).

Shaping the Staging Craft

The nucleus of Osofisan's theatre philosophy is accessibility. He writes plays that can be done at minimal cost, by ordinary folks and in any form of space. Even though provisions for the use of sophisticated stage machinery are evident in his scripts, he de-emphasises them in production and still adequately reaches the audience with high aesthetic standards. This indeed is a major achievement; creating a theatre that thrives well with or without technical aids. This is made possible by the primary structure and dialogue of his scripts which easily generate spectacle and action. In addition to these, he places premium on suggestive and realistic costumes. These further complement the roles of dialogue and action in his theatre. In Daniel Izevbaye's view,

> His stage-craft is very good. He has a talent for experimenting with form. He has this feel for keeping his audience both in terms of language, action and entertainment (Awodiya 1988: 225).

For instance, when he first produced *Twingle-Twangle, A-Twynning Tayle* as an experimental script and class work with the 1988 set of Diploma students of Theatre Arts at the University of Ibadan, he used a bare stage with a small hut in one corner. This was his scenographic conception for a play script that has lake, seashore, forest and a palace as locales with many interplays of time change. Even Bilisi, a character in the play whom he describes as 'a huge weird figure, belching smoke from its mouth and nostrils, was not aided technically. However, through dialogue and well-co-ordinated actions, all these features were animated.

One of the major reasons he favours a reduction in theatre realism, apart from the circumstances surrounding his theatre career at beginning, is because advanced theatre technology is not yet available in Nigeria. In his opinion, writing with such theatres in mind will therefore be irrational. He further

---

[6] Refer to all the stage directions in Femi Osofisan, *Farewell to a Cannibal Rage* (Nigeria: Evans Brothers Limited, 1986).

informs this writer that he deliberately wrote *Another Raft*[7] (which depends so much on stage equipment) to experiment with stage technology but had to turn the production around because of failed sponsorship promises. However, he succeeded significantly with a similar experiment on an earlier play, *Esu and the Vagabond Minstrels*.

The play as produced at the Obafemi Awolowo University Ile-Ife in 1986 had the backing of the Departments of Dramatic Arts, Music and Fine Arts, which offered him production support to experiment with a lot of technical and artistic aids. In the production, silhouettes were created by back lighting the actors dancing behind a screen whenever Esu and his entourage came on stage. According to the script, 'Esu just emerges from nowhere.' In the production, an explosion brought Esu on to the stage in a cloud of smoke. The explosion effect was created with gunpowder stuffed into a metal container connected to electric current. Smoke effect was also created using similar devices. These are rather crude means of achieving these effects. In countries where theatre technology is well developed, these effects can effortlessly be created with equipment already designed for such purposes.

Tine again, Osofisan manifests production styles that are less anchored on technical conventions. He casts and re-casts his plays, rehearses them, costumes his players, builds and strikes his sets all in the presence of his audience. This unorthodox attitude he believes is a means of driving home his message more forcefully by glaringly shocking the audience with living reality. In *Midnight Hotel* for example, he creates an illusion of two rooms and equally makes actors break into that illusion, thereby heightening the comic nuances of the play.

Osofisan's theatre is further underscored by his commitment to reachable play scripting and fine directorial ability. He sees these two arts of the theatre as one: 'For me, I don't separate the two as far as my own work goes' (Ododo 1988). This position explains why he personally directs the premiere productions of his plays in Nigeria, with a few exceptions – *Aringindin and the Nightwatchman* (1988) and *Yungba Yungba and the Dance Contest* (1990) directed by Sunbo Marinho. The creative anxiety of an artiste eager and determined to establish a new form and style probably accounts for this approach. This commitment is further strengthened by the fact that he runs two semi-professional theatre troupe – Kakaun Sela Kompany and Opon Ifa Players. The troupes are committed to the training of actors and theatre personnel through active participation in production process. They are not profit-making oriented. As non-resident theatres therefore, the affairs of the outfits are conducted anywhere – his car, his office, classrooms, the Arts Theatre when available, his house, even the University Staff Club.

---

[7] *Another Raft* was first produced in 1987 at the Arts Theatre of the University of Ibadan, Ibadan by Femi Osofisan.

Conclusion

A stocktaking of Osofisan's theatre reveals that the novelty of his practice is a product of surmounting experimental challenges. It is in unorthodox use of space and iconic utility of stagecraft that the shape, the sound and the sense of his theatre are to be located, while Dapo Adelugba's conclusion that 'the strength of his work is in the coaching of actors to do what would work in the theatre'[8] is also to be respected. It is even believed that some of his scripts are consciously written to fit the acting abilities and natural nuances of some of his key actors. Partly attesting to this belief is the fact that to date all Osofisan's scripts are treated as working scripts until they have been performed.

Properly viewed altogether, the hallmark of Osofisan's theatre is its simplicity, which makes it accessible to the literate, the not-too-literate and the illiterate, unlike his forerunners, Wole Soyinka and John Pepper Clark Beckederemo. These two especially have been described as being too elitist in their theatrical approach unlike Ola Rotimi who tries to liberalise his approach through language and indigenous theatre techniques. However, Osofisan emerged to pitch a tent between Wole Soyinka and Ola Rotimi, creating a more accessible theatre with aesthetic sophistication that thrives on realism and presentational skills, and re-creative deployment of indigenous production elements. These artistic strategies account for the intense popularity his theatre enjoys in Nigeria today.

References

Adedeji, J. 1978. 'Alarinjo': The Traditional Yoruba Travelling Theatre', in O. Ogunba and A. Irele (eds.), *Theatre in Africa* (Ibadan: Ibadan University Press, pp. 27-51).

Adelugba, D. and O. Obafemi (with additional material by S. Adeyemi). 2004. 'Anglophone West Africa: Nigeria' in M. Banham (ed.). *A History of Theatre in Africa* (Cambridge: Cambridge University Press, pp. 138 – 158).

Adelugba, D. 1978. 'Wale Ogunyemi, 'Zulu Sofola and Ola Rotimi: Three Dramatists in Search of a Language', in O. Ogunba and A. Irele (eds.), *Theatre in Africa* (Ibadan: Ibadan University Press, pp. 201 – 220).

Akinwale, A. 1993. 'Theatrical Tradition and Political Culture in Post-Independence Nigeria', in J. Malomo and S. Gbilekaa (eds.), *Theatre and Politics in Nigeria* (Ibadan: Caltop Publications (Nigeria) Limited, pp. 12 – 36).

Amankulor, J. N. 1982. 'Odo: The Mass Return of the Masked Dead among the Nsukka-Igbo'. *TDR* 26, 4 (T96): 46-58.

---

[8] Interview with Professor Dapo Adelugba, Ibadan, 1st August, 1988. Full text of the interview can be found in Ododo (1988).

Amankulor, J. N. 1977. 'The Concept and Practice of Traditional African Festival Theatre'. Diss. The University of California, Los Angeles: UMI 2421, vol. 38/05 – A.

Awodiya, M. P. 1995. *The Drama of Femi Osofisan: A Critical Perspective* (Ibadan: Kraft Books Ltd.).

Banham, M. 1998. *Dances in the Forest: Five West African Playwrights* (Cambridge: Cambridge University Press).

Bodunde, C. 2000. 'Olu Obafemi as a Literary Theorist: The Transposition of Cultural Materialism', in D. Oni and S. Enessi Ododo (eds.), *Larger than His Frame: Critical Studies and Reflections on Olu Obafemi* (Lagos: CBAAC, pp. 69 – 81).

Clark, J. P. 1981. 1981. 'Aspects of Nigerian Drama' in Y. Ogunbiyi (ed.), *Drama and Theatre in Nigeria: A Critical Source Book* (Lagos: Nigeria Magazine, pp. 57 – 74).

Drewal, H. J and M. T. Drewal. 1983. *Gelede: Art and Female Power among the Yoruba* (Bloomington and Indianapolis: Indiana University Press).

Drewal, M. T. 1992. *Yoruba Ritual: Performers, Play, Agency* (Bloomington and Indianapolis: Indiana University Press).

Dunton, C. 1992. *Make Man Talk True: Nigerian Drama in English Since 1970* (London: Hans Zell).

Dunton, C. 1997. 'Plays with Passion', *West Africa*, 8 April – 4 May, p. 693.

Dunton, C. 1998. *Nigerian Drama in English* (London: Hans Zell).

Echeruo, M.J.C. 1981. 'Concert and Theatre in Late Nineteenth Century Lagos', in Y. Ogunbiyi (ed.), *Drama and Theatre in Nigeria: A Critical Source Book* (Lagos: Nigeria Magazine, pp. 357 – 369).

Etherton, M. 1982. *The Development of African Drama* (London: Hutchinson University Library for Africa).

Gbilekaa, S. 1997. *Radical Theatre in Nigeria* (Ibadan: Caltop Publications (Nigeria) Limited).

Hagher, I. H. 1987. *The Tiv Kwagh-Hir* (Lagos: CBAAC).

Horn, A. 1981. 'Ritual Drama and the Theatrical: The Case of Bori Spirit Mediumship', in Y. Ogunbiyi (ed.), *Drama and Theatre in Nigeria: A Critical Source Book* (Lagos: Nigeria Magazine, pp. 181-202).

Ibitokun, B. M. 1993. *Dance as Ritual Drama and Entertainment in the Gelede of the Ketu-Yoruba Subgroup in West Africa: A Study in Traditional African Feminism* (Ile-Ife: Obafemi Awolowo University Press Ltd.).

Ibitokun, B. M. 1995. *African Drama and the Yoruba World-View* (Ibadan: Ibadan University Press).

Kirby, E. T. 1974. 'Indigenous African Theatre'. *The Drama Review* ('indigenous theatre issue') XVIII (4).

Kofoworola, Z. O. and Y. Lateef. 1987. *Hausa Performing Arts and Music* (Lagos: Nigeria Magazine).

Malick, J. 1995. *Toward a Theatre of the Oppressed* (Ann Arbor: The University of Michigan Press).

Nunley, J. W. 1987. *Moving with the Face of the Devil* (Urbana and Chicago: University of Illinois Press).

O'Connor, A. 1989. *Raymond Williams: Writing, Culture and Politics* (Oxford: Basil Blackwell Ltd).

Obafemi, O. 1982. 'Revolutionary Aesthetics in Recent Nigerian Drama'. *African Literature Today* 12: 118-136.

Obafemi, O. 1996. *Contemporary Nigerian Theatre: Cultural Heritage and Social Vision* (Bayreuth: Bayreuth African Studies).

Obafemi, O. 2001. 'Globe Formation: Aesthetics and Identities through Theatre in Africa'. *Daily Times*, August 29, p. 21.

Obafemi, O. and A. Yerima. 2004. *Ideology and Stage-Craft in the Nigerian Theatre* (Lagos: Booksplus Nigeria Limited).

Ogunba, O. 1978. 'Traditional African Festival Drama', in Oyin Ogunba and Abiola Irele (eds.), *Theatre in Africa* (Ibadan: Ibadan University Press, pp. 3-26).

Osofisan, F. 1980. *Once Upon Four Robbers* (Ibadan: BIO Educational Publications).

Osofisan, F. 1984. *No More the Wasted Breed*, in *Morountodun and other Plays* (Lagos: Longman).

Osofisan, F. 1988. *Another Raft* (Lagos: Malthouse Press).

Osofisan, F. 1993. *Twingle Twangle, A-Twynning Tayle* (Ikeja: Longman Nigeria PLC).

Osofisan, F. 1996. *Esu and The Vagabond Minstrels*, in *The Oriki of a Grasshopper and other Plays* (Washington: Howard University Press).

Osofisan, F. 1998. *Tegonni, an African Antigone* in *Recent Outings I* (Ibadan: Opon Ifa Readers).

Osofisan, F. 2001. *One Legend, Many* Seasons (Ibadan: Opon Ifa Reader).

Ottenberg, S. 1975a. 'Illusion, Communication and Psychology in West African Masquerades'. *Ethos* 10(2): 149-185.

Ottenberg, S. 1975b. *Masked Rituals of Afikpo: The Context of an African Art* (Seattle and London: University of Washington Press for the Henry Art Gallery).

Richards, S. L. 1987. 'Nigerian Independence Onstage: Responses from 'Second Generation Playwrights'. *Theatre Journal* 39(2): 215-227.

Richards, S. 1996. *Ancient Songs Set Ablaze: The Theatre of Femi Osofisan* (Washington: Howard University Press).

Rotimi, O. 1981. 'The Drama in African Ritual Display', Y. Ogunbiyi (ed.), *Drama and Theatre in Nigeria: A Critical Source Book* (Lagos: Nigeria Magazine, pp. 77 – 80).

Ukala, S. 2001. 'Politics of Aesthetics', in M. Banham, J. Gibbs and F. Osofisan (eds.), *African Theatre (Playwrights and Politics)* (Oxford: James Currey Ltd. Pp. 29 – 41).

Williams, R. 1978. *Culture and Society 1780-1950* (Harmondswoth: Penguin Books).

NOTES ON CONTRIBUTORS

ABDULLAHI ABUBAKAR is a senior lecturer in the department of English, University of Ilorin, Nigeria.

SOLA ADEYEMI studied theatre arts at the University of Ibadan, Nigeria and cultural and performance studies at the University of Natal, South Africa. He is currently working on identity and politics in the writing of Femi Osofisan.

VICTOR AIRE is Professor of Linguistics in the department of Languages and Linguistics, University of Jos, Nigeria.

MUYIWA AWODIYA is the current head of department of Theatre Arts, University of Benin, Nigeria. He is the editor of three volumes of critical essays on Femi Osofisan.

MARTIN BANHAM is Emeritus Professor of Drama and Theatre Studies, University of Leeds, England. He is also the editor of *The Cambridge Guide to Theatre* (1988) and *A History of Theatre in Africa* (2004).

FELIX BUDELMANN is of the department of Classical Studies, The Open University (Milton Keynes), United Kingdom. He is currently working on an edition with commentary of a selection from Greek lyric, and on a project about the Anacreontic tradition.

CHRIS DUNTON is Professor of English at the National University of Lesotho. Among his publications are *Make Man Talk True: Nigerian Drama in English since 1970* (1992) and *Nigerian Theatre in English: A Critical Bibliography* (1998).

HARRY GARUBA is an Associate Professor of English and African Studies at the University of Cape Town, South Africa. His current academic interests are in African literary studies and the literatures of the African Diaspora.

JAMES GIBBS has taught at the Universities of Ghana, Malawi, Ibadan and Liège and is currently a senior lecturer at the University of the West of England, Bristol. He has published widely on African literature and is co-editor, with Martin Banham and Femi Osofisan, of the annual journal, *African Theatre*.

BARBARA GOFF is a senior lecturer at the University of Reading. Her interests focus on Greek tragedy and its reception, women in antiquity and literary theory. She is currently working on the realtions between classics and colonialism.

YVETTE HUTCHISON is a South African teaching at the University of Winchester, UK. She is assistant editor of the *South African Theatre Journal*. Her doctorate was on the relationship between theatre, myth and history in post-1960s Kenya, Nigeria and South Africa.

BIODUN JEYIFO is Professor of English at Cornell University, Ithaca, USA. Among his publications are *Wole Soyinka Politics, Poetics, Postcolonialism* (2003) and *The Truthful Lie: Essays in a Sociology of African Drama* (1985).

AYO KEHINDE teaches African Literature (oral and written), Literature in English and Literary Theory at the Obafemi Awolowo University, Ile-Ife, Nigeria.

OLU OBAFEMI is Professor of English at the University of Ilorin, Nigeria, and a playwright, theatre director and critic. His critical works include a major study entitled *Contemporary Nigerian Theatre* (1996).

SUNDAY ENESSI ODODO teaches Technical Theatre and Performing Arts at the University of Ilorin, Nigeria, where he is the current head of department.

TEJUMOLA OLANIYAN is Professor of African and African Diaspora Cultural Studies, University of Wisconsin-Madion, USA. He wrote *Scars of Conquest/Masks of Resistance: The Invention of Cultural Identities in African, African-American and Caribbean Drama* (1995) and is currently co-editor, *West Africa Review*.

JANE PLASTOW is Deputy Director of the Workshop Theatre and Director of the Centre for African Studies at the University of Leeds. She has published widely on African theatre and theatre for development, including *African Theatre and Politics* (1996) and *Contemporary African Plays* (with Martin Banham, 1999).

ALAIN RICARD is Research Professor with the French National Centre for Scientific Research (CNRS) in the group Language and Cultures of Africa (LLACAN) and he teaches in the Institut National des Langues et Civilisations Orientales, University of Bordeaux 1, France.

KANCHANA UGBABE is a senior lecturer in the department of English, University of Jos, Nigeria. His publications include *Chukwuemeka Ike: A Critical Reader* (2001).

AMEN UHUNMWANGBO is a senior lecturer of Stylistics at the Ambrose Alli University, Ekpoma, Nigeria.

VICTOR UKAEGBU is a lecturer of drama at the University of Northampton, England. His published works include *The Composite Scene: The Aesthetics of Igbo Mask Theatre* (1996).